MONEY RULES

Also by Gail Vaz-Oxlade

It's Your Money
Money-Smart Kids
Never Too Late
Debt-Free Forever

MONEY RULES

RULES

Rule Your Money or
Your Money Will Rule You

GAIL VAZ-OXLADE

Collins

Money Rules
Copyright © 2012 by Gail Vaz-Oxlade.
All rights reserved.

Published by Collins, an imprint of HarperCollins Publishers Ltd

First published by Collins in an original trade paperback edition: 2012
This trade paperback edition: 2015

HarperCollins books may be purchased for educational, business,
or sales promotional use through our Special Markets Department.

HarperCollins Publishers Ltd
2 Bloor Street East, 20th Floor
Toronto, Ontario
M4W 1A8

www.harpercollins.ca

Library and Archives Canada Cataloguing in Publication

Vaz-Oxlade, Gail E., 1959–
Money Rules: Rule Your Money or Your Money Will Rule You / Gail Vaz-Oxlade.

ISBN: 978-1-44340-896-7

Printed and bound in the United States of America
RRD 9 8 7 6 5 4 3

This book is dedicated to all the mothers, fathers, grandmothers, and grandfathers who wish they'd done more to help their kids figure money out. With this book of rules, you have a road map for future discussions.

To all the young'uns who just want some way of figuring out what's true and what's a load of bullsh*t, here it is, just for you. Now you know. You can't use ignorance as an excuse for making the same mistakes your parents made.

To my son, Malcolm, who could care less about money. This is for when you're ready.

INTRODUCTION

Figure Out How Money Works

For all the people who have said,

"I just can't figure out my money."

"I can't get a budget to work."

"I wish I weren't in debt."

"That damn bank screwed me."

"I thought he was MY advisor."

"My credit card company won't cut me any slack."

"I didn't really understand ..."

"Hey, everyone's in debt."

"I don't have the time to sort out my finances."

I want you to do the following:

- Get several pieces of newspaper and a black marker.
- Write with the black marker on the newspaper:
  It's my money.
- Write it 100 times.

- Roll up the newspaper as if you were making a tube.
- Beat yourself over the head with it.

YOUR money is YOUR responsibility. If you won't take the time to figure out how it works, you shouldn't be surprised when it doesn't work for YOU.

A lot of people out there are going to try to get your money to work for THEM.

Retailers want you to spend it. Bankers want you to borrow and pay them interest. Investment advisors want you to put your money where it does their sales targets the most good. Insurance salespeople want you to buy whatever they're selling, regardless of YOUR needs. As for the credit card system and the credit scoring travesty, if you don't understand them, you'll climb on a hamster wheel and run your little *tuchas* off without ever getting anywhere.

You're working hard for your money. And you're going to work a long, long time. If you make minimum wage and work 40 hours a week from age 25 to 65, you'll earn over $800,000. In all likelihood, over the course of your life you'll earn much more than that. Don't you want to put that money to use for YOU? Don't you want it to serve YOUR needs and wants?

If you have a savings account at a regular bank that's earning 0.25% interest on your balance, is that really serving YOUR needs? If you have a pile of debt and you're paying 11%, 17%, 28% interest on the balance, is that really serving YOUR needs? If you've got a student loan and some Joe has talked you into paying only the minimum because it's "cheap" or because of the "interest tax deduction," is that really serving YOUR needs?

People out there don't care whether you're financially stable or successful. Really, they don't. If you think they do, grow up! If you aren't willing to take control of your money and your life, then you can't whine when things go off the rails.

If you're determined to be in charge of your money, grab a piece of paper and a pen and make a list of all the things you don't understand about how money works or how to make it work for you. From creating a filing system for your financial paperwork to starting a spending journal, from making a budget—a real one, not a pretend one where you just pull numbers out of the air—to creating a debt repayment plan, from setting up an educational savings plan for the kids to making a will and executing powers of attorney, you'll figure out all the things you have to do, write 'em down, and then get busy crossing stuff off your list.

If you don't know what should be on your list, start with the rules in this book. As you read each rule, add the steps you must take to your list. With each rule you'll be one step closer to financial independence.

This book isn't about the "how-to's." There are other books for that. *Debt-Free Forever* will teach you how to get rid of your debt once and for all. *Never Too Late* will show you how to plan for retirement. *Money-Smart Kids* will help you teach your children about money. *It's Your Money* shows how to make a financial plan and then adjust the plan as you move through your life. (*It's Your Money* was written for women, but if you're a guy, it won't make your penis fall off.)

If you need to figure out how a specific investment works, what the rules are for RESPs, or what to consider when buying insurance, the Internet is full of information. Find a couple of websites you like and read up.

If you need some hands-on help, ask for it. Squeeze all you can out of your banker, your investment advisor, your best friend, your insurance agent, your lawyer, your mom, your dad, your sister-in-law, your accountant . . . anyone who knows something you don't. Ask loads of questions. Take notes. Keep learning about money.

Money Rules is the truth about what you need to know about money and who's going to try to pull one over on you. Some of these rules debunk older rules that should never have been rules because they're wrong. Some are misunderstandings that we think are rules because they're repeated so often. And some of the rules are plain ol' common sense. *I want to show you how to turn common sense into money in the bank.*

The Money Rules I've presented here are in no particular order. I've done that on purpose so you can't just turn to a section of the book and read all the rules related to a particular topic. (I figure you'll learn stuff just by having to read all the rule titles!) If you think a rule doesn't apply to you now—maybe you don't have kids, so RESPs hold no interest for you—you could just skip the rule. But keep in mind that every time you skip a rule, you're passing up knowledge you might need down the road.

You're paying for 272 Money Rules in this book. You might as well read 'em!

RULE #1: RENTING IS NOT A WASTE OF MONEY

You don't have to own to have a home. While the common mantra is "Buy and build equity," that's true only if you can afford to buy. So Rule #1 replaces the old rule "People should all own their own homes."

I know there is a stigma attached to renting. But renting or owning is a personal choice. It has nothing to do with how smart, ambitious, or financially savvy you are. If all your ducks line up and you want to buy, then buy. If they don't, you should not be squeezing yourself into home ownership because you think that with it comes some magical financial stability you can't get if you don't own.

People twist themselves into knots trying to own their own homes. They overextend themselves. They buy with little or no down payment just to get into the market. They squeeze their cash flows and have to turn to credit to make ends meet.

Home ownership can be a big ol' pain in the arse. Like when your shingles blow off in a windstorm. Or the furnace breaks. Or you're trying to sell and no one wants to buy, so you can't move and get on with your life. Yes, there are moments of joy and pride that come with home ownership, but it's not for everyone.

So, who should NOT own?

YOU if you haven't done a realistic budget. Don't fall for the crap that home ownership costs the same as renting. It does not. According to the Stats Man, homeowners spend an average of $57,649 a year on shelter-related costs compared with renters, who spend $32,536. That's a difference of over $25,000. Just being able to make the mortgage payments isn't enough. If your budget doesn't include all the other costs—property insurance, utilities (which will be higher than if you were renting), property taxes, and maintenance, you may find yourself tapping your credit cards and lines of credit just to make ends meet.

YOU if you have a variable income. If your income has some slow periods when you have trouble making ends meet, taking on a home may be the straw that breaks your cash flow's back. Most people with a variable income, unless it's very high, find budgeting difficult. Taking on home ownership means taking on a ton of stress.

YOU if you work in an industry where employment is seasonal or erratic. Ditto above. Unless you really sock it away while you are working, you may find it hard to keep up with the financial demands of ownership.

YOU if you don't have the time, skills, desire, or cash to deal with home maintenance. There is always something to be done around a house: a garden to be weeded, walls to be painted, lawns to be cut, plumbing to be fixed, curtains to be replaced, a roof to be repaired, snow to be shovelled, carpets to be cleaned, a furnace to be maintained . . . the list goes on and on and on. Home maintenance can be expensive. Estimate 3% of the value of your home, not including the property; look at your home replacement insurance for this since it doesn't include the land. That means on a $200,000 house, you'd need to include about $500 a month in your budget for maintenance. If you can do it yourself, you'll save on labour, so you can put away a little less. If you must pay someone else, your costs will be higher, so don't skimp on your maintenance budget.

YOU if you'll wipe out all your savings. Would you do ANYTHING to get into a home of your own? Would you take money from your retirement savings plans? Would you tap your tax-free savings accounts (TFSAs)? Would you annihilate your emergency funds? Wipe out all your savings and you could find that once you're in your new home, expenses start cropping up, and you have no safety net in place to see you through. If buying a house gobbles every red cent you've managed to squirrel away, you should wait until you can own a house AND have a safety net.

YOU if you move often. If you work in a career that has you relocating often, the costs of buying and selling may be prohibitive. Nomads live in tents for a reason. Getting in and out of home ownership (sales commission, closing costs, legal fees, land transfer taxes) can wipe out any equity you've built up, assuming the market has been going up in your area. And if the market has taken a turn for the worse just when you're pulling up roots again, you'll eat the loss.

YOU if you can't afford to own in an area in which you would like to live. For the sake of home ownership, would you move far away from friends and family, from your job, from the life you love? It makes no sense to become house-poor in a place you don't even want to live. And if you add huge commuting costs—which you never calculate into your home-buying decision—both in terms of money and time, you'll end up rueing the decision to buy.

YOU if you're not financially responsible. You'd think this would be a given, wouldn't you? Not so much. Loads of people who are clueless about their money have bought homes. If you haven't had the discipline to save up a healthy down payment, what makes you think you're ready for home ownership? If you don't even know for sure how much you make each month, you're climbing out on a rotten limb. And if you haven't given a thought to what you'll have to do to keep the place from falling down, you're delusional about what home ownership involves. In the end, you'll rely on credit to see you through, and have to tap your home equity to pay down your consumer debt.

YOU if you're carrying any consumer debt. You couldn't afford to pay off that credit card or line of credit while you were paying less for housing. What magic do you think is going to make it easier to pay that debt off now that you're making a bigger financial commitment to ownership? Are you nuts?

YOU if you love being able to write a cheque for rent and then not sweat the details. If you're a gadabout or hate routine, home ownership may not be for you. Ditto if you'd rather travel than buy furnace filters, shop for shoes than snow shovels, or go back to school than refinish the floors. If home ownership is going to get in the way of the other things you want to do with your life and your money, you'll only end up resenting your house. So if Saturday morning in a café with a latte is more attractive than heading out to cut the lawn, stick with renting.

RULE #2: DON'T MARRY A MONEY MORON

This rule replaces the old rule "Love conquers all." That one might have been fine when you were in high school (no, not really), but now that you're a grown-up, there are more things to consider than how much your tummy flips and how lucky you are to have landed such a hottie!

If you fall in love, get married, and wake up to find that you're hitched to someone who is spending money without thinking about it, taps the savings account every time there's more than a buck sixty-two in it, or is using credit like it's "free money," you're married to a money moron.

The easiest way to not fall into the trap of always having to clean up someone else's financial caca is to steer clear of the money moron to begin with. So how do you know if you're getting involved with a money moron? Here are 24 questions to answer honestly. If you answer yes to more than three, run for the hills.

FAMILY

DOES YOUR DARLING . . . ?

		Y	N
1.	fail to pay the card balance off in full each month	☐	☐
2.	stay in overdraft for more than a day or two each month	☐	☐
3.	pay more than $30 a month for bank fees	☐	☐
4.	go to a pay-advance store, EVER	☐	☐
5.	have no savings	☐	☐

6. throw bills in a drawer and say, "I'll get to them later." ❑ ❑

7. insist on picking up the bill for everyone whenever you go out in a group ❑ ❑

8. believe she or he "deserves" to have a new car, a vacation, a new TV, even if it means having to put it on credit ❑ ❑

9. have no idea how much he or she makes, or spends, or owes ❑ ❑

10. love to spend money on clothes, entertainment, pleasure, without thinking about how to pay when the bill comes in ❑ ❑

11. work only sporadically, change jobs often, or frequently skip work to play ❑ ❑

12. live at home without paying rent, letting Mommy cook and do the laundry, and have not a red cent saved ❑ ❑

13. frequently tap friends and family for money "until I get paid." ❑ ❑

14. whine about how they wish they could have better stuff ❑ ❑

15. buy stuff to show off ❑ ❑

16. like to gamble ❑ ❑

17. complain about child support obligations ❑ ❑

18. buy you expensive presents you're not sure are affordable ❑ ❑

19. want you to pay for stuff most of the time ❑ ❑

20. frequently let friends pick up his or her share of the tab ❑ ❑

21. drive too fast, drink too much, and spend on   ❑ ❑
    impulse

22. get angry or secretive if you ask about his or her   ❑ ❑
    financial situation

As life would have it, we often fall for people for no rhyme or reason. We just fall. And if all you're doing is fooling around and having fun, hey, what the heck! But getting into a permanent relationship that is destined for disaster because your mate is a money moron is dumb!

If you are determined to have a relationship with a money moron, protect yourself. Do NOT get married to one. Do NOT cohabit. You can sleep together as much as you want, as long as the money moron has a separate address for mail and stuff. The minute you agree to a more permanent relationship, you'll be putting yourself at risk.

While your buddy may not have had any financial smarts up to this point, the fact that your mate-to-be wants to make a commitment to you should mean they're ready to mend their ways financially. If the person you love isn't prepared to change from money moron to something more acceptable, then they don't love you as much as they say they do. Cut your losses and move on.

If you're already married to a money moron, see Rule #138: Protect Yourself from a Money Moron.

RULE #3: YOU MUST HAVE A WILL

This replaces the old rule "Only rich people need estate plans."

More than half of us don't have a will. Really? You're never going to die? Or is it that you think God is holding you by your pompom? Grow up. Without a will, you have no say on who gets your money. Without a will, you can't plan to minimize your taxes. Without a will, you're leaving your family in the lurch. Suck it up and do the tough stuff. Make a will. And get an estate planning professional to do it so your family isn't left unravelling a legal mess.

While those do-it-yourself will kits may look like a good idea, they're not. Yes, they're cheap. But you know what they say: "You get what you pay for." The problem with will kits (regardless of who tells you they're a good idea) is that they are "standard" and can't take into account the peculiarities of your region (wills come under provincial legislation) or your unique circumstances. You are unique, aren't you? I thought so.

It boils down to this: cheap-out now and your estate could end up in court or costing your family in extra taxes. Pay now (anywhere from $300 to $600 for a well-thought-out and professionally drawn will) and save your family the aggravation down the road.

Make a will. You're going to die quickly if you're lucky. If you aren't so lucky, you'll just become incompetent and someone else will have to make all your decisions for you while you sit in the corner drooling. Read Rule #4: You Must Have POAs.

RULE #4: YOU MUST HAVE POAS

This replaces the old rule "My partner knows what I want." Maybe, but if you don't have powers of attorney in place, he or she can't do a thing about it.

Dying is easy, at least for the person who croaks. Not dying and becoming incapacitated—that really sucks. And if you don't have all your i's dotted and t's crossed, it'll suck even more.

A power of attorney, or POA, is a legal document that authorizes someone else to act on your behalf. One type of POA deals with property and gives the person you choose the legal authority to manage your assets. Another type lets you appoint a body to make medical and personal care decisions on your behalf.

Just because you're married, don't assume that means you can make decisions for your partner. That's what Kathryn and Mark assumed, until Mark had an accident on his motorcycle and ended up in a coma for three months. Since he had never executed POAs, Kathryn couldn't touch his bank account, even as the disability payments rolled in. She was desperate as she tried to keep the mortgage paid and buy food for the three kids. Thank goodness for her family and friends; without them Kathryn and the kids might have lost their home.

If you do not execute both a financial and a personal care power of attorney, you're short-sighted, ignorant, or irresponsible. If you were to be involved in an accident and couldn't sign your own name, your family wouldn't be able to touch the money going into your bank account, renew the mortgage on the family home, or even arrange your care and treatment.

If you became ill or physically incapacitated, how would your bills get paid? Who would be able to access your bank accounts to take care of your needs and those of your children, partner, or aging parents? Who would manage your investments, pay your taxes, keep things running? And, ultimately, who would be able to speak for you on medical care issues if you're unable to speak for yourself?

If you haven't yet done this, today's the day you grow up and start acting like the responsible adult you claim to be. Set up an appointment with an estate lawyer to make your powers of attorney. At the very least, go to the Ministry of the Attorney General website for your province or territory and download the powers of attorney kit offered, read the documentation thoroughly, and execute your POAs this week.

RULE #5: FIGURE OUT WHAT'S REALLY IMPORTANT TO YOU

One of the biggest problems people have is their inability to pick something they want and work steadily towards that goal. It's so easy to get sidetracked by dinner out with friends or those snappy new shoes. Inevitably, the big goal gets sidelined for those smaller indulgences.

People spend a lot of time daydreaming about how their lives could be different. They wish they could escape from whatever trap they feel caught in, be it debt, a crappy job, or a miserable life. They wish they could afford to buy a home. They wish they weren't always worried about their money.

If you really, really want something, you can have it. But only if you really, really want it. If you're in the least bit wishy-washy in your commitment to your goal, don't expect to get there any time soon.

Examples of wishy-washy dreaming abound. There are the folks who wish they could save a down payment on a home, but instead of squirrelling away every extra penny for their dream, they eat out four nights a week. Or the people who say they're tired of being in debt, but put their next vacation on their line of credit or credit card. Or the folks who bemoan having no money saved for the future, but who do the drive-thru thing twice a day.

Really, really wanting something means nailing down the goal with a timeline and steps to get you there. If you don't know how to set a goal, read Rule #6: Set Some Goals.

RULE #6: SET SOME GOALS

Have you ever set a goal and then ended up beating yourself up because you missed by a mile? Are you still setting goals, or do you figure it's totally pointless?

You can't give up trying. Setting goals is one of those skills that you'll get better and better at if you just keep practising. Even if the first few times you feel the process is stilted, keep practising. It'll come more naturally every time you set another goal. The first time you drove a car the process didn't feel natural, right? But with time driving got easier; the process became smooth.

If you don't know what you want, if you don't lay a plan for getting from one point in your life to another, you're just wandering in the woods blindfolded. You're probably going to tumble down a steep slope, trip over some roots, or fall in a hole. You will get hurt. And then you'll be angry, frustrated, sad. Wouldn't it just be easier to take off the blindfold?

Becoming debt-free, buying a home, having and raising children, building a safety net, creating a retirement account with enough money to live on when you stop working . . . these are all goals. You may not have thought of them as such, which means you've been walking around with the blindfold on. When you take it off and delineate what it is you want, you'll stop missing by a mile and driving yourself into apathy.

The first step is to write down your goal. It should be so clear that any Tom, Dick, or Harriette could look at what you're trying to achieve and be able to measure your success. After all, if you don't know exactly where it is you're going, how will you know when you get there?

If you haven't been successful setting goals—or you haven't yet tried—then practise with very short-term goals first. Grab a pen and a piece of paper and write down a list of what you want to accomplish today. Eventually, you'll learn to set goals with longer time frames, but starting short helps keep you focused.

Next, pick one big thing you want to do over the next six months or so, and write it down as a goal. To be a SMART goal, it has to be:

Specific. A general goal would be "Pay off my debt." A specific goal would be "I want to be debt-free, so I will pay off my debt, repaying my most expensive debt first, and having all my consumer debt paid off in three years or less."

Measurable. Establishing concrete criteria for measuring your progress will help you to stay on track, reach your target dates, and experience the exhilaration of achievement that spurs you on to reach your goal. To determine if your goal is measurable, ask: How will I know when I've accomplished this?

Attainable. If the goal is too big, frustration will get in the way. Expecting to have the same house, same car, same lifestyle as the millionaires you see on TV isn't attainable. Let's face it: on your income it's just not going to happen. Figuring out how much you can afford to spend on a house based on YOUR income makes the goal attainable.

Realistic. You are the only one who can decide just how high your goal should be. But planning to have your emergency fund saved in three months when you make just $10 an hour isn't realistic. It may take a year or even longer to save six months' worth of essential expenses. Don't sabotage yourself by setting unrealistic goals.

Timely. A goal must be grounded within a time frame. With no time frame, there's no sense of urgency. If you want to save $1,000 for an emergency, when do you want to save it by? "Someday" won't work. But if you anchor it within a time frame, "by August 1," then you've set parameters within which you're working.

A plan followed blindly is as bad as no plan at all. And yet, sometimes when we set a goal for ourselves, we become so slavishly committed to meeting that goal that we can't see the damage we're doing to ourselves elsewhere in our lives. We rack up credit card debt because we're determined to pay off the mortgage in 10 years or less. We ruin our relationships with partners because we're so committed to being debt-free that we become uncaring about other people's needs and whatever else is happening around us. We have our hearts so set on a summer wedding that we are unwilling to delay for even a few months to avoid putting the party on credit.

That's not to say that every change in our circumstances means another path to take. A change simply means we must pause to THINK, to re-evaluate. Sometimes sticking with the original plan and avoiding distractions is what will get us to our goals. Sometimes a slight adjustment in the plan will suffice. Sometimes a whole rewrite is necessary. Ultimately, however, if you have a clear goal, you'll figure out where to correct for the winds and turbulence with which you're faced.

RULE #7: YOUR BANKER IS NOT YOUR FRIEND

If you are under the impression that the folks you deal with at the bank are there to "help" you, you're a sap. (Those ads are working on you, aren't they?)

While once upon a time financial advisors had a fiduciary responsibility—they were required to put the customer's best interests first—that "fiduciary responsibility" has gone the way of the dodo. If you still think your lender, your banker, your insurance agent, or your investment advisor is your "friend," you need to give your head a serious shake.

Banks (and all other financial institutions) exist to make money. Just like car dealerships and electronics retailers, they expect their people to shovel as much product as they can. And they're not too fussy about who is upset or negatively affected by their profit manoeuvres. Hey, it's a dog-eat-dog world, so "Buyer Beware!" applies when you walk into a bank, just as it does when you walk onto a used car lot.

Stop thinking (and acting) as if your banker is your friend. You may have a good advisor, a real professional who is knowledgeable and capable. He is not your friend. You may have an advisor who is empathetic and encouraging. She is not your friend. You are a customer.

Banking is no different from any other retail transaction. If you went into a shoe store and bought a pair of shoes that ended up giving you blisters, would you blame the shoe store salesperson? How about if you went into a restaurant and ordered the double chocolate cheesecake; would it be the

REALITY BITES

waiter's responsibility to point out that you're gonna get fat? And if you walked onto a car lot . . . well, you get my drift.

When you're dealing with a bank, insurance company, investment advisor, or lender, the SALESPERSON is under no obligation to offer you alternatives or tell you about options that will save you money. She's working for a company that is focused on making a profit. YOU should be equally focused on ensuring YOU get what YOU need.

Since you are a customer, you should be demanding all you deserve as a customer. Stop cutting the bank slack because "they are nice to you." They're supposed to be nice to you; you're the customer. And stop thinking that the bank would actually put your needs first. As with every other "purchase" you make, do your research, know what you're buying, and work to get the very best deal. And if your bank is blowing it, walk away.

RULE #8: EVERYONE NEEDS
AN EMERGENCY FUND

This rule replaces the delusion "Bad things don't happen to good people."

An emergency fund is indispensable as your first line of defence against the unexpected things life will throw at you. Money in the bank gives you options and the means to deal with life's lumps. Your son breaks his arm; you have the means—the money—to take a day off work, get him to the hospital, and cope in whatever other ways you must. Your partner is downsized; you have the means to pay the mortgage and keep food on the table until he finds new ways of bringing home the bacon. You bang up your car, watch your shingles blow off in a windstorm, or find yourself in the throes of a divorce, and you have the means to keep the financial boat afloat while you find ways to cope with all the other stress in your life.

Without an emergency fund, you'd have to turn to credit to fill the holes. No, a line of credit is not an emergency fund. It's debt waiting to happen. If you hit a wall and end up racking up tens of thousands in debt on an LOC, how is that diverting disaster? After all, if you can't save $10,000 in an emergency fund, how are you going to pay off $10,000 plus all the interest building up on that LOC?

You need to have cash in the bank. How much cash? Work towards accumulating six months' worth of essential expenses. (Cable is not an essential expense!)

But Gail, I can hardly manage on the money I'm making now. Where am I supposed to get the money? Wouldn't having $1,000 be enough?

An emergency fund of $1,000 may be enough if you live under a rock. If your home is paid for, if you have no debt, if you walk everywhere you go, and if you're happy eating ketchup soup three nights a week, you'll need less. If you want a realistic emergency fund—one that actually gets you though the rough—figure out your monthly essential expenses and multiply by six. That's how much you need. (Essential expenses are those that keep body and soul together: rent or mortgage payment, basic food, basic utilities, transportation, minimum payments on your debt so your credit history doesn't go into the crapper and end up costing you more money.)

But Gail, I'll get Employment Insurance if I lose my job, so that means I won't need such a big emergency fund.

EI may help fill the gap if you lose your job, but it doesn't go very far. And unemployment isn't the worst emergency you may face. Get sick and watch your money evaporate. Even if you have good health and disability insurance plans, your cash flow will still take a kicking until your benefits click on.

When you add up what it costs to keep your family going for six months, you might be intimidated by the amount you have to accumulate in your emergency fund. Six months of essential emergency expenses can be an enormous goal. So start small. Make your initial goal $500. Once you reach that benchmark, set your next goal.

Make your savings automatic. If you decide to save $50 a month, have that amount auto-debited from your main banking account to your high-interest savings account every month. You'll get used to living without that money in no time flat.

Here's a great tip I picked up from a regular visitor to my website, which she calls the Tit-for-Tat approach to savings. Each time she buys herself something she considers a WANT, she contributes an equal amount to her savings account. Not only does it make her really think about whether she's going to spend the money—because in essence whatever she buys is going to cost her cash flow twice as much—but she's also saving for the future while she enjoys her todays.

If the next words out of your mouth are "I can't see the point of letting money sit earning next to nothing in a savings account for an emergency that may never happen," remember that an emergency fund isn't about building wealth; it's about mitigating risks. While it can be a really sad thing to watch thousands of dollars earning very little in a savings account, return isn't the priority with an emergency fund. Access is. Stick that money into the market and it may not be there when you need it most. Stick it in a high-interest savings account and, while you may be irked by the pittance you're earning in interest, the emergency fund will be at the ready when you hit the wall. The point is to have some wiggle room when the unexpected happens.

Don't fall into the trap of using every excuse to tap your emergency fund. Tires need to be replaced? You couldn't see that coming? Roof is leaking. Gosh, you mean a roof has a life expectancy too? It makes no sense to label every financial setback an "emergency" and then bleed your emergency fund as you reach for the quickest solution.

Your emergency fund is meant to hold you through the toughest of times, not scratch every replacement itch you get. Leave it alone so it can grow.

RULE #9: CALCULATE YOUR OWN DEBT REPAYMENT PLAN

If you have debt and you want it gone, then you have to take control of the process. Here's how to calculate how much you need to pay each month to get your debt gone within a specific amount of time:

1. Take your outstanding balance and multiply it by the interest rate. Then divide by 12. That's the monthly interest. So if you have a credit card that charges 18% and you have a $1,465 balance, your calculation would look like this:

   $$1,465 \times 18 \div 100 = 263.70 \div 12 = \$21.98*$$

   That means you have to pay $21.98 in interest every month.

2. Decide how long you want to take to pay off your debt.

3. Take the outstanding balance and divide by the number of months in which you want to be out of debt. So if you want that credit card balance of

---

*Note: Interest is usually calculated on a declining balance—as you pay down your debt every month, what you owe keeps going down, which means that the interest amount will get a little smaller with each payment. But for this rule I've simplified this calculation. If you want a more accurate figure, find a loan calculator on the Internet and put in your numbers. You should still do the exercise here because it's good for you to understand how to determine your own payments.

$1,465 gone in six months, your calculation would look like this:

$1,465 ÷ 6 = $244.17

That means you will be paying $244.17 against what you owe (your principal) every month.

4. Add the two totals (interest and principal) together to get your monthly payment.

$21.98 (in interest) + $244.17 (principal) = $266.15 (total monthly payment)

5. If your total monthly payment is too high and you just can't work it into your cash flow, you have two choices: either make more money or extend the number of months for the principal repayment calculation. If you decide to extend the time it will take to pay off your debt from six months to nine months, your calculation will look like this:

$1,465 ÷ 9 = $162.78 + $21.98 (in interest) = $184.76 (total monthly payment)

Just remember, the longer you take to pay off the loan, the more months you'll be paying that interest, so the more it will end up costing you.

RULE #10: YOUR FINANCIAL EDUCATION IS YOUR RESPONSIBILITY (PART 1)

Your financial well-being has to be at least as important as learning to drive a car or learning to cook. You spent some time reading, practising, getting better and better, until you felt proficient at those things, right? So why wouldn't you take the same approach with your money?

While it's fine to turn to specialists for help with certain aspects of money—never buy disability insurance from anyone other than a disability expert—abdicating responsibility to the expert is the wrong thing to do. You must use the expert to educate yourself so that you can make sound, well-informed decisions. It's your money, so it's your decision to make. And if you don't make it—if you let someone else make the choice instead—you shouldn't be surprised when you find out it wasn't the right decision for you.

If you think learning about money is hard, you're right. There's a lot of really complex stuff, especially when you get into things like investing and insurance. But most of the basics are readily available in books and on the Internet. Read, read, and read some more. If you're not the type who learns well from reading, sign up for a basic personal finance class at a local community college. Or ask your friends for help.

If you throw your arms up and say, "Oh, I just don't have a head for money," you're wrong. **You *do* have "a head for money"—you just don't want to use it.** How tough is it to understand that "You can't spend more money than you make"? If you are unwilling—UNWILLING—to accept that truth, this isn't a "can't understand" issue; it's a "don't wanna understand" issue.

If you've decided to be done with being ignorant, begin with the basics. Tackle budgeting, and then move on from there to deal with:

- emergency funds
- cash management
- renting or owning
- your credit identity
- saving
- investing
- insurance
- taxes
- estate planning

Cover all the parts of a sound financial plan one at a time, making sure you understand exactly what you're doing as you go. If you don't understand something well enough to explain it to a teenager, ask more questions or do more research.

Your financial education is your responsibility. Nobody else is going to make sure you learn what you need to know. But you can be damn sure others will be more than happy to take advantage of your ignorance.

Do you feel financially literate? If you don't, what are you doing about it?

RULE #11: HOME OWNERSHIP DOESN'T GUARANTEE AN EASY RETIREMENT

If you're under the impression that buying a home will make your retirement easier—you've heard the saying "My home is my nest egg"—it's time to get a new impression.

Home ownership isn't a panacea for having saved no money for the future. If you feel you're running out of time and desperately want to own a home—maybe you're in your forties or early fifties and have only just started to think about the future—know that if that home can't be paid off before you retire, those mortgage payments will become an albatross around your neck.

Home ownership is one way of *reducing* costs when you retire if—and only if—your mortgage is paid off. Even then, there are still substantial costs associated with home ownership: property taxes, utilities, insurance, maintenance and upkeep. I live in a small home in a small town. My taxes run to almost $300 a month, utilities add another $210, insurance is about $100, maintenance and upkeep about $340. So even owning my house outright, it's costing me almost $950 a month to keep a roof over my head. Those costs won't go away just because I retire.

Home ownership does not mean you eliminate housing costs in retirement. People need to stop seeing home ownership as The Answer. Home ownership makes sense if you like where you live and want to stay there. And it makes sense if you can reduce your costs by eliminating the mortgage before you retire. Otherwise, rent.

RULE #12: COMPARE YOUR STUDENT LOAN INTEREST RATE WITH REGULAR LOAN RATES

Old rule: The government wants to do right by students.

Reality: You may be paying way more interest than you have to.

There are a whole bunch of things you may not know about government student loans programs. True or false?

T F

1. The six-month, no-payment grace period ☐ ☐
   students are given when they leave school
   comes interest-free.

2. The interest rate on student loans is ☐ ☐
   comparable to what's available at the bank.

3. You should use the student loan default ☐ ☐
   repayment schedule to pay off your student
   loan.

False is the correct answer for all three. Surprised? Did you really think that after years of giving you money for free, the government wasn't going to find a way to get its pound of flesh?

The six-month grace period comes with a cost: interest. While you don't have to make a payment, the whole time you don't, your debt continues to grow. If you're a student in the Maritimes, you'll graduate with an average debt of about $28,000, and that six-month deferral could cost you as much

INSURANCE

as $1,000 in additional interest. You'll have the option of paying it in a lump sum. But most people just add it to their principal and end up paying interest on interest. Talk about putting compounding to work AGAINST you.

The interest rates on student loans are actually higher than you can get at a bank. Why? Well, remember all those years you or your kids were in school, using the government's money and paying not one red cent in interest? The interest rate clock was completely off. Since the government is going to get its money back one way or another, student loans come with a hefty price tag once the interest rate clock is turned on. In fact, if you choose a variable interest rate, you'll pay prime plus 2.5%, while the fixed rate loan charges prime plus 5%. Whew!

If you use the student loan default repayment schedule, it will take you almost 10 years to pay off your student loan. The student loan system default repayment term is 114 months, and most people go with the default without giving a second's thought to the cost of the loan. A graduate with $27,000 in student loans who goes for the default repayment schedule at 2015's fixed rates will pay $12,310 in interest.

Want to pay less interest? Once you've got a steady job, consolidate your student loans with an aggressive repayment schedule. That'll mean convincing a bank to give you a loan at a lower interest rate than you're paying in your student loan. Plan to take 3 to 5 years to pay off an undergrad degree, 5 to 7 years for a master's, and 7 to 10 years if your mommy gets to call you "doctor."

To figure out how to calculate your repayment schedule, read Rule #9: Calculate Your Own Debt Repayment Plan.

RULE #13: TERM INSURANCE IS NOT BETTER THAN PERMANENT

The "term versus permanent insurance" debate has raged since Joan Rivers was a teenager. Proponents on both sides like to slag the other for trying to steal your money. In the end, they've just made consumers wary about buying any kind of life insurance because it all feels like a rip-off. It's not. Life insurance is an important part of your financial foundation. And only you can decide what the right type of insurance is for YOU.

Term insurance, which covers you for a specified time frame, costs less because the payout is limited to a death benefit alone. It may be the best fit for those who are older—say 45 years and over—for whom permanent insurance would cost way too much or for those who need a whopping amount of insurance for a specific period of time—say, 10 to 25 years. Think protecting a young family. Think paying off a mortgage or other debt. Term insurance is an expense, like rent. While it will give you comfort and peace of mind, it accumulates no residual value.

If you want insurance coverage to last your lifetime, permanent insurance, including whole and universal life, is a better choice. Permanent insurance not only provides you with a death benefit that does not expire, it also includes a savings portion through which you can build up a cash value. Later you can borrow against that cash value or withdraw the cash value to help meet some future goal. If term insurance is rent, then permanent insurance is more like a mortgage payment;

in the early years there isn't a lot of asset accumulation, but over the long term the money pot will grow.

While it's true that term insurance is cheaper than permanent insurance, that's because the statistics are in favour of the insurance company not having to make a payout. With permanent insurance the company will have to pay; it's only a matter of when.

I bought my life insurance when I was 30. It's a whole life plan, and many people scoffed at me. At the time I had a mortgage but no husband or kids, so I just wanted to make sure I'd have insurance if I ever needed it. I've been paying just under $90 a month for $200,000 in coverage. By the time I turn 65, I will have paid $37,800 in premiums, but my policy will have a guaranteed cash value of $32,000. That means 35 years of life insurance coverage will have cost me $5,800, or $13.81 a month.

Don't pick a particular type of insurance just because you've heard it's what everyone should buy. Figure out what you need in coverage and how long you have to keep that coverage in place. Then shop for the policy that best addresses your specific issues. And please, please don't confuse the illustrations—or financial examples—you'll get on permanent insurance with reality. Life insurance illustrations are designed to show how much cash value a policy will build over time. But illustrations are only projections of what might happen; they are not guarantees. If the underlying investments don't perform as illustrated, you'll end up with less, so don't count your chickens before they hatch.

RULE #14: DON'T LET YOUR LENDER DECIDE HOW MUCH HOME YOU SHOULD BUY

This replaces the rule "Your lender wouldn't give you more than you could afford to repay." Ha!

It's all very well and good to go get prequalified for a mortgage. But letting your lender decide how much you can afford to borrow is a little like putting a fox in charge of the hen house. You do know the lender wants to make money, right? And if he's doing it on your back—hey, you're the buyer, and you know the saying: Buyer Beware!

It doesn't matter how much mortgage you qualify for; that should NOT be the determining factor in how much home you buy. I am more than a little surprised at the amounts that lenders have been throwing at people over the past decade. Since normal lending criteria have gone out the window, apparently just the desire to win the business drives the decision. And since so many people are taking on homes with down payments of less than 20% and have to be insured by the Canadian Mortgage and Housing Corporation (CMHC) anyway, there's absolutely no risk to the bank in giving you more mortgage than you can manage. You know who will end up covering CMHC's butt if the lenders start collecting on defaulted mortgages, don't you? Yup, YOU, the taxpayer!

I'm not exaggerating when I say that lenders are perfectly happy to lend you far more than you can afford to repay. In 2011, a study came out showing that 700,000 Canadians couldn't handle a $200 per month increase in their mortgage payments, while another 200,000 Canadians couldn't manage ANY increase at all. With interest rates at historical lows, there's only one way for rates and payments to go: Up!

The rule of thumb is to not spend more than 35% of your net income on housing expenses, including mortgage payments, property taxes, insurance, utilities, and maintenance.

If you bring home $3,750 and your mate earns $4,225 NET (after taxes) a month, you have a total net income of $7,975. Multiply by 35 and divide that by 100 ($7,975 × 35 ÷ 100 = $2,791). That gives you $2,791 you can afford to spend on shelter.

What's it going to cost for your property taxes? It'll depend on where you live, but let's say it'll be about $300 a month. How about your home insurance? A hundred dollars a month should be about right. Then there are utilities: heating, electricity, water, sewage. Mine cost me about $225 a month. And home maintenance? If you pay condo fees, use those plus an additional $200 a month for stuff you have to do inside your unit. No condo fees? Estimate 3% of the value of the home, sans property. For the sake of a projection, start with an estimate of $500 a month for maintenance. Add up all those costs. That's a whopping $1,125—NOT including the mortgage payment. That's what we'll have to figure out next.

So, if you have $2,791 to spend on shelter, and you're spending $1,125 on everything but your mortgage, you have up to $1,666 to spend on your mortgage payment. Time to head over to a mortgage calculator to play with the numbers to see how much mortgage you can afford.

Plug in different mortgage amounts and change your amortization—how long you'll take to pay the mortgage off in full—to see which number comes closest to what you can afford. Don't squeeze yourself into the biggest mortgage you can theoretically manage, particularly if rates are going to go up and a renewal down the road will take your mortgage payment higher. As a rule of thumb, use the five-year mortgage rate for your calculation, even if you're choosing a shorter term.

If you're over your head on housing, it means having very little life. It can also mean having to use credit to supplement your cash flow, digging yourself a hole that'll just add to your misery. If you must spend more than 35% because home prices are so high where you live, you better have no consumer debt so you can use that allotment (15%) to make your home a manageable expense. And you better be prepared to spend less money on just about everything else in your life.

RULE #15: DON'T WAIT TO INVEST

Old rule: "I'll invest when I know more about the market."

Stop procrastinating. Sure, it may feel scary and it may take some work to figure out how to make your money work as hard as you do. But figure it out you must.

Investing is anything you do to make your money earn more money. If you put your money in a savings account earning 0.25%, it's invested. Not well, since competitive savings accounts will pay you 1% more, but it's earning money. If you buy a GIC, a mutual fund, a stock, bond, or index, you are investing. The investment world is HUGE, but the only way to get a handle on it is to start. NOW.

Do you think some magical can opener is going to come out of the sky, open up your skull, and pour in everything you need to know to get comfortable with investing? If you aren't putting your money to work, you need to find a course, read a book, follow a blog or three, and learn. Learn. LEARN. Remaining ignorant isn't the answer. The two biggest things that affect how much money you'll have in the future are

1. how long you have for the money to grow, and
2. how much return your investments earn.

You should also practise a little before you leap whole hog into investing. There are dozens of sites on the Web that will let you create an imaginary stock portfolio, track and trade your investments, and develop some skills as an investor. Go to Google, search "investment simulator online," and see what pops up. Your bank's direct investing website may also offer a practice account you can sign up to use until you're ready for the real thing.

The objective of playing before paying is to make some of the mistakes beginners inevitably make—through ignorance, excitement, or fear—while you're still using pretend money. I'm talking about things like becoming overconfident because you've been on a "winning streak," going with a "tip," and bailing at exactly the wrong time because you're scared. Get the novice mistakes out of your system and you'll lose a lot less money when you finally do hit that trade button.

Avoid online stock market games, since they tend to reward players for making the most money in the shortest period of time and teach very little about the long-term skill of investing. To win at one of those games, you'll likely have to assume an extremely aggressive investment style, which has no bearing on how you'll choose to invest when you're doing so with your own hard-earned money.

So how long should you practise before you jump into investing real money? Does six months sound like a long time? Think of all the years of training and experience most money managers have. Six months is a blink of an eye. You must create a long enough time frame while you're in practice mode to experience some market volatility and see how you feel about it. If the market takes a plunge, do you feel okay or do you sigh with relief because it isn't real money? That should tell you something about your risk profile. And if you can't keep up with the news, the re-evaluation of company fundamentals, the monitoring necessary to manage your own investment portfolio, you might think twice about taking it on as one of your jobs in real life. And then, of course, you might just stink at it, in which case you need a guide to help you.

Would it surprise you to learn that I have an investment guy (we'll call him Patrick, because that's his name) who does my investing for me? Hey, do I look like I have the time to keep my eyes glued to the markets? That doesn't negate the need for me to know what the hell Patrick is talking about when he calls me up and says, "Gail, you know what we should do?" But I'm smart enough to know that it's Patrick's job to watch the markets, and my job to ensure I know that what Patrick is suggesting fits my style, investment horizon, and risk profile.

If you are going to become an investor, you must know at least as much as you would expect a broker to know. Yup . . . that's a lot. But if you're taking on the role of advisor to yourself, you better be able to answer all the questions correctly.

Go slowly. Now that you're determined to become educated so you can take control of your money, commit the time and effort necessary to become an expert. Understand your investment goals, clearly define your investment time horizons, and know how much risk you can afford to take before choosing your investments. And keep learning.

RULE #16: DON'T PUT ONE GUY IN CHARGE OF THE MONEY

It's not unusual for one person in a relationship to assume the nitty-gritty of managing the daily finances. Maybe it's because one partner is more inclined towards these tasks. Or maybe one is just more interested, or has more time. But when the other mate is excluded or totally abdicates responsibility, things can turn ugly. Your partner may sail your love boat onto a reef or grow resentful at always having to do the detail. If you're in a relationship and you want it to last, each of you should not only feel involved in the big financial decisions but also understand the day-to-day details.

Take turns managing the spending journal or your budget and have regular conversations so that both of you are clear about what's going on. Then you'll both be in the know and working to the same ends. Taking turns also means that one person doesn't have to deal with all the crap, while the other merrily laughs off the stress and frustration with "You're managing the money, so this is your problem to deal with."

FAMILY

RULE #17: NEEDS MUST COME BEFORE WANTS

Needs are the things we must have to keep body and soul together. We need a roof over our heads, we need food in our bellies, we need to be loved.

Wants are the things we really like. While we need a roof, we want a four-bedroom, three-bathroom house on a nice lot, with parking, schools close by, and not too much traffic. And while we need food, we want the chicken stuffed with goat's cheese and sundried tomatoes in a lovely basil-tomato sauce.

If you believe that you need a vacation, a full-out cable package and a cell phone, you're confusing wants with needs. None of these things stand between you and a grave. They aren't needs, plain and simple, no matter how often you say they are.

Wants are fine. It's not a matter of only satisfying your needs and leaving all your wants to wilt from a lack of attention. It's a matter of making sure your needs—your must-haves—are dealt with first.

You need to keep a roof over your head, but you don't need to live in a McMansion. If your cost of accommodation is pushing your budget out of whack and there's nowhere to cut back, it may be time to call the movers!

A good rule of thumb to follow is to spend 50% of your net income on needs and 25% on wants. (The rest goes to debt repayment and savings.)

If you spend far more money on wants than on needs—leaving needs unattended—you're a glutton. And if you're putting your desire to go out for dinner before your need for savings, you're a money moron.

CASH
MANAGEMENT

RULE #18: CREDIT IS GOOD—DEBT IS BAD

Credit isn't evil. It's a tool that must be used carefully. Know the rules and you can use credit to your advantage. Have no self-control and credit will turn into debt and eat your future.

It's all well and good to go out and put a $120 dinner on a credit card, but if you don't pay that balance off in full when the bill comes in, you're just dumb. Why? Well, you had a nice dinner, right? Then you went home and pooped! Dinner is gone. But the balance you're carrying lives on. That's bad debt.

Think of credit as a tool that can help you achieve your goals. Want to go to school to increase your earning power? Student loans can help. Want to buy a home? You're probably going to need a mortgage. Need a car to get that job? Not my favourite use of credit, but acceptable if you manage the costs. Want to put in that new kitchen, take a trip with the fam, get those new appliances? DON'T USE CREDIT.

It's easy to use credit to buy consumables that we think we must have TODAY! But if you can't afford to pay for them in full TODAY, then you're indulging yourself and turning credit into bad debt. And debt has a way of haunting you for eons.

Outside of the things that will outlast the credit you may have to use, like a car or a house, don't step into the quagmire of debt. Instead, use credit to build a good history so when there are things for which you must borrow, you can do it on the best terms.

RULE #19: WRITE DOWN WHAT YOU'RE SPENDING

Whenever I introduce the idea of keeping a spending journal, people rush at me with a dozen reasons why nailing themselves down on money isn't something they want to do. They claim there's no passion, no spontaneity in chronicling their every purchase. To have a fun and breezy life, they must be able to buy on a whim an ice-cream cone or a few magazines, a cup of tea or a new pair of shoes. Writing down every purchase would actually make them "consumed" by money, rather than financially liberated. Oh, give me a break!

It's not a matter of being consumed with money. Your money is a tool. It's a resource and it's your job to manage it. You frickin' haul your sorry ass out of bed every day, drag yourself to work, and bust your butt to make a dollar. Why wouldn't you write down where you spend it? If you want to go and buy some magazines, buy 'em. Write it down in your spending journal and you have held yourself accountable.

At the end of the month when you add up all the money you spent on magazines (you can substitute any other purchase for "magazines" here) and see that you spent $76.24, either you'll say, "Great, I'm so glad I did that," or you'll say, "Lord love a duck!" Either way, you will KNOW. You are not being unconscious about where your money is going.

Today, buy yourself a notebook and start writing down every penny you spend. Write the current balance in your bank account at the top of each page.

Each time you use your credit or debit card, write a cheque, or take a cash withdrawal, enter the amount you have spent and deduct it from your balance.

Every time you make a deposit, add it to your balance.

Remember to debit the automatic withdrawals that come out of your account: your mortgage or rent payments, car loan, savings, retirement account deposit, utilities, car insurance, and the like.

When your credit card bill and bank statements come in, check the transactions against your list in your spending journal. If there's something on your statement that's not your doing, call right away and identify the wayward transaction.

You can carry your notebook around, or you can bring home your receipts and enter them at the end of the day (which is the way I do it). Account for every cent you spend so you know what you're really doing with your money.

Here's what a set of spending journal entries might look like:

JUNE		CREDIT	DEBIT	BALANCE
1	Pay	1,875.00		1,875.00
2	Rent		-825.00	1,050.00
3	Car Insurance		-222.36	827.64
4	Emergency savings		-25.00	802.64
5	RRSP		-50.00	752.64
6	Debit: Groceries		-36.72	715.92
7	Cell (conf# 0071)		-57.77	658.15
8	Debit: Groceries		-23.24	634.91
9	CC: New Pants		-39.99	594.92
10	CC: Birthday present		-27.65	567.27
11	HST Rebate	60.76		628.03
12	Cheq #18 Mag Sub		-18.99	609.04

Thoughts about some of the entries: First, I don't actually number the entries; I've just done it so I can refer to them here. If you're meticulous, you'll date your entries, but that's not a must.

Lines 1, 11: When you deposit money, you add it to your balance. Sometimes this will be a paycheque; sometimes it may be an expense reimbursement or a government rebate. Everything you deposit into your account is entered as a credit. When you are carrying a balance from one month to the next, you enter that number at the top of the new month's worksheet.

Lines 2, 3: Money that's automatically deducted from your account is entered first so you aren't tempted to spend the money and then bounce the debit. If you have several auto-debits and are paid a couple of times a month or more, you'll have to match your debits to your pays.

Lines 4, 5: Savings are deducted automatically. If you wait until you see what you have left to save, you'll never have anything left.

Lines 6, 8: Debits are deducted when you do them.

Line 7: Note any online bill payment confirmation numbers.

Lines 9, 10: Credit card charges are also deducted when you make your purchase. When your bill comes in, check the statement against the charges you've deducted to make sure everything is there. The way I handle payments on my credit card is to write a letter in my spending journal beside everything that's come in on a single statement. So for June, I might use the letter "F" and write an "F" beside all the credit card charges I'm paying. Then I'd create a single-line entry in the spending journal:

Paid Credit Card $67.64 Conf# 1234254 June 28/12

This entry won't change the balance in your spending journal because the charges made have already been deducted. But having all the info in one place makes it really easy to check back later on.

Keep in mind that not all credit card charges may come through in a single month. You may have an entry you've deducted that doesn't have a letter beside it in your spending journal. When the next statement comes in, the charge should show up. But you don't have to worry about having forgotten that dinner you had with your sister, because you deducted it when you ate the food, so the money has been set aside to pay the bill. See how swell this system is?

Line 12: If you write a cheque, you include it in your spending journal (you can do away with the chequebook register) noting the cheque number and what the cheque was for. If the person you wrote the cheque to doesn't cash the cheque immediately, it won't mess with your money management system because you've already made the deduction, so the money is "gone" and you can't spend it twice.

Money is a tool. Use it wisely and you can have everything you want. Misuse it and you'll find yourself up to your armpits in alligators. It may take a while before you feel them snapping at your throat, but I guarantee you will. If you aren't writing down what you're spending, you have no idea whether you're being wise with your money or not.

RULE #20: KEEP LEARNING—KEEP GROWING

Once upon a time we thought that our brains hit a peak at some arbitrary age we had chosen and proceeded to decline from there. We know better now. New learning makes new connections in the brain, keeping us sharp. But the learning has to be NEW; the brain gets bored quickly, and so new and increasingly challenging experiences are important to keep it hopping.

When was the last time you challenged yourself to do something new? Learn a new skill? Cook a new recipe with ingredients you can barely pronounce? Take a new road to an old destination? When was the last time you opened your mind to something completely new?

There are always new things to learn about when it comes to your money. There are investments to investigate, tax tactics to tweak, and debt-repayment strategies to digest. Doing things differently won't always be easy. And taking in new knowledge can sometimes make your brain ache. But it's good for you. So do it.

Growth is hard. Change is hard. And doing something different—even something that's good for you—isn't always comfortable. Accept the discomfort as the first sign that you are thinking (and acting?) differently, and give yourself room to grow. Don't be too hard on yourself; mistakes happen. Just recognize them and move on. And when you're successful, look at what you did that worked and incorporate that approach into your next challenge.

FINDING
BALANCE

RULE #21: IT'S NOT HOW MUCH YOU MAKE—IT'S HOW MUCH YOU KEEP

Saving is a habit. Either you get into the habit of saving and have something in the future, or you don't. If you wait until you earn "enough" money to start this habit, you'll never start. If you spend every red cent you make, it doesn't matter how much you make—you'll never have anything.

Saving is the act of "not spending." It is a conscious decision to take money you could have used to buy stuff and set it aside for some future need. When you save—when you accumulate a stash of cash for some point down the road—you give yourself options. Having savings gives you the flexibility to cope with whatever crap life throws your way. No savings—no options.

Start with as little as a dollar a day. Set up an automatic transfer of money from your chequing account to a high-interest savings account every month. As you earn more, set aside part of your new earnings to boost your savings. If you don't, your lifestyle will inflate—you'll get used to spending more money— and you'll have nothing to show for your hard work later on.

While it might be easy to save when times are good, the real test will be to do without something you really want so you can keep saving even when the money is thin. And since you can be sure times won't always be good, having something set aside for the leaner months or years can save your butt.

Saving is an investment in your future. Money in the bank gives you choices. Nothing in life makes you feel more in control than having choices.

SAVING

RULE #22: EVERYBODY NEEDS A BUDGET

I don't care who tells you that budgets don't work, that making a budget is stupid, or that they'd rather get a root canal than tie themselves to a budget. EVERYBODY NEEDS A BUDGET.

Sure, you may be able to get to the end of the month before you get to the end of the money because you make a whack of cash and you live a simple life, but that is no reason not to have a budget. Only people who are LAZY and can't be bothered think a budget is a waste of time. Ask those who live on a budget and they'll tell you a budget creates a sense of freedom. Since you have a plan for how you will spend your money, executing the plan is easy peasy.

Well, not always. Sometimes expenses jump up and bite you in your budget. But at least you have a place to start when trying to decide which Peter you'll have to steal from to pay Paul. Without a budget, you'll grab money from any pool to cover your butt, likely creating another crisis down the road.

I have a budget. I'm a big ol' TV star and I make enough money to not have to think about it, but I do. I use a spending journal. I track my spending against my budget every frickin' month, not because I love it, but because I work hard for my money and I'm not going to let it slip through my fingers. I never know when this gravy train will end and I'm going to make sure I have enough money socked away so that when it does I don't look back and say wistfully, "Gosh, I wish I'd saved more of my money instead of spending it on stupid stuff." (Said in a whiny, singsong voice.)

When you hear people, including experts, say that budgets

don't work, it means they don't want to do the work entailed in keeping a budget balanced. If you think you can do better without a budget—a written-down and paid-attention-to budget—none of the rest of the rules in this book will be of much use, so stop now and pass this book on to someone who is smarter than you.

If you're ready to make a budget, go on to Rule #23: Make a Budget.

RULE #23: MAKE A BUDGET

Whether paper-based or electronic, the discipline of managing your budget will help to keep you organized. Annual bills, such as car insurance, won't surprise you, sending shock waves through your cash flow. And unexpected expenses, which have a category in a spending plan, won't throw you for a loop.

A budget consists of two parts: income and expenses. Income is the money that comes in: your salary, commission, dividends or interest income, alimony, child support, pension, or disability income. It doesn't include money you think you might get. So, if your bonus is not guaranteed, don't include it in your budget. Keep it in reserve to boost your RRSP or take you to the sunshine next winter.

Expenses are the items you have to pay. Some expenses are fixed: think rent or mortgage payment, car payment, telephone bill and home insurance. (Divide annual bills, such as insurance, by 12 to come up with a monthly amount.) Some expenses are variable: think food, gas, entertainment, and clothing.

Don't take shortcuts when trying to build a budget, guessing at how much you spend and then blaming the budget when it's off because you used inaccurate data or ignored less regular expenses (insurance, hockey fees, property taxes). Hey, you've heard the term "garbage in, garbage out." It's dead true for budgeting. And if you're not prepared to do the work to come up with a realistic budget, and to tweak the budget as your life changes, forgedaboutit!

The best way to figure out your expenses is to look at what you've been spending. Collect your bank statements, credit card bills, and whatever other records you have of where your money went over the past six months. Put each bill in an appropriate category—such as utilities, food, clothing, child care, gifts—total the figures for each category, and divide by six. That's your monthly average. Add the categories together. That's what you've been spending. Here's how to do it:

1. **Get yourself a budget worksheet.** You can use the Interactive Budget on my website (under Resources), download a budget worksheet from the Web, or make your own spreadsheet.

2. **Put in your fixed expenses.** Put them all in, but know that some are must-haves (like rent or mortgage payments) and some are nice-to-haves (like cable and cell phone.) You may have to sacrifice those nice-to-haves if you can't get your budget to balance.

3. **Saving, debt repayment, and emergency savings are must-haves.** While you may be tempted to ignore savings if your budget is tight, don't. Even $25 a month gets you on the right path. Totally ignoring savings until "things get better" means you're stuck in Never Never Saving Land. Just a little is all it takes to cross the border.

4. **Drop in the variable expenses.** Again, some are must-haves and some are nice-to-haves. You have to eat, and

you have to be able to get to work. But whether you can afford to munch organic or ride in a cab will be determined by how much money you have available.

5. **Look at bottom line.** If the budget still doesn't balance, you'll have to find places to cut back. Start with your variable expenses, adjusting the amounts down. Some things you may have to get rid of completely. If you're in debt, you can't afford booze, cigarettes, manies and pedies, haircuts, coffee, lunches out, or video games. You will have a very limited entertainment budget, and you'll have to have all your fun (sports included) out of that money. Food gets chopped back: you can afford ground beef, not filet mignon. It's important that everyone eat healthily, but you're going to be very careful, shop only for what is in season, use coupons, and make every last bite count. And no one gets to eat out!

6. **Then look at your nice-to-have fixed expenses.** Cut your cable. Cut your phone bill. Cut your utilities. Consolidate your car and home insurance, raise your deductible and cut your insurance premiums. Sometimes there's a crossover between must-haves and nice-to-haves, such as when your only pair of winter boots is no longer serviceable; then that "clothing" item becomes a must have. This is particularly true if you have kids who will insist on growing. In this case, you put in a must-have number to cover the basic needs, and then upgrade it

to a nice-to-have number for all the extra things you will want. If you have to cut back later on, the nice-to-haves have got to go!

7. **Be realistic.** If you cut back on a category to get the budget to balance, knowing full well that you'll have to spend the money even if it's not in the budget, you're playing a game, not making a budget. If you leave out categories like clothing, home maintenance, fun, family gifts, medical expenses, and car repairs, you're not being realistic.

8. **Be prepared to adapt on the fly.** Crap happens and sometimes you need to spend money you didn't plan on spending. If your "car repair" money hasn't built up enough to cover the cost of the new tires you had to buy, you may have to "borrow" money from your home maintenance fund in the short term.

The bottom line is that you can't spend more money than you make. If you can't get the budget to balance, you either cut costs or make more money. Debt has to be repaid. And you have to save something both for emergencies and for the long term.

If you think you can keep flying by the seat of your pants forever, good luck with that. If you've decided to take control of your financial future, congratulations. Create a budget that balances and you've taken a big step towards making your money work for you.

I swear by my budget; it's what keeps me honest. When I review what I've been spending, I can reassess if those expenses are true indications of a change in my circumstances or me just not paying attention. I'm not a slave to my budget. If I go nuts on entertainment one month because there's a lot happening, I just look for places elsewhere to trim back. I make choices. Conscious choices. I'd much rather know I'm blowing my travel budget and make some adjustments elsewhere than be surprised with a credit card balance I can't pay off.

RULE #24: CALCULATE YOUR TAXES TO AVOID A TAX BILL

No, I'm not talking about filing your tax return by the deadline. I'm talking about knowing how much you're going to have to pay in taxes so you're sure the right amount is being deducted and you don't end up with a tax bill.

Whether you're working a second job, off on maternity or parental leave, or withdrawing money from an RRSP or RRIF, you need to account for all the income you receive to accurately determine how much you should be paying in taxes. It isn't your employer's job, the government's job, or the financial institution's job to make sure your taxes are paid in full. It's your job.

Let's take the example of Cathy, who was planning to go on maternity leave in June. As a well-paid social worker, Cathy will have already earned half her $67,000 (gross) salary by the time she leaves her job. That's a gross income up to her maternity leave of $33,500. While on maternity leave, she'll receive $485 a week, so she'll earn another $12,610 by the end of the year. Since the Employment Insurance (EI) system only cares about the EI money paid to Cathy, it'll deduct taxes on her mat leave income as if that's her only income, taking far less than she will actually owe once her before mat-leave income is factored in.

Here's what I told Cathy to do:

1. Add up the income you'll earn before you go on maternity leave (or after your maternity leave, if you'll be returning to work mid-year.) In Cathy's case, that's a gross income up to her maternity leave of $33,500.

2. Add up the gross income you'll receive from EI. Cathy will receive $12,610.

3. Add the two numbers together. Cathy's total gross income: $46,110.

4. Now add up all the taxes that have been deducted from all your income. If it's not clear from your paperwork what you've paid in taxes on your income so far, call your payroll department to get the specific amount for your calculations. You'll need to wait for your first maternity cheque to see just how much tax has been withheld on it. Cathy had $7,300 deducted at work, and would have another $1,200 deducted on her maternity benefits, for a total tax paid of $8,500.

5. Go to an online tax calculation website (make sure it's Canadian; one I really like is http://lsminsurance.ca /calculators/canada/income-tax) and enter your total gross income. See how much tax the calculator says you'll owe. Since Cathy lives in Manitoba, she'd actually owe $9,990 in income tax.

6. Deduct the amount that's already being withheld from the amount you'll owe. So Cathy will have a tax shortfall of $1,490.

7. Set aside the difference in an "I must pay my taxes account" so when the time comes to file your return, you'll have the money ready. Over the remaining six months, Cathy will have to save $249 a month to make sure she has enough to pay her taxes.

Remember, if your maternity leave runs over two calendar years, you'll have to do this calculation twice.

Regardless of where you're getting your income, you need to do the math to make sure you're setting aside enough for taxes and don't end up with a bill that throws your financial plan off track.

RULE #25: NEVER IMPULSE-SHOP

Back-to-school, Christmas, weddings, vacations, birthdays—any kind of special event—prompts us to blow our brains out on stuff we think we must buy. The only way to avoid the seasonal shopping trap is to figure out how much you have to spend. Yes 'um, that means making a budget. (See Rule #23: Make a Budget.)

Regardless of the season and how good a reason you have to go shopping, make a list of what you need and want. Write an N or W beside each item on your list to help prioritize.

Inventory what you already have so you aren't re-buying stuff you own. Cross the things you have at home off your shopping list.

Shop the sales. Look at flyers. Comparison-shop using the Internet. Find the best deal going.

If you must go over your "budgeted" shopping amount—hey, sometimes you underestimate and get caught—you can only do so if you decide where you're going to trim elsewhere in your budget that month. Carrying the difference on your credit card is not the solution.

RULE #26: DON'T HAVE YOUR CREDIT WITH THE BANK THAT HAS YOUR DEPOSITS

This replaces the old rule "Consolidate all your business and get a better deal."

Polly wrote me in distress. When her husband was laid off, she did her level best to keep the bills up-to-date on a third of the family's regular income. She cut the cable, quit the gym, and made every single meal at home, chopping her grocery bill in half. But they had several credit cards with balances, and after a few months Polly couldn't even make the minimum payments anymore. She stopped paying her department store card bill first, then her bank credit card. She was stunned when she found out that the bank just went into her account and took the balance she owed on her credit card. "Can they do that?" she asked me. "They made my mortgage payment at another bank bounce, so now I'm in even more trouble. What am I going to do now?"

Yes, Polly, they can do that.

Banks have a clause in their client agreements that gives them the right to dip into your account to recover money you owe them. I've often talked about how the Tax Man can do this, but he's not the only wolf at your door. If you owe your bank money—on a credit card, on a line of credit, on overdraft—it can decide it wants its money back and dip into any account you may hold there to get it. Boing, boing . . . that's your mortgage payment bouncing!

Most people don't realize that revolving credit such as credit cards, lines of credit, and overdraft protection is callable credit: banks can "call it," or ask for it back, at any time and you'll HAVE to give it to them. Well, if they ask nicely, right? Not necessarily. If you have accounts with positive balances at the same place, you are carrying your debt. They can just take it!

Can this happen to you? You betcha. All you need are the right circumstances: a tough economy, a tight credit market, a "let's get our money back" decision from on high at the bank.

The only way to protect yourself is to NEVER have your credit card or line of credit with the same bank in which you keep your deposits.

RULE #27: DON'T TITHE IF YOU OWE MONEY

Are you in debt and tithing or giving money to charity? That's not your money to give, so stop.

I have nothing against tithing if it makes you happy. After all, it's your money and you should do with it as you wish. *But it has to be your money.* That's the line I draw on the tithing and charitable-giving thing. If it isn't your money, you shouldn't be tithing. So I do have a BIG problem with tithing when you're in debt.

For the people who believe they have to tithe—that it is an integral part of their belief system, part of who they are— then heads up: it's time to start deferring your own pleasures and needs in order to give. Pass on the coffee, say no to the vacation, skip the new sweater. Give YOUR money from your heart. If sacrifice is required, so be it.

To give with real spirit, as opposed to by rote or by rule, is to take what you HAVE and share it to someone else. It is about prioritizing the needs of others over our own wants. It requires thinking about how you will spend your money so that you can also afford to give some of that money in support of your beliefs.

If you are in debt, you aren't actually tithing your own money. Your "gift" is being supported by lenders far and wide who are making lots 'n lots of money on your donation.

If you can't afford to live within your means, you aren't demonstrating responsible living and you don't have the right to salve your conscience by tithing. Only solvent people have the right to tithe, and if you don't have your crap together yet, you shouldn't be doing it. Tithing 10% and then putting $500 a month on your line of credit is hypocritical because you are not giving what YOU have.

I'm all for sharing. If you must tithe to keep within your religious guidelines, then you must also make the commitment to tithe from your resources. If you can't afford to do that, you must rethink your decision.

Sharing doesn't have to be money. You can share your experience. You can share your time. You can share your goods . . . all that stuff you bought that got you into debt in the first place. What are you prepared to give up so that someone else can have some?

RULE #28: DON'T USE PREPAID CARDS

When prepaid credit and debit cards first came on the scene, they were heralded as a huge convenience. You could load up your food money for a month and use the card to stay on budget. Or you could send your kid off to school with spending money that was safer than cash. But at what cost?

Some prepaid cards come with a slew of fees: activation fees, withdrawal fees, fees for statements, even dormancy fees. Some cards charge a one-time activation fee of up to $9.95. Others charge a lower activation fee—say, $2—but then have monthly fees that kick in down the road. A card might come with a purchase price of just $3.95 but then have an inactivity fee of $1.50 a month if you're not using the card. Really. They're charging you for NOT using the card. And they'll charge you to receive statements, which means you'll have to pay to see if your card was double-swiped. While you might think a prepaid card is safer than cash, if it is stolen, the money could be gone for good, since the zero liability protection offered on traditional credit cards is more limited on prepaid cards.

Prepaid cards also do squat to build your credit history. Since no "payment" is required, no history is being built. These cards are pretty much just transactional tools, like gift cards. Prepaid cards feel like money already spent, giving the user license to shop. This is particularly true for young 'uns just starting out.

Prepaid cards are yet one more costly way to distance you from using cash. If you don't trust yourself with plastic, prepaid cards aren't the answer. Cash is.

RULE #29: YOU *CAN* HAVE IT ALL, JUST NOT ALL AT THE SAME TIME

Life is about making choices. You choose to have children. You choose to go back to school. You choose to buy a home. With those choices come gains, but also things you must give up. If you choose to have children, you won't have a single shirt without food stains for at least six months. Choose to go back to school full-time and you give up some of your income and what that money could buy. Choose to buy a home and you give up eating out in restaurants because you have less money, not to mention less time for yourself, because the time you would have spent reading, you now have to use to cut the lawn and change the furnace filter.

Everything in life comes with a cost. And while you can eventually have it all, it takes a whole lifetime to achieve that goal. In the short term, you must make choices about what you'll give up to get the thing that's at the top of your "I really want this" list.

If you believe you can have it all at the same time, you won't be able to do anything with the focus it takes to do it well. And in trying to have it all, you'll wear yourself out completely. Having it all is just not possible. If you've bought the bull that you can, you're likely always wondering why you don't measure up.

Stop. Today, figure out what's at the top of your "I really want this" list. Focus on that. Recognize what you may have to give up. Reconcile yourself to the changes you'll have to make. Then go get what you want.

This reckoning is something you'll have to do all the time. It's not a one-off exercise. Each time you're faced with change, with a choice, with new opportunity, you must go through the exercise of deciding what you're prepared to give up to get what you want.

Managed right, over time, you'll have the sense that you have had it all. That's a well-lived life!

RULE #30: EVEN CHICKENS CAN INVEST SAFELY

If you think you can't be an investor because you have no appetite for risk, think again. There ARE ways to make sure your capital is safe while earning potentially more than in a GIC. But you have to be willing to swallow some higher fees.

If you're determined to protect your capital, but you want to partake of the feast being served up in equity markets around the world, try this:

First, invest your money in a monthly pay GIC—one that gives you your interest every month. While you may earn up to 0.25% less in interest, your principal will be guaranteed. Each month, take the interest you're earning and invest in an aggressive, growth-oriented mutual fund. Your principal will be safe, and over the long term, you'll be able to participate in growth in equities to increase the overall return on your investment.

Another alternative would be to invest in a combination of strip bonds and equity investments. Strip bonds are bought at a discount and guaranteed to mature at a specific amount. Use some of your investment dollars to buy a strip bond that matures at the full value of your original capital. If you were investing $20,000, for example, you'd buy a strip that would mature at $20,000 in 10 years. Use the rest of your investment dollars to buy the index, or individual stocks, as long as you know what you're buying (and can explain it to a teenager).

If you need a guarantee to get into the market so you don't panic and jump out should there be a nasty spill, check out a segregated fund. Seg funds look like mutual funds and taste like mutual funds, but the icing on the seg fund cake is the principal guarantee—a promise that you'll get back 75% to 100% of your capital after 10 years even if the market has gone down the sewer. The guarantee also becomes effective if you die before the 10 years are up, so your heirs won't be left holding a plate of crumbs. This guarantee comes with a price: seg funds are served up with a higher management expense ratio (MER) than are mutual funds, which have no guarantee. Here's the question only you can answer: "Is the guarantee worth it?" Maybe so if you wouldn't have begun investing without it.

Just because your primary focus is on the preservation of your capital—keeping your money safe—it doesn't mean you have to miss out completely on the potentially higher returns the stock market offers. You just have to show some creativity!

RULE #31: ENROL IN YOUR COMPANY PENSION PLAN

About half the people who have access to company pension plans don't bother to sign up. Really? Your employer wants to give you more money and you won't take it?

Often people say they can't be bothered to fill out the paperwork. That's a lie. The real reason is that people don't want to have to match their employers' contributions. Unwilling to give up a nickel in spending money, people forgo the matching their employers would do—and turn their backs on perfectly good money.

Hello, that's like walking away from a raise.

If you're living so close to the edge that you simply can't afford to give up the money that would be your contribution to the plan, you need to take a good look at your spending. That fancy-dancy cable or cell phone package is not worth your future.

If the thought of going without your small indulgences for the sake of having some money 20, 30, or 40 years in the future just doesn't seem worth it, think about what your life will be like when you retire and have no money saved. Not spending money today means you'll have some in the future. If you think the future will take care of itself, you're deluding yourself.

If you work for a company that offers a savings matching retirement program, go and sign up. Today!

SAVING

RULE #32: ENJOY YOUR MONEY ONCE YOU'RE BACK IN THE BLACK

So you've balanced your budget, paid off your debt, and you've got your emergency fund stashed away somewhere safe. You're saving for retirement, you've got the kids' educational savings set up, and you've established some goals for yourself. Life is good.

You have a bit of cash left every month and you're trying to decide what to do with it. Sure, you could boost your savings even further, but you're thinking maybe there are better things you could do with that money.

If you've been single-minded about balancing your budget and creating a sound financial foundation, you may have forgotten just how much fun FUN is. Maybe you miss hunting through flea markets with your bestie, sipping coffee with your sister, or experimenting in the kitchen. Haven't been skiing in dogs' years? Want to make that new quilt you've been talking about but are reluctant to shell out money to start? Hey, this may be the perfect time to do those things that bring you joy, teach you something new, or let you share with someone you love.

Use your money to strengthen bonds with family and friends. It's a great way to increase your happiness quotient. Studies show that close relationships have a lot to do with how happy we feel. Spring for a trip to see your old high-school chums or university roommate. Offer to bring your sister and her family to your place for a visit. Your saying "My treat" lets people who are themselves financially strapped consider doing things that they'd love to do but simply couldn't afford.

Use your money to reduce your stress. If you and your partner are working hard, busy with the kids, and can't find time to do the vacuuming, paying to have a clean house may be just the ticket. And if you're tired of yelling at your mate to get the garage, the basement, the shed cleaned up, hiring someone to do the dirty work would eliminate the need to nag.

Use your money on someone else. Making other people happy has this fabulous rebound effect. If you could help ease someone else's burden or just bring a little unexpected joy to another's very difficult life, the gift you give will be returned to you in spades. Would your child's teacher appreciate some new books? Would the elderly in the local home appreciate a bunch of new movies to while away the hours? How about building a treat basket for less advantaged neighbours and leaving it on the doorstep with a note that says, "I'm having a great day. Hope you have one too!"

Whatever you decide to do with your money, it should be something that will truly make YOU happy. Never mind what turns anyone else's crank; this is about using your money to fill your life with joy. Figure out what makes you happy, and then use your money to fill your life full.

RULE #33: SAVE WHILE YOU PAY OFF YOUR DEBT

Debt repayment is important. But so is establishing the savings habit. Debt-free isn't the Holy Grail. It's simply one step along the way to finding financial balance. If you don't have a balanced approach to your financial life, you're going to be off-kilter.

Never mind what The Spurts say about focusing all your extra money on debt repayment until you're out of debt. Being financially balanced is more important than rushing to debt-free. After all, you want to be debt-free forever, right? That takes a plan. And it takes balance.

Doing anything whole hog to the detriment of the other parts of your financial life is shortsighted. Not building your emergency fund means you'll be pushed back to using credit when the caca hits the fan. Not saving means you're delaying establishing a very good habit. Is there really ever a convenient time to start saving?

The right time to start saving is TODAY! And if that means you're putting aside $1 a day, so be it. Start. As for getting your debt paid off as fast as possible, don't do it to the detriment of the rest of your financial plan: your goals, spending plan, emergency fund, insurance, and estate plan. If you're serious about getting out of debt and you want it to happen quick like a bunny, get a second job, get a third job, get a better job, and get the debt gone. Bust your arse. Don't sacrifice your savings.

SAVING

RULE #34: WATCHING YOUR PENNIES DOESN'T MAKE YOU "CHEAP"!

I have known some cheap people. They are the folks who show up at a party with two bottles of beer and then drink a dozen. They are the people who leave the tax and tipping to everyone else at the table by throwing down the bare minimum to cover their tab. They are the dopes who are always bumming a ride, bumming a meal, bumming a drink with an "I'll get you next time."

Hey, nobody likes a tightwad, which is why jokes about being cheap make us laugh. Ever heard the one about being tighter than paper on the wall? How about the one about squeezing a nickel till the beaver poops!

Once upon a time, thrift was a virtue, and it needs to be thought of as virtuous again. If you've been erroneously associating thrift with being cheap, you need to reorient your thinking. The root of the word "thrift" is "thrive." Thrift isn't about being stingy. It's about building prosperity through careful management of resources. It isn't about being miserly. It's about embracing a way of life that lets ordinary people have a good life while they save and share.

Watching where your money is going and being mindful of how you're spending it doesn't make you cheap. It makes you smart!

RULE #35: DON'T OBSESS
ABOUT YOUR CREDIT SCORE

CREDIT

This replaces the old rule "Do anything to have the highest possible credit score."

I do not have the highest possible credit score. Does that surprise you? If you understand how the FICO score is calculated and the extent to which it is based on you doing the wrong thing with your credit, you'd get why I don't have the highest score. And you wouldn't want the highest score either.

The way to get a great credit score is to have access to lots of different forms of credit, leaving yourself overexposed to identity theft and fraud. You should also have nice high credit limits so you never get above the 30 to 50% mark with your spending, providing tons of opportunity to dig a huge debt hole. And you should make only the minimum payment on your credit, so you pay lots 'n lotsa interest. Yup, having a high credit score means you are a very, very profitable customer.

The very things that give you a high score—that make you a profitable customer—are completely counter to sound money management. Let's look at each one in a little more detail.

Lots of different types of credit. Credit scores award you for using different types of credit: credit cards, lines of credit, instalment loans. If you limit the amount and type of credit you use—which makes sense in a world full of ID fraud and computer glitches—your credit score will suffer. Lenders want you to make full use of their wide range of products, so they give you more points on your FICO score for using a variety of credit.

High credit limits. Under the credit scoring rules, you shouldn't have a credit-to-debt ratio (also referred to as your credit utilization) of more than 30 to 50% (depending on who you talk to, because the credit scoring system is a BIG secret) to collect the most points under the credit scoring system.

The credit-to-debt ratio is calculated like this:

Debt Used ÷ by Available Credit × 100 = Debt Load

So if you're carrying a $600 balance on a credit card with a limit of $2,000, your calculation looks like this:

$600 ÷ $2,000 × 100 = 30%

Now here's the kicker: *Just because you pay off your balance in full every month, it does not mean that the credit scoring system will rank you as a good customer.* The point—from the credit score (and lender's profitability) perspective—is for you to have lots and lots of credit. Really, it's about making sure you have enough rope to hang yourself. So despite the fact that you zero your card every month, the credit scoring system will penalize you if it randomly checks your credit utilization and you're up too high, even if you pay your balance off in full every single month. No one can predict the exact point when the credit scoring system checks your balance, so you could be at or close to your limit just before you plan to pay off the balance and you'd lose points big-time.

Minimum payments. If you carry a balance on your cards, paying only the minimum each month, you get more credit score points for being profitable than if you pay your balance off in full each month. Again, not exactly conducive to sound financial management.

The credit scoring system is a racket designed by lenders for self-serving purposes. It gives more points to people who are irresponsible because they have too much access to credit and are more focused on paying their minimum than on getting to debt-free. And it penalizes responsible borrowers so that when it comes time to borrow for a good reason—like a mortgage—lenders are justified in charging you a higher rate of interest because your credit score isn't as high as it could be.

If you aren't convinced yet, wrap your head around this: I worked with a 21-year-old earning $24,000 a year who was approved for a credit card limit of $15,000. He had neither the character (age and maturity), capacity (income), nor credit history (he was too young) to justify that kind of limit. But he had a GREAT credit score because he always paid his minimum on his previous credit card.

Not only does the credit score identify profitable customers (read "people who will pay lots 'n lots of interest), it can be used to make customers more profitable. Just ask all the folks who watched their limits arbitrarily cut (yah, they don't even have to tell you), and their credit utilization skyrocket. The next thing that happened was their credit scores dropped. And that justified credit card companies hiking their rates because those all-important credit scores had fallen.

Instead of using a credit scoring system that rewards borrowers who only pay their minimums, we should create a system that's based on financial sustainability. (We had one, but we threw it out the window when the easy-peasy credit score came along. Lazy lenders!) If we force lenders to do their jobs—assess each client's ability to actually handle the credit they are being given—instead of relying on the credit score, how can that be bad for business?

If you think this system sucks and you want things to be different, you'll need to become active in fighting against the use of the FICO system for granting credit. You can write to your Member of Parliament and demand that the rules be changed. Maybe ask MPs how they would feel about you checking their credit scores before you voted for them. (Go to my website and look under Resources for a letter you can use to communicate the issue to your MP.)

As for YOUR business and your money, quit chasing the highest credit score. Focus on managing your money smartly and getting to debt-free. Then your credit score won't matter a whit!

RULE #36: DANCE YOUR WAY TO WHAT YOU WANT

I believe with all my heart that we can each do anything we want if we want it badly enough and have some gumption. But you have to believe that you are the author of your fate. You have to KNOW that you are going to achieve what it is you've set your heart on.

No one ever said getting what you want is easy. Sometimes it's damn hard. Follow these five dance steps and you're much more likely to succeed:

D—Decide. What do you really, really want? You must be clear and absolutely committed.

A—Act. Nothing will happen if you aren't prepared to do whatever it takes.

N—Notice. What are you doing? Is it working? What isn't working?

C—Change. You must be adaptable. You must be willing to accept new information and alter course if that will get you to where you want to be.

E—Evaluate. Measure your success. Take pride in your accomplishments. Decide if you are still on the right track.

Did you notice that we're back to DECIDE? Yup, the whole process is a cycle, a pirouette of turns. Sometimes you'll dip. Sometimes you'll slip. You need to stay committed, practising your steps and perfecting your promenade. DANCE and the world dances with you!

RULE #37: KNOW YOUR TIME HORIZON

This is one of Three Golden Rules of Investing. (For the other two, see Rule #74: Don't Buy What You Don't Know, and Rule #79: Know Your Risk Tolerance.)

This is such a simple rule I can't believe how many people just blow it off. It goes like this: You've got to take into account when you'll need to use the money before you decide what kind of investment to buy. Seems like a no-brainer, right? Then explain to me why so many people who are only a stone's throw away from needing to use their money are in equity investments.

If you'll need to use your money in 3 years or less, you have a short-term time horizon. So no equities for you.

If you'll need to use your money in under 10 years, you have a medium-term time horizon, but still no equities for you.

If you won't need your money for more than 10 years, you have a long-term time horizon, and you can put money into equities.

Markets have a tendency to go up and down. The last thing you want is for the market to be on the downside of the cycle when you need to cash in. The longer you have until you will need to use the money, the more time your investment has to even out its return.

As you get closer to using the money, your time horizon shortens and your investment choices must change. Sure, you had a long-term horizon when Baby Girl was born and wouldn't need her educational savings until she was 18. But now that she's turning 12 and in grade six, your investment time horizon has shortened and your choice of investments needs to change.

Ditto as you get closer to using your retirement savings. Notice that I said "closer to using" the money, not to your retirement date itself. If you retire at 65 and think you'll live until you're 85, you won't need some of that money for more than 10 years, so you still have a long-term time horizon for the part you're going to not spend, which is why you need some variety in your investment holdings.

Every time you invest money, decide how long it'll be before you'll need to use that money. And every year, review your portfolio and see if your time horizon has changed, so you can adjust your portfolio accordingly.

RULE #38: MORE WON'T MAKE YOU HAPPIER

Everywhere you turn, the message is that more is the key to happiness. If you don't like your job, ask for a raise; more money will make it better. If you don't like your home, buy a bigger one; more space will make it better. And if you're unhappy about anything, go shopping; more toys, more clothes, more entertainment will make you feel better.

While you do need more money if you can't take care of your most basic needs and put your financial boat to rights, for most people more doesn't slay the dragons or blow away the mist of insecurity. Pay raises get eaten up by higher expenses, space gets filled, and toys . . . well, the thrill of new wears off and you're left measuring your life by what you don't have.

It doesn't really matter how much you're paid; if you hate your work, you're not going to be happy. And if your relationship, your family, your sense of personal space, isn't working for you, then buying more physical space isn't going to do you a bit of good. Happy people are happy with what they have; they don't spend their lives pining for greener grass.

In today's world of constantly new and improved, it takes a concerted effort to stay focused on what you have, instead of what everyone else tells you is missing.

So how do you swim against the cultural current for more?

Look at what you value, and find a way to compensate for what may be missing without substituting stuff for what's really important to you.

Unhappy with your job? If it's because you wish you were

making a contribution and you just don't get that feeling at work, volunteering may be one way to get what you're looking for. If it's because you wish you could do something different, make a plan to get the skills you need to change your job and change your life. If you value your family's security and safety, changing jobs can feel decidedly risky. Perhaps you'll move to a smaller home to give yourself some financial breathing room while you change careers. And if you want a great education but loathe the idea of taking on a ton of student debt, playing the role of poor student even after you get your new job will get your debt paid off lickety-split and give you what you're looking for.

Unhappy with where you live? Are you prepared to give up a bigger house for a shorter commute? No, a nicer car to commute in won't make your life better. It's not really about the "drive," is it? So what is it about? Is it worth it to live closer to work in a small home so you can spend more time with your partner or your kids?

Unhappy with yourself? A monthly wardrobe makeover won't make you happier. Nor will a big ring, snappy new carpeting, or a fancy coffee machine. You have to decide what makes you really happy and why you're substituting stuff.

If you remain caught in the trap of chasing MORE in the belief that it'll make you happier, it's going to cost you a lot of money, but it won't bring you a dime's worth of peace. As you work to change your life so that you're moving closer to what you value, focus on the good you have: the time to enjoy your family, your friends, the clean air, your personal freedom, the access to healthy food, all the blessings already in your life. You may find yourself happier than if you spend every spare moment of your time trying to cram in "more."

RULE #39: *YOU* ARE IN CHARGE

Once upon a time, there was a young lady named Molly. Molly travelled to visit her girlfriend Callie for the weekend. Over the weekend Molly's wallet was stolen. Molly was stuck away from home, no money, no identification.

Molly went to the local branch of her bank. She needed money. When she told the bank representative her wallet had been stolen, the rep said there was nothing she could do to help. Molly wasn't taking no for an answer. She wanted her money. She asked for the manager.

When the manager came over, Molly explained the situation again. She needed money from her account. She said, "Tell me what I have to do to prove to you who I am so you can give me $100 from my account."

The manger put her through her paces. What was her address, her telephone number, her account number? Molly answered all the questions.

"What's the last thing you purchased with your debit card?" asked the manager. Molly told her. She also told her the three things she had purchased before that.

The manager hummed and hawed. Molly said, "Listen, unless someone has been stalking me, there's no way they could know all this stuff. I am clearly me. Give me my money." The banker agreed.

Molly travelled home. But she was still without a debit card because without ID no bank under the sun will replace your debit card. So the next day Molly grabbed her passport and headed to the bank.

She explained what had happened. She provided her information and showed her passport. The banker said, "You're only 17."

Molly said, "Yes, I know that."

The banker said, "We can't give you a replacement card without a parent present."

Molly said, "My mother lives in another town. She can't be here. This account is in my name."

"Yes," said the banker, "but that's our policy."

Molly gritted her teeth. "Okay," she said, "in the next five minutes one of two things is going to happen. Either you will give me a replacement card, or you will give me all the money in BOTH my accounts (she had a chequing account, and a savings account with over $10,000 in it to pay for school) and I'll go across the street, where they'll give me a debit card."

Molly got her debit card.

The moral? Don't take no for an answer. You are the customer. The bank is there to serve your needs, and "policy" means "guideline." If you can't get what you want, escalate the issue to someone with more power. If you still can't get what you want, be prepared to move your business. But, for heaven's sake, don't take guff from an employee who doesn't really give a crap how complicated your life is. That employee is there to serve your needs. If that employee can't do the job, find one who can.

BTW, Molly is my nickname for Alex, my daughter. She called me up after these encounters and said, "Mom, I felt like I was channelling you!" I'm very proud of her for standing up for herself.

Hey, if a 17-year-old can get a bank to do what she wants, you can too!

RULE #40: FIGURE OUT YOUR MONEY SET POINT

Everyone has a money set point. When you reach yours, you feel "rich" and stop paying attention to the details. It may be a low set point—just $500 is all it takes to make you think you're invincible. Or you may have a high set point; you need to have $3,500 in your bank account to not feel like you're standing on the edge of a precipice.

It's important that you figure out your money set point. You do this by watching your chequing and savings account balances and recognizing when your "keep piling up the money" button clicks off. This may take a few weeks or even a few months. And it will definitely take conscious attention. When you get the feeling "Oh, that's a lot of money" or "That's enough" or "Let's go shopping!" you will know what your money set point is.

My money set point is $5,000. If I have that much money in one place, it feels like a lot to me (hey, I'm old and I remember making $150 a week). But I'm also a money accumulator by nature, so having money in the bank feels good to me. My savings button doesn't turn off. However, if my bank balance drops below $5,000, I go into austerity mode and look for ways to cut back so I can get the balance back up over my money set point. Heaven help the kids if they try to hit me up for money when I'm in austerity mode!

Some people's savings buttons click off early so they can never get their emergency funds up as high as they need to be. Some people feel they can jet off on vacation every time they get their credit card balances down to a specific point. If you don't know what your money set point is, you're never going to understand why just as you're making progress you do something to set yourself back to where you were.

If you can't change your money set point (and many people can't), then you'll have to work around it. Saving a problem? Try using multiple savings accounts. Each time you get close to your money set point, walk away from one bank account and open another. It may not be convenient or efficient, but it'll work. Ditto RRSPs, TFSAs, RESPs. These are all ways to pile up money in different pools so you don't feel "rich" and reach your savings set point.

My money set point for debt is zero. Any consumer debt makes me twitch. I don't even have a line of credit because the idea of potential debt makes me squirm. I'm fine with my credit cards because I know I'm using them for points and for convenience and I never spend money I don't already have in the bank.

If you have a money set point that's higher than zero for debt, add all your debt together. While keeping your savings in separate piles works in your favour, keeping your debt in separate piles will get you further and further in the hole.

Find a way to reset your debt set point or you'll always be in debt. Consider writing your total debt on a big sign and hanging it on your fridge. Spray-paint it across your car (it doesn't have to be in permanent paint). Put it on the mirror in your bathroom. Put that debt in your face so you have to deal with it day in and day out. And as you bring it down, reward yourself. In the best of all worlds, as you bring your debt down, your debt set point will come down too.

RULE #41: DON'T PLAY THE KEEPING UP GAME

Comparing yourself to your friends, family, co-workers, or neighbours is a bad habit that can get you in trouble financially. If you're always trying to keep up—damn the costs—then you'll be willing to use credit to acquire what you need to stay ahead of the pack. And trying to keep up with other people's lifestyles is a game that will suck you dry financially.

Ever heard two boys bragging about their latest electronic acquisition? Ever felt that your phone, your car, your kitchen countertops were just not good enough anymore because your sister-in-law showed up and showed off her new and sparkly?

One of the biggest struggles for the newly independent is the sense that life was so much better when you lived at home, where you had the full run of a very nicely appointed house. The cold shower of independence may leave you a little nostalgic for what you had. You may even feel you're entitled to the same big-screen TV, upper-middle-class diet, and STUFF to which you grew accustomed. Hey, if you don't have the means to pay for that lifestyle, you are not entitled to it . . . yet. You'll get there. It'll take some time and some concerted effort. But you have the power to make the life you want.

I met a woman not so long ago who said, "It's so hard to see my friends and co-workers going on trips, buying new cars, and eating out all the time, and not want that stuff too." This woman was completely honest about how much she struggled with the idea of keeping up with the Joneses. "My next-door neighbour just redid her kitchen," she went on. "I walked into her house and immediately started salivating over her new granite counters and her fabulous appliances."

I asked her if she had any debt. "Just my mortgage, and I'm about 10 years to the end of that." I looked at her and guessed her age to be about 37.

"So you'll be mortgage-free before you're 50?" I asked.

"Yup," she said proudly.

"And your neighbour?" I asked.

"Oh, I don't know. I think they just refinanced," she said.

Here's what I told her: Life is hard enough without also beating yourself up because you're measuring yourself against someone else's stick.

People hide all sorts of things. They hide their credit card debt. They hide their overdraft protection. They hide their lack of an emergency fund. You can't see what they don't have. All you can see is what they're spending their money on.

Imagine if we all had to wear T-shirts that declared our level of indebtedness so we could see the flip side of all that keeping up.

We can't judge our lives by what other people do with their money. We can only know that we're doing what works for us. That's the thought to hold front and centre in your mind the next time your sister-in-law drops by to show off her latest bling.

RULE #42: TALK TO YOUR PARENTS ABOUT THEIR MONEY

When was the last time you talked to your parents about money? It may be time for a chit-chat about what can be a very touchy subject. Should your parents die or become incapacitated without the appropriate paperwork in place, you'll be in for a nasty shock if you try to assume control of their assets or their medical care.

If your parents are of the generation where they don't talk about money—not with friends and certainly not with their children—you may have quite the challenge on your hands. It's not easy to begin talking about issues as emotional as dying or becoming incapacitated. Point out that you want to follow through on their wishes should your parents not be able to speak on their own behalf. And those wishes have to be documented so it's clear that you have your parents' blessing to act for them. Talk about your own estate plan or the recent death of a friend or relative as a way of opening up the conversation.

FAMILY

"Hey, Mom, did you hear the total disaster poor Julia has to deal with? Aunty Barb's money is a huge mess, and now Julia has to figure it all out to make sure Aunty Barb gets the help she needs. If you do that to me, I'm going to move you into my basement and use you as a plant stand!"

If your parents resist the chat, don't give up. You may have to try a time or three. It will be far worse if you do end up having to step in and you don't have a clue where anything is, or worse, if there's no documentation in place.

If your parents look at you a little bewildered when you ask if they have a financial and a personal care power of attorney, you've got some 'splaining to do. (See Rule #4: You Must Have POAs.)

Some parents worry that their kids are butting into their financial affairs or want to take control. To reassure them that you're not trying to take over, tell them, "I don't need to know what's in the will, Dad. I just need to know where the will is."

At the other end of this spectrum are parents and children who are completely in sync financially. Being jointly signed on everything lulls them into a false sense of security. But joint ownership doesn't negate the need for parents to have powers of attorney. Even with joint ownership of assets, such as a home, without powers of attorney children cannot make changes (i.e., sell the home) until someone is appointed to represent the parents' interest.

Ask your parents to think about getting help once they hit the point where they can't do everything on their own. Would they be willing to turn the bill paying over to someone else?

If you've had this conversation with your parents already, good for you. Still trying to figure out how to broach the subject? You could always rip out this page and leave it on the kitchen table the next time you visit your folks.

RULE #43: YOU *CAN* USE YOUR RRSP AS COLLATERAL

This replaces the old rule "RRSPs cannot be used as collateral for a loan."

Even banks don't understand this one! There are no rules that say RRSP assets can't be pledged as collateral, although your RRSP provider will likely tell you there are. However, there are consequences. If you borrow against your RRSP, the fair market value of the RRSP assets pledged are included in your income for tax purposes at the end of that year. When the plan's assets are no longer pledged, you may deduct the amount previously included in your income, minus any loss resulting from using the plan's assets as collateral.

So why would a person do this?

Well, let's say you suddenly find yourself without a job and need to take money out of your RRSP to keep body and soul together. Once you do, there's no way to put that money back into the plan. Even if you found yourself out of the cash flow squeeze, what's been withdrawn stays withdrawn and that's that.

Patrick and Suzanne were in the middle of some pretty big home renovations when Patrick lost his job in June. "We had an $18,000 bill sitting on the desk and one income," said Suzanne.

"I knew I'd be back to work quickly," said Patrick, "but I didn't want to put the whole weight of this on Sue's shoulders."

Patrick transferred $26,000 from his existing RRSP to an

RRSP with the bank he wanted to get the loan from. Since he wasn't working, this would help him "secure" the loan. He then got a loan using the RRSP as collateral. That meant that the RRSP was "de-registered" for tax purposes, but the money was still in the plan. The money would not affect his income unless the plan remained de-registered through the end of the year, at which point the money would be part of his income.

Patrick paid the bills and helped Sue manage for the next few months. In October, Patrick was offered another position. He went to the bank and, with a secure job, had the loan uncollateralized. The RRSP was "re-registered."

So instead of making a cash withdrawal from his RRSP, Patrick used his RRSP assets as collateral for a loan, and the plan was treated as if it had been de-registered and the money included in his income at the end of the year. However, because he re-registered the RRSP by taking off the collateralization before year end, his RRSP assets were once again safely tucked away and he'll have lost nothing.

If Patrick had not found a job until February of the following year, he would have had to take the $26,000 into income at the end of the year and there would have been a tax bill. (You would never use this strategy without talking to a tax advisor about the tax implications first.) However, once the loan was repaid or the security was released, the amount previously included in his income could be deducted once again.

RULE #44: PROTECT YOUR FINANCIAL IDENTITY

Identity theft is a huge problem in the U.S. and a growing problem in Canada. According to a 2006* study done at McMaster University, 6.5% of Canadian adults suffered some form of ID theft.

Be sensible about what you do with your financial garbage. Shred your financial paperwork. Dumpster-diving has become a favourite way for fraudsters to find information they can use to apply for loans or credit cards in someone else's name, so buy a cross-shredder and make your financial paperwork into confetti. (It's great if you have to pad boxes for shipping prezzies at Christmas.)

Don't share your PIN with anyone. NOT ANYONE. I don't care how much you love and trust the person. No sharing! When choosing a PIN, don't make it too obvious: a phone number, address, birthdate. Periodically change your PINs. If you're having trouble remembering your multitude of PINs and passwords, take a page from my girlfriend: she carries a telephone book around that has her PINs and passwords concealed among all the other names and numbers.

If you are contacted by phone, never give out information. And don't respond to emails requesting personal information. Your bank would never send an email requesting log-in information or call and ask for information.

*Susan Sproule and Norm Archer, "Measuring Identity Theft in Canada, 2006 Consumer Survey," Working Paper #21, McMaster eBusiness Research Centre.

Be careful when you shop online. Use reputable retailers. And apply for a credit card with a very low balance that you use only for online purchases.

If you bank by computer, clear the cache after every transaction if someone else has access to the computer. And for heaven's sake, don't let your friends watch as you check your online accounts, particularly if you live in shared accommodations. Yes, students, I'm talking to you about your besties.

It won't always be a stranger who steals your identity. At a book signing for *It's Your Money*, a woman told me that her ID had been stolen and a credit card ordered in her name and run up to the hilt. The culprit? Her husband.

"Did you charge him with ID theft?" I asked.

"No, I couldn't," she said, shrugging. "I'm still living with him."

Damn!

RULE #45: MEASURE YOUR PROGRESS

Have you ever noticed that when you start something new, you're all gung-ho, but as time goes by your energy and effort wane? Hey, it's human. Once you lose your initial lust for your goal, it turns into something that feels more like concrete shoes.

When you're working towards a goal, staying focused on what you've achieved so you can keep going can be a huge challenge. Having knocked a $2,000 credit card balance back to zero, you may find your motivation to attack that student loan waning. It can feel like a long haul to debt-free forever when you start to discount what you've achieved and look only at the hole you're in.

There are things you can do to keep the blush on the rose. Measuring your progress is one way to stay focused and keep yourself motivated.

By recording how you're doing, you can look at a picture that reflects your reality, not what you think is your reality. You can appreciate what you have—what you've accomplished in moving towards your goal. And you can see how you're doing, measuring your improvement and tweaking your plan to keep moving forward.

I can hear some of you moaning now . . . "But Gail, all that measuring takes time I don't have." Really? You're trying to achieve a goal that you've said is important, but you don't have time to check in and see how you're doing? Or is it that you're afraid you're going to miss the mark and would rather keep your head buried in your delusion?

If you make a habit of checking up on your progress, in no time at all it'll become second nature and it won't feel like a chore. When measuring your progress becomes part of your routine, you'll find moving towards your goals—particularly the big ones that take longer to come to fruition—a smoother process.

If you can't even set aside 15 minutes a week to measure how you're doing, maybe your goal isn't really all that important to you. Save yourself the aggravation; stop wasting mental energy thinking about it. If you find that what you wanted to achieve lingers as a concern in your mind, then maybe it does matter to you and it's time to put some real energy into achieving your goal, including measuring your progress.

If you find yourself hugely resistant to keeping a financial log to monitor your spending, it may be that you're not yet committed to change. Writing down your spending means making a deal with yourself to do something that has results. If you're not writing it down, there's no deal, and you're off the hook. 'Course, it also means you're going to keep doing what you know isn't working. But hey, if you want to hang on to your delusions, that's a choice you get to make. Just stop whining!

RULE #46: DON'T PUT YOURSELF AT RISK TO HELP OTHERS

You should never, NEVER put yourself at risk financially to help someone else. I don't care if it's your mother, father, sister, brother, child, best friend, or lover. It makes no sense for two people to be in a mess. Or two families.

No matter how much you love a body, putting your own financial foundation at risk is not the answer. Help in ways that you can, but don't risk your own financial independence. Even if you fear people might be drowning, if it feels like you are "bailing" them out, don't. They're going to have to learn to put some of their feast money away for famine days eventually. It might as well start now.

I know it's tough not to step in and save the people you love. Here's the gist of a letter I got from Catherine that talked about how worried she was about her parents. I've shortened it.

My parents are 62 years old and have practically nothing saved for retirement. They sold their house and didn't save any of the money. My parents are hard-working, but have never been able to save a dime in their lives and have always been impulsive. I have not said a word about their retirement in over two years because I gave up on them, but now I am so upset and angry. They make jokes about parking in our driveway and living in their camper, which I don't find particularly funny. Because of the nature of their work (condo supers), if one of them gets ill or passes away, the other is most likely out of a job and a place to live. It angers me that they are not confronting reality. I also get upset when I think my oldest brother and I will probably have to take care of them at some point. I feel if I don't do something now, it'll be worse when a crisis hits. I feel that the crisis is looming . . .

Here's what I said to Catherine:

It's time for you to start treating your parents like the grown-ups that they are. This is not your problem to fix. Whatever money you've already given them, consider it written off. It's gone. But there will be NO MORE money gifts. You must deal with your life and your parents must deal with theirs. You can't be responsible for other people (unless they are your minor kids or have come to need through no fault of their own). If you continue to "enable" them, you have only yourself to blame for your anger and disquiet. Love them. Hug them. Don't give 'em another cent!

If you have anyone in your life who is irresponsible with money, parents who are trying to guilt you into providing for them as they did for you as a child, siblings who seem to have not one iota of common sense and no plan for the future, a best friend who is always trying to hit you up for a loan, you need to recognize this is NOT your problem. Above all, you cannot help anyone if that help necessitates putting yourself at risk. All that does is create more problems.

How do you say no to someone you love? It's hard, but it goes something like this:

"I know you're in a tough spot. I would be happy to help you figure out how you're going to change what you're doing so things can get better. And if you want me to help you find a professional to help, I will. But I'm afraid I don't have the financial means to bail you out. I need to take care of my family and myself so I don't end up where you are right now. I must keep my financial house in order. Please let me help you figure out what you have to change. I love you and want to help, but not with money."

RULE #47: PAY ATTENTION TO YOUR CREDIT CARD COSTS

This rule replaces the old one that says "Know your APR" for people who don't pay off their balances in full every month.

Your APR is your annual percentage rate, or the cost of the money you are borrowing as a percentage. When you look at your credit card statement, it's the 6.7%, 14.9%, or 29.9% that should be clearly shown there. (This number isn't always as apparent as it should be.)

It's important to know your APR and not just what your monthly payment will be, so that you're not being overcharged in interest. But if you know your APR and then become totally complacent about the cost of using your credit cards, you defeat the purpose. Especially if you don't pay off your credit card balances in full by the due date.

APRs get a lot of attention in the media, but knowing your APR isn't going to do you a bit of good if you don't calculate what your credit card is costing when all the additional fees are added up. Sure, you may know your interest rate, but have you translated that into the actual dollars you're spending? And how about what you're being charged as an annual fee, in over-limit fees, credit insurance fees, and inactive-account fees—all those extra charges credit card companies like to load in?

I'll bet dollars to donuts that you haven't read your credit card agreement. Can't handle the mouse print? Hey, I feel your pain. Maybe it's because the language the credit card agreement uses is total bafflegab, designed to obfuscate and confuse. Who wants to read it?

According to www.consumer-action.org, 94% of credit cards charge over-limit fees ranging from $20 to $39 monthly. The average late fee is about $28. And penalty interest rates can run as high as 32%.

Penalty interest? What the hell is that?

Some credit card companies change at the drop of a hat the interest rate they charge, so the interest rate you thought you were paying may be far less than what you're actually forking over. If you miss your due date by even one day on a low-interest introductory rate, you'll find yourself paying a much higher percentage in interest. And if your credit card company arbitrarily lowers your credit limit, pushing you closer to the top of your credit utilization (see Rule #35: Don't Obsess about Your Credit Score), that will likely trigger a drop in your credit score, which is all your credit card company needs to justify jacking up your interest rate.

If you are disorganized enough to go over your credit card limit, your credit card company is under no obligation to turn away your transaction or send you an alert. Nope, they just charge you a penalty. And if you don't use your credit card, some companies will try to get their pound of flesh through an "inactivity" fee. Lord love a duck!

So why do you pony up and pay? Why would you use a card charging 18%, or 24%, or 29% in interest, and then add on an "over-limit fee" or an "account balance premium," never mind the credit insurance that's a total rip-off? Two reasons:

1. You commit to a card because it offers points, travel miles, or some other incentive and then stop paying attention to the costs.
2. Your don't read your statements.

If you're buying credit, you should shop around. You can't go whining about how much the credit card companies are ripping you off if you're too lazy to find a better alternative. And if you don't even know what you're paying, how will you know when you've become the sucker every credit card company loves to have as a customer?

RULE #48: IT'S NOT YOUR MONEY
UNTIL IT'S IN THE BANK

I've been disappointed a few times by projects that didn't come through, plans that fell apart, and jobs that didn't turn out to be all they could be. What I've never done is spend the money before it hit the bank.

I've seen freelancers spend money before they've cut an invoice; the project falls through and there's no money. I've seen people spend their bonus money before they get it; hey, just because you got a bonus last year doesn't mean you're guaranteed one this year. I've seen people spend their future income because they're banking on a raise; the economy turns south, the raise (and sometimes the job) evaporates, and they're stuck owing money. Perhaps the worst example of an optimistic spender is the body who is banking on an inheritance to clean up all their financial woes. Really? You're waiting for people to die?

It's not your money to spend until it's gone into your account. Up until then, it's pie-in-the-sky. And it's just as likely to disappear as show up.

RULE #49: YOUR KIDS' FINANCIAL EDUCATION IS YOUR RESPONSIBILITY

This replaces the rule "The best place for kids to learn about money is at school."

For kids to understand how money works—not just to KNOW but actually be able to DO—they need to have some money to work with. Not just pretend money, like in a Monopoly game. (If we could pretend our way to brilliance, we'd all be real estate moguls.) For money lessons to work, parents have to put some real money into their kids' hands and deliver sound financial messages at home. Give them an allowance, set some expectations for how that money will be handled, and talk, talk, talk, talk, talk about everything to do with money.

You also have to walk the talk. If you want your children to value saving, you have to do more than say, "Saving is important." You have to demonstrate how easy it is to save—as easy as it is to use a credit card, and ten times as beneficial in the long run. And you have to break the money lessons you're teaching into very small, very manageable bites that can be easily digested. Don't even know where to start? Go get a copy of *Money-Smart Kids*. I've laid it all out for you.

The best place for kids to learn about how money works and the role it should play in their lives is at home. You are their best teacher. If you worry you're not up to the job, study up. Think about what you want your children to know about money. Don't abdicate! This is part of your job as a parent.

RULE #50: YOU'RE ENTITLED!

There, I've said it. There is something you're ENTITLED to and it's about time you started demanding it. **You're entitled to good advice that meets your needs and that you can rely on.**

It's a real shame that we don't know who we can trust when it comes to our money management. Once upon a time financial institutions took their "fiduciary" responsibilities seriously and knew the importance of giving sound customer-focused advice. Sure, they were a little paternalistic. But they never handed credit to anyone who couldn't pay it back, and they never suggested people invest in things they didn't understand. Now with KYC (Know Your Client) forms all checked off and their butts covered, today's institutions let the blind lead the blind.

Good financial advisors want to form long-lasting relationships, so they give advice they'll be happy to stand behind. You can tell you've found them when they have customers who are happy to refer friends and family. They're damn good at their jobs and don't have to justify their existence to anyone. They take real pleasure from helping their customers and they—and their clients—know they are trustworthy. But for every one of them there are a dozen Joes who are doing it for the commission or to meet the sales targets.

Because you're ENTITLED to good advice, you need to stop taking crap. When you feel you've received bad advice, don't just walk away grumbling. Whether you feel you're being pushed into a decision you're uncomfortable with or you find out that you were not sold the appropriate product or service for your needs, escalate the issue to the next level of management and demand good service. If you have to go all the way to the executive vice-president, do it! The only way institutions will stop putting ineffectual representatives in your way is if you make 'em. So stop buying the bull. Demand the best. You work hard for your money. You're ENTITLED to sound advice!

RULE #51: YOUR MONEY SAYS A LOT ABOUT YOU

When you look at your net worth, where your money goes every month, and how you're doing on the whole, what picture do you see?

If you've racked up a wicked amount of debt on consumables—on your credit cards and lines of credit, or debt you've hidden in your mortgage when you consolidated consumer debt—that may speak to a lack of self-control. Or maybe you're just way bad at planning. Or you're a gambler, a drunk, or a junkie. Maybe food is your drug. Maybe shopping is your aerobic workout.

If you haven't looked at how you're spending your money, maybe you're an ostrich in denial about the mess you're making of your life. Maybe you're refusing to take a good hard look because you're so afraid it'll mean that you're going to have to do things differently and, spoiled baby that you are, you just don't wanna.

Maybe you're doing a great job: your budget balances, you've got little or no consumer debt, and you've dotted all your i's and crossed all your t's when it comes to creating a sound financial plan. You can pat yourself on the back and keep on keeping on.

How we manage our money is a reflection of who we are in life. I'm a planner, so I don't do anything, including spending money, without a plan. And I'm a buttoned-down, detail-oriented girl, so I don't like to guesstimate. I'm organized

25 out of 30 days—NO ONE is perfect—and that shows in my money management. When I go off track, I give myself a stern talking-to and fix what I messed up PDQ. And I'm completely risk-averse, so I don't carry debt, I'm well insured, and I've got my will in place.

What does your money say about you?

	Y	N
1. I'm saving regularly for retirement.	☐	☐
2. I pay all my bills in full every month.	☐	☐
3. I have checked my credit history in the past six months.	☐	☐
4. I always shop with a list.	☐	☐
5. I have enough insurance.	☐	☐
6. My children receive an allowance.	☐	☐
7. I pay no fees for ATM withdrawals.	☐	☐
8. I have an up-to-date will and powers of attorney.	☐	☐
9. I'm building up (or have) six months' essential expenses in an emergency fund.	☐	☐
10. My bank costs are less than $20 a month.	☐	☐
11. I have a plan to be consumer debt-free in three years or less.	☐	☐
12. I know to the penny how much I make and how much I spend every month.	☐	☐
13. I spend at least 30 minutes every month reviewing my finances.	☐	☐
14. I talk openly about money.	☐	☐

If you're not happy with how you've done so far, if there are questions you could not say yes to in all good conscience, what are you going to do differently?

It's all well and good to say, "Hey, I'm not a planner—that's just not who I am. I can't do this budget thing." But if the rest of your life has gone to hell in a handbasket because you refuse to do any planning, that approach just isn't working. It's time to take stock and make some changes.

I know it's hard. It's always hard going against your "nature" to do something differently. But if your child's nature was to only eat sweets and never touch a vegetable with a 10-foot pole, would you say, "Oh well, that's just how she is"? Or would you teach her how important it is to eat well and give her incentives to add a couple of bites of veggies to every meal?

"That's just not me" is a very childish thing to say. It's how teenagers respond to things they can't imagine because they have very limited life experiences. But we grown-ups know there are lots of things we must do that wouldn't be a first choice. From cleaning up puke to wiping dirty bums, from washing the kitchen floor AGAIN because of the gravy slopped on the way to the dinner table, to rewashing just-washed sheets because the cat peed, we do thousands of things we wish we never had to do. We do it because we know we must.

The same holds true for how we deal with our money. Today, take a good look at the picture your money paints of you and your life. What do you see? Are you happy with the picture? If not, it's time to make a plan and do something differently so that you're happy with what your money says about you.

RULE #52: SET UP A CURVEBALL ACCOUNT

Despite the best-laid plans of mice and men, there are times the unforeseeable just waltzes into your life and poops on your budget. Sure, you have a budget of $400 a month for groceries, but your brother and sister-in-law and their four kids came to visit for a week. Your best friend announces she's getting married and you have to find a way to pay for a $200 dress. Your kid is failing math and the only way to pull his butt out of the fire is with a tutor who will cost you $60 a week.

One of the best ways to cope with life's constant financial challenges is to have a "curveball" account. This is not your emergency fund, which you need for major disasters like losing your job, becoming ill, or some other calamity that affects your ability to make money. Your curveball account is a slush fund from which you can draw when unexpected expenses come whizzing at you at 60 miles per hour and you don't want to throw your budget totally off track. Whether you deposit a little or a lot into this account every month, it can be a real budget saver. And if you move all the money you "save" by shopping smartly into this account right after you haven't spent it, it'll grow even faster. So the next time you save 50¢ on a coupon, go home and drop that 50¢ into an "I'm a smart shopper" jar, and then deposit all those savings to your curveball account at the end of the month.

Want some more ideas to build up your curveball account?

- Use those points you've accumulated on loyalty cards for things you would normally have to buy, so you can use the extra money to start or boost your curveball account.

- Carpool for a month, or park the car and take transit, so you can transfer the savings to your curveball account.

- Pack your lunch: Save $5 a day × 20 days a month and you'll have $100 a month for your curveball account.

- Give up ONE vice for ONE month: no wine, no beer, no ciggies, no candy bars, no potato chips, no _____ (insert your weakness here). Once you have the $75, or the $150, or the $500, you think you need in your curveball account, you can go back to your vice if you really want to.

You don't need a lot of money in your curveball account: Somewhere between $100 and $500 should do it, depending on the kind of crises you tend to have. Remember, this isn't a category you tap regularly. If you have recurring expenses, you need to add a new category to your budget. Your curveball account is for things that pop up unexpectedly. Think back over the last year. How many times would an extra $100 or $200 have helped you smooth out your cash flow? That curveball account will not only buy your budget some flexibility, it'll also buy you peace of mind.

RULE #53: DON'T BUY THE
MINIMUM PAYMENTS BULLSH*T

Old Rule: Make your minimum payment on your credit cards every month so you keep your credit score nice and shiny.

Did you know that if there was no minimum payment on your credit card statement, you'd likely pay off your debt faster?

In a study* conducted by Dr. Neil Stewart, a psychology researcher at the University of Warwick, in Coventry, England, two test groups were given credit card bills with $700 balances. The first group's bills had no minimum payment listed. The second group's bills did. On average, the first group made a payment of $280, the equivalent of 40% of the balance. The second group paid an average of $161, or 23% of their balance.

The lower the required minimum payment on the statement, the lower the actual payment you'll make. Minimum payments distort your behaviour to increase the credit card company's profits.

Credit card minimum payments are meant to keep you in debt for as long as possible so that credit card companies can make loads and loads of profit from interest charges. The credit scoring system even awards more points for making only the minimum payment, so lenders can grind every last cent of interest out of you. (See Rule #35: Don't Obsess about Your Credit Score.)

---

* N. Stewart, "The Cost of Anchoring on Credit Card Minimum Payments," *Psychological Science* 20 (2009): 39–41.

Want to stop the credit card company from messin' with your mind? Get yourself on a debt repayment plan of your own making, and stick with it. (See Rule #9: Calculate Your Own Debt Repayment Plan.) The only thing the minimum payment amount is good for is keeping your account in good standing while you focus on paying off the debt with the highest interest rate first. If you're using that minimum amount as a guide for how much to pay, even if you're paying more than the minimum, you're being had.

RULE #54: STAND ON YOUR OWN TWO FEET

People are under the delusion that if they have a partner, life is easier and more stable, at least financially.

Yes, there may be some things that initially seem easier to manage in partnership, such as home ownership. But for the most part, the sense that life is easier as a couple is only a matter of perception. When you nail it down, there's no greater safety in numbers.

Some people consider their partners to be their emergency funds or their disability-insurance plans. So, you can live on one partner's income and nothing bad could ever happen to your buddy? (Are you still holding on to the idea that bad things don't happen to good people? Grow up!) Besides, since most people jack their expenses up to gobble both incomes, any change in income creates problems.

The only way to know you are safe is to stand on your own two feet financially. Even if you have a partner, you must be able to take care of yourself (and your kids, if you have them) should circumstances arise that force you into the role of sole provider.

But what if you're the non-working parent in a family? Well, you better make sure that your butt is covered by a big, fat emergency fund and a lot of the right kinds of insurance. Don't let your buddy talk you into being completely dependent on his or her income. Crap happens and life can change in a heartbeat. You have to KNOW you are safe by knowing everything about where the family money goes and by having a rock-solid foundation. You must be able to manage on your own so that your "dependence" on a buddy doesn't turn into a pair of handcuffs or give you the illusion of safety. And if you're a one-income family, you better make damn sure that one income is insured seven ways from Sunday.

RULE #55: A MATE IS NOT A PREREQUISITE FOR HOME OWNERSHIP

Being single doesn't negate your ability to own a home. Sure, you may find it easier to qualify for and buy a home when there are two incomes. But it's not just getting into the home, is it? It's being able to keep the home, regardless of what life throws at you. There is always a risk, but if you're determined to own a home, you've got to make a plan and take your shot. Partnership won't solve the risk problem. After all, how would you keep that home if it takes both incomes to hang on and one of you loses your job or gets sick?

My girlfriend Jazz bought herself a home when she was in her twenties, did a load of work on it (much of it herself) and sold it for a nice profit. She rolled that into the next property she bought: a duplex, which gave her both a place to live and the ability to generate some income to pay off the mortgage faster. And she did it as a single mom.

I bought my first home as a single woman just before I turned 31. Back then I was self-employed and had to jump through hoops to prove my creditworthiness to a lender. And I had to have 25% down to avoid going high-ratio. So I made do without a lot of stuff to scrounge up the money.

I'll give you that it may be cheaper to live in a joint household since a lot of expenses can be shared: telephone, heat, rent, cable. But again, who says that just because you're single you have to live alone?

If you *choose* to live by yourself, your expenses may be

higher proportionate to your income, but you're exchanging money for privacy. You don't have to pick up after anybody, fight over who gets the bathroom first, or seethe because buddy left the sink full of dirty dishes.

If you don't make enough to live comfortably on your own, there is always the option of getting a roommate, finding a shared accommodation, or buying a house with another body to make the life you want. Think *Golden Girls*.

RULE #56: LEVERAGING ISN'T FOR EVERYBODY

While the rule that's bandied about is "Double your profits by using credit," it's a red herring. You should NEVER leverage unless

1. you're an experienced and knowledgeable investor, and
2. you're prepared to lose money.

Whenever you borrow to invest, you are "leveraging" your investments. Whether you're told to take a mortgage on your home and use the money for investments, or you're offered an RRSP loan so you can catch up on missed contributions and grow your retirement savings exponentially, you're playing the leverage game. When you leverage, you increase your potential for return. You also increase your exposure to risk. If you don't understand the upsides and downsides of leveraging and you do it, you're a fool.

Buying on margin is one of the easiest ways to leverage. When you buy on margin, you borrow cash from the investment broker to buy more than you could afford on your own. Your brokerage house gives you a limit and you can borrow as much or as little as you need, up to that limit. So here is how you might use your margin account, and the implications.

Let's say you have an account at ABC Brokerage, and you have an existing investment portfolio of $100,000. They offer you the option of opening a margin account. You'll have to invest 50% of your own money for anything you decide to buy on margin, but they'll lend you the other 50%, no questions asked, at whatever their going interest rate is.

You get a tip that The Best Supermarket Ever is bringing out an earnings report to beat the band. The stock price is sure to jump 5% from $30 to $31.50. You have $12,000 in cash that you're ready to invest, so you could buy 400 shares and make a profit of $600. However, if you used your leverage account, you could buy 800 shares and make a profit of $1,200. You'd double your money and your cost would be just the interest on the $12,000 until you sold . . . pretty cool.

Problem is, the shares don't go up in value; they tank. Seems that a major lawsuit has just been filed against The Best Supermarket Ever and the stock price drops by 20%. Now you're out $6 a share on 800 shares, which means you've lost—at least on paper—$4,800. Ouch! Sure, you can hold on to the shares and hope they go back up, or you can hold on to the shares and ride them all the way down, but that's not really the point. The point is that by leveraging your investment, you increased your potential upside, but you also increased your exposure to risk. Now you not only owe interest on the $12,000 you've borrowed to leverage, but you'll have to cover your margin—pay back a portion of the loan you've been given—because the value of your investment has fallen from $24,000 to $19,200. If that forces you to sell, you'll "crystallize," or "make real," your loss.

Leveraging is usually sold on the fact that the interest on investment loans is tax-deductible. If you pay $100 in interest, you can deduct that $100 from any profit you make on your investments before you have to start paying tax. That's one reason things like the Smith Manoeuvre, which is a fancy-dancy leveraging option, and home equity lines of credit for investment purposes became such hot topics of conversation. They were presented as a way to grow your money faster because investing a larger amount means compounding has more to work with. They were also presented as a way to make your mortgage interest tax-deductible, which always has been a carrot for donkeys who will do anything to beat the Tax Man.

The big question you have to ask yourself is this: Am I prepared to lose more than I have to invest?

If you use your own cash to purchase an investment, any gain or loss will equal the gain or loss of the investment itself. However, if you use borrowed money to purchase an investment, the gain or loss you experience will be greater.

One of the most deceptive techniques used to demonstrate the benefits of leveraged investing is to use the historical performance of the market as a whole to compare a non-leveraged and a leveraged investment portfolio. Brochures show graphically how much better you would have done if you'd been "smart" enough to leverage, as opposed to using the tried-and-true "investing what you can afford to lose." Problem is, no one ever "buys the market"—even indexed investing isn't the whole market—so the example is a red herring.

Hey, I have nothing against leveraged investing for people who understand the implications and how the markets work. But this strategy is sold to people who don't have Clue One about the risks they are taking. (If you've written to me to ask if it's a good idea, you're exactly the person I'm talking to.) And even people who know what's what need to be careful that they don't overextend themselves. The last thing you want is to be forced to cash out early because of an unforeseen change in your ability to make interest payments or cover your losses. Make sure you borrow less than you can afford so that you can comfortably absorb whatever blows the investment world may throw your way.

RULE #57: LEARN FROM YOUR MISTAKES

Whether you've decided you want to be debt-free, own your own home, or have a big pot of money for retirement, don't think you can just do it without flagging or faltering. Life hardly ever happens that way. Having unrealistic expectations means that when there's a slip or a slide, you may throw up your arms and quit. Just because you make a decision to change doesn't mean your path will be smooth. Most paths have some rocks, a few holes, and the odd dragon. But giving up isn't going to get you anywhere. If you're afraid of failing, you've got to feel the fear and move forward regardless. Don't you dare let that fear stop you—it's in your head. Change your thoughts and move through the fear to where you want to be.

Sometimes the first road we choose isn't the one we actually want to end up on. Try out a road to see if it's going the right way, and adjust your direction as you go. If you miss your mark the first time, correct your trajectory and try again. Miss again and you'll have even more experience, more information to go on for the next attempt.

Our mistakes should not define us. They contribute to who we are, but they are not who we are. If you try something one way and it doesn't work, change how you're doing it. Experiment. Learn. Eventually, you'll find the way that works best.

Don't stop trying new things. (See Rule #20: Keep Learning—Keep Growing.) Complacency is the nemesis of success. Stay focused. Stay sharp. Keep making mistakes. It means you're growing and getting better.

FINDING BALANCE

RULE #58: DON'T LET EMOTIONS MAKE YOUR DECISIONS

We are part logical, part emotional creatures. You may swing more to one side of the scale than the other. But letting your emotions drive your money decisions is a recipe for regret.

People end up in more home than they can afford because they're so anxious about getting into the housing market before it leaves them behind that they throw all caution to the wind. They buy without enough of a down payment, triggering mortgage insurance premiums on top of their mortgage, adding to their costs. They use credit cards and lines of credit for their down payments. (Once upon a time this wasn't allowed by lenders, but now lenders seem to be looking at their shoes.) Buyers don't have money set aside for closing and end up tapping other sources of credit. They get into bidding wars, spending more than they originally planned because they HAVE to have THAT home. Anxiety pushes them to do the dumbest things.

Fear is a powerful emotion that can be used to manipulate us. When we're afraid, we will do just about anything to feel safer. Each enterprising salesperson who suggests you buy an extended warranty is using fear to make the sale. In fact, in the language of sales, there is a "Fear of Loss Close" that is actually used to motivate you to buy. You've heard it: "This sale will only be on today." "This is the last one we have and we don't know if we're getting any more." Acting from a place of fear means you're not making a well-thought-out decision.

And allowing fear to paralyze you—I'm so afraid of what will happen I'd rather do nothing—isn't the answer.

Falling in love can be a problem too. Whether it's with the "perfect" house or the "perfect" partner, the wealth of emotion washes away good ol' common sense. This is the root of the bidding war phenomenon. Dumb! A house may be a great deal at $350,000. But at $500,000 you're a sucker! Do you really think there are no other houses anywhere? As for marrying a money moron (see Rule #2: Don't Marry a Money Moron), do you actually think that if your buddy refuses to change before you hook up, you'll have any luck at all once you've tied the knot?

The next time you have to make a decision that involves money, stop and breathe. Take some time to examine the situation logically, giving yourself the space to get over the emotion or at least push it aside while you think. Make a budget, make a list, make a plan. Do your research so you're responding to sales pressure from a place of knowledge, not letting people tug your emotional strings. You have a heart and a head. Use them both.

RULE #59: NEVER SIGN UP FOR IN-STORE CREDIT CARD OFFERS

This replaces the old rule "Take your discount wherever you can get it."

If you've ever signed up for an immediate 10 to 20% off your day's purchases by applying in-store for a store credit card, you're a sucker. Yes, you think you got the right end of the deal, but you didn't. You was had.

While store credit cards come with the enticement of the initial discount, and some offer ongoing discounts and exclusive shopping experiences, they come with very high interest rates. If you ever carry a balance—and lots of folks do, which is how those cards can afford such heady enticements—you'll give back far more in interest than your initial discount.

Since an application for a new credit card means a "hard inquiry" on your credit report, it'll be reflected in your credit score, potentially pushing it down, and pushing up the cost of borrowing on other forms of credit. A hard inquiry is the check a lender does to see if you're creditworthy. (A soft inquiry is when you check your own credit history, and it doesn't count against you.)

Store credit cards can also be pretty tough to negotiate with should you run into any kind of problem on your statement. I once reported a department store credit card lost, only to have further charges go through on the card and be billed to me. When I tried to explain that there was a mistake, I was stonewalled by the credit card department. And when I asked the credit bureau to verify, it simply asked the credit card company what happened and took the company's side of the story. (Yes, that's what actually happened.) I refused to pay the charge and my credit score took a big hit. But I never carry a balance, so I didn't care when my interest rates went up on every other card I had.

Store credit card issuers don't follow the same rules as bank credit cards. And no discount is worth having your hands tied behind your back as you watch your credit go into the dumper!

RULE #60: NEVER BUY
MORTGAGE LIFE INSURANCE

When you apply for a mortgage, one of the things your lender will try to sell you is mortgage life insurance. Don't buy it.

Mortgage life insurance should really be called "group creditor insurance" since the creditor is the person who is protected by the policy. You pay the premiums and your lender is protected, because if you die, the lender gets the money to clear your debt.

The premiums are not only significantly higher than an equivalent amount of term life insurance, but they remain the same even as the benefit goes down because mortgage balance decreases.

Not convinced yet? How about the fact that when it comes time to make a claim on your bank-sold mortgage life insurance, there may be no payout. Have I got your attention now?

Bank employees selling mortgage insurance are unlicensed and rarely trained to explain the details and legalities of what you're buying. The result: you could end up paying premiums and think you're covered, only to find out later that you're not. Since there is no underwriting (which is what insurance companies do to actually qualify you for the insurance) at the time of purchase, the insurance company has the right to determine that you're NOT eligible, even after you've paid your premiums for years. And claims have been denied more times than you'd like to think.

What's your option? Use "decreasing term" insurance purchased from a licensed insurance broker. Your policy will be underwritten when you buy it, so you know you're covered. The "decreasing term" means the insurance will be cheaper because it's based on your insurance needs getting smaller and smaller over time. Or you could buy regular term insurance, and your beneficiaries will get the full amount you purchased. Your beneficiaries. Not the lender.

RULE #61: MAKE YOUR OWN
OVERDRAFT PROTECTION

Overdraft protection should really be called "Too Lazy to Keep Track Protection." Designed for people who don't want to be bothered with making sure they have enough money before they go shopping, overdraft protection protects your credit history from becoming bruised because you bounce a payment. Some people consider OD permission to live beyond their means.

While overdraft protection is positioned as a big ol' favour the bank is doing you to ensure you don't blemish your credit history, the bank is, in fact, selling you credit. And you'll pay dearly, both in fees and interest charges. Like credit cards and lines of credit, OD is "callable" credit, which means the bank can withdraw it at a moment's notice.

Overdraft is meant to be a short-term solution to a financial misstep. During the last credit crisis, banks started demanding that people who had been in overdraft for months repay their overdrafts quick like a bunny. Those customers were faced with having to take advances from their credit cards to repay their overdrafts. Some folks even found their bank accounts frozen because the bank wanted its money back and it wasn't taking no for an answer. People couldn't make deposits, withdraw cash, or write cheques. The next thing they knew, their "debt" had been sent off to collections for being delinquent.

Can the bank do this? You betcha, bubba. Didn't you read your overdraft agreement before you signed it?

Want a better option than OD? Create a buffer in your

chequing account to prevent overdrafts by keeping a few hundred dollars that you never allow yourself to spend. If your balance dips into your DIY OD, you stop spending until you put more money into the account.

Deep in overdraft and can't figure out how to get out? Go read Rule #253: Get Out of Overdraft!

RULE #62: UNDERSTAND OPPORTUNITY COST

If you spend $50 on dinner, you can't spend the same $50 for those fabulous shoes that are on sale today only! That's the "opportunity cost" of having used the money. The opportunity cost of spending $5 on coffee every day over 35 years is the $113,000 you'll have to give up in retirement savings, $71,000 of which will come from compounding return (at an average rate of just 5%).

You may be under the impression that you can have your stuff and your money too. You can't. This is one of the first lessons to learn about money. If you spend it, then you give up what else you could have bought (or had, in terms of savings).

"Opportunity cost" sounds complex, but it isn't. A six-year-old can understand it if it's explained carefully. She gives her toonie to the cashier in exchange for a Popsicle, and you say, "Okay, sweetie, now you have the Popsicle. But that means you can't have the chips, the can of pop, or whatever else you might next want to buy, because you've used the money. Got it?"

Easy access to credit has blurred the lines around opportunity cost because you can use your money to buy what you want and then use the bank's money to buy whatever else you want. If you're doing this, you need to understand that you're spending money you haven't yet earned. You may be spending tomorrow's Needs money on today's Wants!

Using credit lulls you into a world with no opportunity cost. Unless, of course, you count all the money you're going to have to shell out in interest payments, which you could have spent on things like saving for the future and going on vacation.

RULE #63: MAKE SPOUSAL RRSP CONTRIBUTIONS BY DECEMBER

While RRSP contributions for a spousal plan can be made up to 60 days into the new year, don't use the 60-day grace period. Why? On the off chance that you may have to make a withdrawal from the spousal plan, it matters a lot when the money goes in. The spousal RRSP withdrawal rules are based on "calendar" years.

If you make a contribution for 2011 by December 2011 and then no further contributions, your mate will be able to withdraw money and have it taxed in his or her hands as soon as January 2014.

Make that contribution sometime in the first 60 days of 2012 and your mate will have to wait until January 2015—a whole year later—before withdrawals are taxed solely in his or her hands.

RULE #64: PLAN LIKE A PESSIMIST

Take into account all the downsides of life so you can focus on the good stuff.

Every step you take, from building an emergency fund to buying enough insurance, from saving money for the future to executing a well-thought-out estate plan, gets you closer to a place where you don't have to worry. Planning like a pessimist means considering all the downsides of life and putting a safety net in place so you're able to deal with the worst if it does happen.

Here's a checklist you can use to see if you're planning like a pessimist. Whatever you say no to has to go on your to-do list.

REALITY BITES

	Y	N
1. Do you have an up-to-date resumé?	❏	❏
2. Have you checked your credit report in the past year and fixed any errors?	❏	❏
3. Are you building an emergency fund?	❏	❏
4. Do you have enough life insurance?	❏	❏
5. Do you have individual disability insurance or critical-illness insurance?	❏	❏
6. Have you executed a will?	❏	❏
7. Have you put powers of attorney in place for both your financial and medical needs?	❏	❏
8. Have you designated a guardian for your children?	❏	❏
9. Are you setting aside enough for retirement?	❏	❏
10. Do you know when you'll be debt-free?	❏	❏

Just worrying about the anvil falling on your head is a waste of energy; using that image to motivate you to plan for the worst—to plan like a pessimist—means you can stop worrying because you've done all you can. You can live like an optimist.

Once you've got all your ducks in a row, you need only do a periodic review to see that you're still on track. Semi-annually, or each time there's a significant change in your circumstances, go over your Pessimist's Checklist to make sure everything is still ticketyboo, or make the changes you need to put things back in order.

RULE #65: JUST BECAUSE YOU HAVE A VARIABLE INCOME DOESN'T MEAN YOU CAN'T BUDGET

If you think that because you don't bring in the same income every month—you can't even predict how much you'll make in a month—budgeting is out of the question, you'd be wrong. Fact is, if you have a variable income, budgeting is more important than ever for you than for the average Paycheque Joe. You just have to do it differently.

Make three budgets:

Budget A covers your most basic needs: rent, food (ground beef, not steak), and the bills you must pay every month, like your car payment, your credit card minimums, and whatever else you've committed to paying. Base your A budget on the very least you need to keep body and soul together. If you must go out and get another job or two to make even the A budget work, you might want to take another look at what you consider "essential" expenses.

Budget B covers things like better food, clothes, and entertainment—nice to have, but you won't die if there's no money for them.

Budget C covers the very nice to have—more clothes, vacations, manies and pedies, and so on.

If you're just starting out with A, B, C budgeting, regardless of how great your income initially is, you need to live on your Budget A for a few months as you build up a stash of cash. On a variable income, you must take care of the potential for a

CASH MANAGEMENT

No-Money Month, which is always a possibility. So have about three months' worth of Budget A expenses in the bank as part of your emergency fund before you start spending on B and C expenses.

When your earnings exceed your Budget A expenses, you can buy some of the things on Budget B. And when you have enough money, you can buy the things on Budget C. The important thing is to always have the basics covered.

A variable income means an emergency fund is very important. (See Rule #8: Everyone Needs an Emergency Fund.)

RULE #66: KNOW THE DIFFERENCE BETWEEN GOOD AND BAD DEBT

Good debt helps you increase your income or build assets. Bad debt doesn't.

A mortgage is good debt, as long as it isn't too much mortgage and doesn't put you at risk of default.

Student debt is good debt as long as you're able to pay it back on the income you'll earn when you graduate.

An RRSP loan is good debt if you can pay off the loan in one year or less, save on taxes, AND make your RRSP contribution for the next year. Otherwise, you've just gotten on the hamster wheel.

Business loans are good debt as long as the business generates income and stands a chance of making a profit.

Investment debt is good debt if you know what you're doing and are prepared for the risks associated with leveraging. (See Rule #56: Leveraging Isn't for Everybody.)

A car loan may be good debt if you need the car to earn your income. But it can't be a big ol' fancy car. And it's got to be paid off as quickly as possible (three years or less).

A line of credit used to finance home improvements that MUST be done to keep the home healthy and safe and is paid off lickety-split isn't technically "good" debt (you should have had a home maintenance fund), but it beats watching your largest asset fall down around your ears.

A consolidation loan isn't "good" debt either, but it's better than the alternative forms of borrowing if the interest rate is lower than you're currently paying on those debts AND if you pay off the loan in three years or less.

Everything else is bad debt: credit card balances, the Buy Now Pay Later plan, the line of credit used for everything from groceries to vacations, furniture loans, home improvement loans for nice-to-have features, leases or loans on cars that take you above the 15% (of net income) guideline for transportation. Oh, I could go on all day. Suffice to say, if you don't fall into any of the categories above for "good" debt, think seriously about why you're borrowing and what you'll "gain." No gain? Don't borrow.

If you're taking on bad debt, I want you to slap yourself on the forehead. Hard. If your debt falls into the "good debt" category and you're being responsible about how you deal with it—keeping your costs low, not dragging out the repayment period—then it's a necessary evil and you shouldn't beat yourself up over it. Just work hard to get it paid off as quickly as you can.

RULE #67: TAKE CARE OF YOUR STUFF

I'm sometimes surprised at how much people are willing to pay for New, but how little effort or money they want to put into keeping their stuff "healthy." It is almost as if once we acquire something we've longed for—and shelled out good money for—it loses its value and our attention. Witness the many people who buy homes and have little or no money in their budgets for home maintenance. Or the people who swoon over the new-car smell but don't bother to do their routine oil changes and regularly scheduled maintenance. Or folks who drop $300 for a new pair of boots but can't be bothered to spend the time or the ten bucks to spray on the leather protector that'll stop those boots from being ruined by salt and snow, or the $15 for a new heel.

Furnace filters need to be changed. Showers need to be recaulked. Tires need to be inflated. Walls need to be painted. Fridge coils need to be cleaned. So do lawn mowers and computer hard drives. When was the last time you washed your makeup brushes or oiled your pneumatic tools? You work hard to buy the stuff you desire. Despite planned obsolescence, most things will last longer with some attention. Take care of your stuff.

SAVING

RULE #68: TIP MONEY IS REAL MONEY

Matthew, my daughter Alex's boyfriend, texted me one day: "What should I do with my tip money?" Good question.

So many people put their tips in their pocket and then spend them willy-nilly. Those fives and tens disappear in no time, leaving no trace. Are ya nuts? Tip money is real money and should form part of your budget. Here's how:

Put all of this month's tip money in a jar. (This will be hard at first because you're so used to spending that money you're going to feel deprived. Get over it.)

Next month, count the money in your tip jar and incorporate it into your budget. You might use it for entertainment or groceries, for clothes or to boost your emergency fund. That'll leave more from your paycheque in the bank to cover other expenses and goals. Every month, use your previous months' tip money, which you stored up in your jar, to pay for specific budget categories. Since you already know how much you earned in tips—they're in the jar—you don't have to guess how much you have available to spend in those categories.

When Matthew asked Alex to count his tip money jar after one month, he was astounded to learn that it was over $300.

"No way," he said.

"Way," said she. "Isn't my mommy smart?"*

*I don't think she actually said this, but she should have.

CASH MANAGEMENT

RULE #69: EI DOESN'T NEGATE THE NEED FOR AN EF

If you've justified not having an emergency fund because you know Employment Insurance will kick in or because you expect you're entitled to a big severance, you're deluding yourself. There are so many scenarios in which EI won't help at all, including the following:

- What if the company you work for becomes insolvent? No severance.
- What if your partner becomes ill and you have to take on full responsibility for paying all the bills? No wiggle room.
- What if your work hours are cut back? No EI.
- What if your child or elderly parent gets sick and you must take time off work? No EI and only a pathetic amount of caregiver support.
- What if you're unemployed for more than a year? EI will run dry.

It is a sad reality that people who have stable jobs in good companies find themselves kicked to the curb with far less than they imagined they would have. And it can take some people a long, long time to find another job. Sometimes you'll find yourself making less. There are so many different ways for an emergency to strike.

Having money in the bank gives you options. And the peace

of mind is worth so much more than just the money in the bank. This is one of the things most people who don't have an emergency fund can't appreciate. If you're without one, it's only a matter of time before you'll be wishing you had one.

No one is ever lucky enough to get all the way through life without some crap hitting the fan. Even if you do qualify for EI, you'll have to wait some time for the first cheque to arrive. You'll need some cash in the bank. Plan like a pessimist and you can reduce the mess.

RULE #70: STOP LETTING YOUR ADULT CHILDREN TAP YOUR WALLET

You've provided for a family and raised happy, healthy children. You should be glowing with pride. Instead, you're riddled with guilt because your adult son or daughter is a mess financially. You're tapped out and you don't know what to do.

Your progeny don't get a free ride just because they are of your loins. You've done your job as a parent. It's time for these adults to learn that if they want something—to go to China, to get a master's degree, to buy a car—they have to find a way to pay for it. I'm all for helping out when the money is there. But if you're tapped out and you need to pull back and figure out what you "want" to do and what you think you "must" do because of parental guilt . . . then lose the guilt.

Make a budget that covers not only your basic needs but some of your wants too. Then sit down with your kids. Tell them how much you love them and how certain you are that they can have the lives they want, but that it's time they started to pay for those lives. You'll help when you can—those are small gifts that you give because you "want" to—but now it's time for you to take care of your future and your present!

Kicking kids off the bankroll isn't easy. I know what it feels like to want to give your kids EVERYTHING! But it's not healthy for them, because until they do for themselves, they don't know they CAN do for themselves. And if your giving is putting you at risk financially, you must stop. (See Rule #46: Don't Put Yourself at Risk to Help Others.)

RULE #71: BE CAREFUL WHEN GIVING OUT YOUR INFO

My friend Megan asked, "Is there any risk to using sites like mint. com when they require all your bank access information?" It's a good question.

Technically, if you give your personal access codes to a third party, banks are off the hook should your account be accessed fraudulently. They don't consider it "fraud" because you willingly gave someone access to your information. I think the courts would take the same position. So you could end up holding a huge bag of crap if there's ever a breach and your information is stolen.

Only you can decide if you trust a third-party aggregator like mint.com with your information. And since their terms of use explicitly say that you agree you're using their service at your own risk, that should be enough of a warning.

Keep in mind the same holds true if you give your partner or your best friend your PIN or password. If you're in a jam and you HAVE to give your info to someone—life happens, right?—change your password or PIN immediately after the favour is done. Leaving anyone with access to your financial world is begging to be screwed.

Giving out your credit card number is fine, as long as you do it without also handing over the three-digit number on the back of your card, unless you're doing a secured transaction. How do you know if the transaction is secured? The website will blast it at you to reassure you. Or there will be a little symbol in your browser telling you so.

REALITY BITES

RULE #72: DON'T AUTOMATICALLY RENEW YOUR MORTGAGE

It may be easier to just sign the renewal document when your mortgage term ends, but that isn't always a good idea. Banks know that it's a major hassle to leave one lender for another. Once they have you hooked, you are likely to stay with them out of convenience. So banks tend to offer great incentives to new buyers, while neglecting their old, loyal customers.

When the mortgage renewal shows up in your mailbox (which will happen even if you work with a mortgage broker), don't assume you've got the best offer out there. Go online and compare rates, and then call your lender to negotiate a better deal. Or call your mortgage broker and have him or her do it for you.

What will a savings of just 0.5% mean in terms of interest you won't have to pay? Well, if you manage to pay 0.5% less on a $200,000 mortgage amortized for 25 years, over a 5-year term you'll save $4,795 in interest. Do it over the life of that mortgage and you'd save $16,879 in interest. Isn't that worth a little negotiating?

RULE #73: TRACK YOUR NET WORTH

Think of your net worth statement as a financial report card. A net worth statement measures the difference between what you own and what you owe to show you where you stand. If you've been patting yourself on the back because you've got a pension plan at work and have a maxed-out TFSA, but you're also carrying a dozen credit cards littered with balances, your net worth statement will make you sit up and pay attention.

The numbers don't lie (unless of course you play loosey-goosey with them). If you work through this process and find you have less than you thought, don't be sad. Knowing where you are right now is just the first step. Take a snapshot of your progress at least once a year to track your progress.

Completing a net worth statement takes a little work because you'll have to gather up all your statements for what you own and what you owe. Unless, of course, you owe nothing, in which case it's straight addition! Well done!

Do NOT guesstimate figures for your net worth statement. If you can't be bothered to do the work, just consider yourself a money moron and move on to some other fun activity.

Once you've got all your paperwork in one place, take the following steps:

1. Add up what you Own. This may include the value of your home, your car (Black Book value), your retirement savings, your TFSA balance, the money in that savings account you hid from yourself.

2. Add up what you Owe. Everything. Your student loans, your credit cards, your car loan, overdraft protection, and the Buy Now Pay Later that's still outstanding, even if it hasn't come due yet.
3. Subtract what you Owe from what you Own. That's your net worth.

If you have a positive number, it means you own more than you owe and you're building assets. If your number is a negative, it means you owe more than you own and you must get busy paying down your debt and building up your assets. Use your net worth statement as a motivator, celebrating as you move from level to level in achieving your goals.

For goodness' sake, don't compare your net worth to anyone else's. Use your net worth statement to compare where you were to where you are and where you want to go next.

RULE #74: DON'T BUY WHAT YOU DON'T KNOW

This is one of Three Golden Rules of Investing. (For the other two, see Rule #37: Know Your Time Horizon, and Rule #80: Know Your Risk Tolerance.)

My biggest criticism of the investment world is its focus on return, with a cursory nod to the potential risks and how an investor may react. Because of this, people get talked into buying investments they don't understand. But it's not enough to THINK you understand. You have to KNOW you understand well enough to explain it to a complete neophyte. The next time you're tempted to buy an investment, find yourself a teenager and see if you can explain it. If you can't, don't buy it until you can.

Investing requires both knowledge and experience. If it were easy to make money in the markets, all those Joes trying to sell you investments would have made their scores and bought themselves financial freedom.

There are fabulous advisors out there. But fabulous advisors don't work for free. If you want to use their brains to make money, you'll have to pay for it. If you aren't willing to do that, stick with buying the index (assuming you know what the index is and can explain how it works to a teenager).

The sad reality is that many of the people who banks put in front of you to sell investments aren't actually qualified to help you. They're pretty much furniture salespeople, and those mutual fund units are chairs and TVs. Bank people are counting on the advertising to draw you in and on your financial ignorance to make them look smart.

RULE #75: PAY OFF CALLABLE DEBT FIRST

This replaces the rule "Pay off your most expensive debt first."

"Callable debt" is credit the bank can demand you repay at their whim. Think credit card debt, lines of credit, and overdraft.

During the last credit crunch, callable credit got called. When Angie phoned me in a panic, it was to say that her bank had arbitrarily lowered the limit on her line of credit. Out of the blue, it reduced her maxed-out credit line from $10,000 to $6,500. "How am I supposed to come up with $3,500? If I had that kind of money lying around, I wouldn't have needed the line of credit, would I?"

Angie was mad. But she was also desperately afraid. She had secured the line of credit as part of a plan for getting her debt paid off, and this would be a major setback. "I'm going to have to take cash advances on my three credit cards to make good on the line of credit." One step forward, two back.

Angie's wasn't the only story I heard. I got calls from people who watched their credit card limits reduced. Then there was the call from Rebecca. Having lived in overdraft for over a year—with her account moving into the black on payday and then right back into the red the minute her rent cheques cleared—Rebecca was surprised to find her bank account frozen. "They said I can't stay in overdraft. I'm only supposed to use it for brief periods."

"They're right," I replied. "Overdraft is supposed to help you out of a tight squeeze, not provide you with $800 of extra money to spend every month."

"But I've been in overdraft for years and nobody complained before."

"I know," I said, "but the credit market has dried up, and lenders and banks are covering their asses."

"They can do this?" she asked plaintively.

"They sure can," I said. "So now where are you going to come up with the money?"

"I'm going to have to miss my rent payment this month," she said. "That's my only option."

If you think that just because your line of credit interest rate is lower than your mortgage interest rate, you should get the mortgage paid off first, think again. Even though the mortgage rate may be higher, you must pay off the line first because it is callable credit.

RULE #76: STOP RATIONALIZING

Are you a master at rationalizing your spending? Have you ever said?

- "It's a really good deal."
- "It's an investment." (referring to a consumable)
- "I'm saving 75%!"
- "Spending $200 on this pair of jeans is okay because they're a better quality and fit."
- "I need it."

FINDING BALANCE

If you find yourself coming up with a "good excuse" for laying out money you hadn't planned on spending, you're probably rationalizing. That's bad. It means you think you need to justify the decision. And that means you're not sure you should be taking the action you're taking.

Most people who rationalize their spending do so to convince themselves that it's okay to part with the money. Hey, does it make sense to buy another pair of jeans, an appliance you'll use once in a blue moon, or a super-expensive designer label when you don't have any savings?

Sure, you have to live. Plus there's got to be some fun in your life. But if you haven't taken steps to create a sound financial foundation, you're deluding yourself into thinking that bad things can't happen to good people. And you're wrong.

The next time you find yourself rationalizing with thoughts like "I work hard—I deserve it" or "It's just . . ." referring to the cost, stop and think. Consider the short-term pleasure you derive over the long-term cost to your future. Also think about the opportunity cost of spending the money. (See Rule #62: Understand Opportunity Cost.) Then decide if you really, really want to buy that something. If you do, buy it.

As long as you have the money and you're sure of your decision, you don't need to rationalize your purchases.

RULE #77: BUILD A STRONG PERSONAL ECONOMY

The news is always full of some financial drama or another. The stock market is skyrocketing. The stock market is diving. The credit world is in meltdown. Savings are in the tank. Inflation is zooming. The economy is suffering from stagflation.

The global economy will always be changing. That's life. But does that breaking news always have an impact on you and your life? Let's face it; if the whole world is on a high and you've just lost your job, can't make your bill payments on time, or have just had to leave work because of an illness, all that good news has little bearing on you. And if the whole world is ready to jump off a bridge and you've got all your ducks in a row, you'll be fine.

If you don't have a strong financial foundation, the global or local economy's woes are likely to have a bigger impact on you than you'd like. But if your personal economy is strong, you'll have a plan, along with the resources and flexibility to make it through the rough patches and take advantage of the highs in the bigger-picture economy.

Focusing on your personal economy means putting into place the pieces that will protect you and give you some financial room to manoeuvre. Having clear financial goals helps. Establishing a well-maintained emergency fund is key. So are using credit wisely (not taking on debt for stupid stuff) and living below your means. And, of course, you have to be saving and investing for the future.

The issues and the impact of the global economy are real, and they can have an impact on your personal economy. Just ask all the folks who have lost jobs, taken pay cuts, or had their hours at work cut back. But if you allow the mind-numbing negative information that flows around you to drive your behaviour, you will not be happy.

You do value "happy" as part of your personal economy, right?

RULE #78: TOO GOOD TO BE TRUE USUALLY IS

Whenever investments pop up promising returns that are significantly higher than the current average rates of return, you have to be VERY careful. I'm talking promises of interest rates far in excess of what's available at a regular bank. I'm talking "guaranteed returns" that are projected to be extremely high.

Extremely high returns—or promises of return—are used to lure novice investors and greedy people into plunging good money into suspect investments. And every year some sucker falls for a scam. If you don't want to be a victim, use your common sense and do some legwork:

- Check with your local securities commission to see if the company and the salesperson are registered and if there are any current or upcoming enforcement proceedings against them.
- Do a Google search: "Is [name of company or investment] a scam?" If you get back rave reviews, it probably is because someone is planting "raves" like worms on hooks to get suckers to nibble.
- Look at the kinds of investments the company is making.
- Ask for and read the company's financial statements.
- Above all, follow Rule #73: Don't Buy What You Don't Know, and never buy what you don't completely understand.

If you are being promised a high rate of return with no risk, or being given "inside" information, rest assured you're being scammed. If you're being asked to make the decision quickly because it's a "one-time opportunity" and you have to "act fast," you're being scammed. If you're being offered a tax-free offshore opportunity, or the chance to get in on something usually available only to the wealthy, you're being scammed.

RULE #79: KEEP TAX-RELATED PAPERWORK FOR SEVEN YEARS

Remember when they said that computers were going to do away with the mountains of paper we have to file? We was lied to. Between investment accounts, bank accounts, credit card statements, and the millions of other pieces of paper the mailman delivers to my mailbox, I am swamped.

Deciding what to file and what to fling boils down to a couple of things:

1. Are you likely to need it again as a reference?

2. Are you obliged to hang onto this piece of paper just in case someone official starts asking questions?

If the answer is yes to either one, the item gets filed. No? Then it joins the ranks of the shredded.

Your home: File real estate paperwork and mortgage contracts. Fling everything but your most recent insurance documents. File all records relating to home improvements, repairs, and additions. Keep six months' worth of utility bills and fling the rest.

Your stuff: File the warranties that came with household appliances or electronics. Fling 'em when they expire.

Your vehicle: File the most recent version of your car insurance along with a copy of your car registration and ownership. If you can write off automobile expenses on your tax return, file every single itty-bitty receipt for gas, oil, repairs, licence fees, and parking.

Your job: File employment contracts, details of benefits packages, group insurance, and pay stubs. (File your pay stubs in your tax file). If you can write off entertainment and travel, keep these receipts. If your boss reimburses you for them, you can't claim them on your personal return.

Your financials: File bank and investment statements chronologically. Fling all the promotional flyers and brochures that arrived with the statements. A good rule of thumb is to keep investment paperwork for six years after you've sold the investment. Keep a year or two's supply of bank statements, cancelled cheques, and credit card statements so that when it's time to review your spending, you have some figures to work with.

Your taxes: CRA says you should keep your supporting documentation for six years from the end of the last year to which your paperwork relates. Just count back seven years from the year of your return and you'll be safe. So, you'll have to keep your 2016 tax paperwork until 2023.

Your estate: File your will, powers of attorney, and a full list of all the key contacts of your financial life somewhere people can find them. If you put them in your safety deposit box, no one will be able to get at them.

Your personal documents: Make colour photocopies of your SIN card, your provincial or territorial health insurance card, your driver's licence, birth certificate, certificate of citizenship, and marriage certificate. File the originals somewhere safe and use only the photocopies when you must produce the documents, unless the original is specifically required.

Your marriage and divorce papers: File them. Don't think that because the marriage is over, you can fling the paperwork. You might need it again down the road if you decide to remarry (and to my shock and horror) if you decide to divorce again. File everything legal relating to the kids.

All it takes to put your paperwork in order is a little time, some file folders, and a willingness to part with the minutiae.

RULE #80: KNOW YOUR RISK TOLERANCE

This is one of Three Golden Rules of Investing. (For the other two, see Rule #37: Know Your Time Horizon, and Rule #74: Don't Buy What You Don't Know.)

Risk tolerance can be a tough thing to measure. If you only think of how you would react to a fall in the value of your investment, it's easy to delude yourself because it's easy to be brave in theory. Let the reality of watching one-third of your portfolio evaporate in a market decline and your actions may tell a whole different story about your risk tolerance. That's why a market downturn results in fools fleeing for their lives and turning their "paper losses" into real losses.

Think of risk as having two faces:

- **Risk tolerance** is how you'll react when the going gets tough.
- **Risk inclination** is how you think you'll react when the going gets tough, which is influenced by the prospect of a higher return on your money.

Not until you answer some very concrete questions will you know what your true risk tolerance is. In the meantime, your risk inclination might get you into trouble.

The standard question asked by most risk profiling questionnaires, or by advisors, is "Are you prepared to take more risk for the opportunity to earn a higher return?" Most people happily say, "Yes." That's risk inclination at work. Sure, you want a higher return. But how much more risk are you willing to take? And how big a loss would you be able to tolerate?

"Life" questions help you to see more clearly how you might respond in "investment" circumstances. Leopards can't change their spots, and if you'd react one way in "life," in all likelihood you'd react the same way in "investing." So, the key to figuring out where you are on the risk inclination/tolerance scale is to think about a variety of circumstances and how you might respond.

Here's an example of what I mean. Let's say you've just saved the money you need for the vacation you've long been planning. You haven't booked anything yet, but the money's in the bank. Then you find out that you're about to lose your job. Would you

a) cancel the vacation?
b) take a more modest trip?
c) go as you planned (you've got the money)?
d) take some extra time and extend the trip, since who knows when you'll get to do this again?

Can you guess what the conservative investor would do? What would you do?

Experience plays a role in increasing your ability to tolerate risk and in helping you clarify your risk inclination. If you've done some investing and you've experienced the markets' ups and downs, that experience will influence your future behaviour. A spate of investment successes might serve to make you feel immune. That's what happens when markets are rising and any fool can make money; people come to believe there's no downside. Ditto when the markets start to dipsy-doodle and folks start likening investing to gambling.

Investing isn't gambling unless you're an idiot and don't understand what you're doing. But many investments do carry significant risk of capital loss. If you don't understand that risk, if you can't balance your inclination with your tolerance, you will be unhappy.

The risk questionnaires in *Never Too Late* are good examples of what you need to know about yourself to figure out your risk tolerance. If you let your risk inclination rule, you could very well end up a very unhappy investor.

RULE #81: AVOID EARLY RENEWAL PENALTIES

SHELTER

Planning to renew your mortgage early? Maybe you're trying to lock in at a lower interest rate because rates have fallen and you want the better rate for a long time. Or perhaps you see that the longer term rates are going up, so you want to lock in now at the existing rate for a longer term so you don't end up paying 2%, or 3%, or 4% more. Regardless of your reason for renewing your mortgage early, paying a penalty can be a bitter pill to swallow.

Sometimes called a "lost interest compensation (LIC)" or an "interest rate differential (IRD)," it's your lender's pound of flesh if you're breaking your mortgage contract.

When the interest rate on a new mortgage is higher than on an existing mortgage (in the case of locking in for a longer term), you'd think lenders would waive the interest rate penalty. Not always. They may still make you pay three months' worth of interest as a penalty.

If the interest rate you're moving to is lower than the current rate you're paying, your lender will definitely make you pay the IRD. The IRD is the difference in the interest payable on your existing mortgage versus that payable on a replacement mortgage, calculated on the time remaining in your existing mortgage term.

If you had a year and seven months left on a $200,000 mortgage at 5% and your new interest rate was 3.75%, you'd end up paying an IRD of about $4,300. Each lender has its own way of calculating the interest penalty if you renew early

MONEY RULES · 163

(or try to pay down your mortgage beyond what's allowed by your principal prepayment clause of your mortgage contract). Most lenders have online calculators that can help you figure out your IRD.

Some people are very willing to eat the LIC, adding it into their mortgage so they can get the lower interest rate for a longer period. They argue that the longer term savings on their mortgage is well worth paying the LIC. But why would you pay something you don't have to pay?

Ask your mortgage provider about a "blend-and-extend" mortgage as an alternative.

With a blend-and-extend, you continue to pay the existing interest rate for the remaining term on your mortgage, but you renew early to lock in the lower rate for the remaining term.

Say you have 19 months to go on your mortgage at 5%. The current 5-year rate is sitting at 3.75%. If you used a blend-and-extend, you'd pay 5% for the first 19 months and 3.75% for the remaining 3.5 years on your new 5-year term. If the lender presents this as a single blended interest rate, ask to see the math to make sure you're getting the deal you think you are getting.

Not everyone understands how a blend-and-extend works. You may have to ask for a more experienced lender to get what you want.

RULE #82: STAY WITHIN CDIC LIMITS

Whenever you're thinking of putting your money on deposit—be it in a savings or chequing account, a term deposit, a GIC, TFSA, RRSP, or RRIF—the first thing you should check is that the company taking your money is a member of Canada Deposit Insurance Corporation (CDIC) and that your deposit is covered.

CDIC is a federal Crown corporation that was created in the late 1960s to protect you in the event that a bank or other financial company in which you held your money failed. The best place to check to see if the company you're dealing with is a member of CDIC is on the CDIC website at www.cdic.ca.

There is a single $100,000 limit for all non-registered accounts with a single bank, including savings and chequing accounts, term deposits (deposits for 30 to 364 days), and GICs (usually deposits of 1 to 5 years). If you're offered a deposit term longer than 5 years, it will NOT be covered by CDIC.

Joint accounts are covered separately up to a $100,000 maximum.

Registered accounts such as RRSPs, RRIFs, and TFSAs are covered separately from non-registered deposits, but only for those deposit products that are CDIC-insurable. So mutual funds, stocks, treasury bills, bonds, and foreign currency accounts are NOT covered.

Your RESPs may not be covered by CDIC. Betcha didn't know that! The *CDIC Act* makes no provision for separate coverage of eligible deposits held in a RESP. So eligible deposits in an RESP may or may not qualify for separate coverage, depending on whether the particular RESP is structured as a trust. You'll have to ask your RESP provider. This is a significant oversight on CDIC's part and should be fixed. It won't be until you yell about it!

RULE #83: CALCULATE THE REAL PROFIT ON YOUR HOME

One of the favourite delusions people like to share with one another is the "I made a b'jillion dollars on the sale of my home." Another version of this delusion is the "My house is worth a b'jillion dollars more than I paid for it."

Your profit isn't just the difference between what you bought your home for and what you sold your home for (or what you paid versus what the house is currently worth).

Here are some of the other things besides selling price that you have to take into account:

- the interest you've paid (through your mortgage payments) thus far;
- the property tax you've paid (or owe);
- the cost of maintenance and upkeep; and
- the costs associated with selling the home, if you choose to liquidate.

While it's lovely to think that you've been very smart, buying a home for $275,000 and then selling it seven years later for $425,000, the $150,000 difference isn't all profit. There are some significant costs thrown in, to which many people choose to turn a blind eye.

Assuming you put 10% down, amortized that puppy for 25 years, and paid an average interest rate of 6.35% (the current 7-year rate as I type this), you would have paid $103,692 in interest over the 7 years. That knocks your "profit" back a bit, doesn't it?

Don't delude yourself into thinking that a home is a great investment. It's a good investment. And there's a wonderful sense of pride for people who genuinely love their homes. Home ownership is not for everyone. And it gives only a modest return on investment.

And for heaven's sake, the next time people tell you how much profit they made on the sale of their home, make sure it's take-home profit after interest, taxes, maintenance, and commissions. Otherwise, you're just buying into their delusion.

RULE #84: KNOW HOW COMPOUNDING WORKS

When it came time to write the rule about understanding how compounding works, I called my editor, Kate. "Do I actually have to write this AGAIN?" I moaned.

"Yes," she said, "it's an important rule."

"Can't we just copy it from one of the other books?"

"No." Long silence. She was probably giving me room to go off on a rant—she claims she was thinking—but I waited to hear what she'd say next. "You actually have to find another way to explain it." I could just hear the glee in her voice. Kate enjoys presenting me with challenges.

So I sat and thought. And thought. And thought. And then I decided, "Y'know, a really useful way to explain this again would be to do it as if I were explaining it to a 10-year-old. Then all the parents out there who haven't a clue how to explain this extremely important concept to their young 'uns would have an example to follow. And all the people who still don't know the rule of compounding would finally get it."

Since we want to make compounding as easy to understand as possible, the first thing we're going to do is accept that we have to use a completely unrealistic rate of interest in our lesson. And since we don't want to take a whole year to explain the idea of compounding, we're going to shorten the time span.

Get two jars—any clean jars will do. You'll also need about 25 loonies, 40 dimes, and 40 pennies.

Here's the talk:

"When you put money in the bank, if you're a smart shopper and choose the right account, the bank will pay you inter-est on your money. I want to demonstrate how that interest can work to earn even more interest.

"Here's a pile of loonies. When I give the go-ahead, you'll put one dollar in the savings jar, which will be our pretend bank account. That's the amount of money you're saving. So go ahead and drop your dollar in the jar.

"The bank looks at the money in your account and decides how much to pay you in interest. Interest is the money the bank pays you for letting it keep YOUR money in ITS account. I'm the bank. I'm looking at your dollar in the savings jar, and I'll pay you 10 cents. I'll drop a dime in the interest jar.

"You could take the dime out and spend it, and you'd still have the dollar in the savings jar. The dime is the interest you would get for that saved dollar for one year.

"If you always took the dime out, then you'd only ever have the money you put in the savings jar. But look what happens when you leave the dime in the interest jar each time.

"Go ahead and drop another dollar in the savings jar, and I'll pay you 10 cents in interest on it. Again, the dime is the interest you would get for that dollar for one year on the money you saved.

"And now you have how much in interest? I've given you two dimes, so now you have 20 cents in interest, and that's money that you didn't have to save.

"Okay, drop in another dollar and I'll give you another dime.

"And another." (All the way to $10.)

"Now let's empty out the jars and count what we have.

"How many loonies are in the savings jar? Ten—good.

"How many dimes are in the interest jar? Ten—good. What do 10 dimes add up to? A dollar. So instead of just the $10 you put into the jar, you now have a total of $11.

"Now here's the magic part: You put all the interest you've earned into your savings jar and you've just 'compounded' your interest . . . as in, left it there to earn more interest.

"Drop another dollar in your jar. Now you have $12 in the jar. As long as you leave all those dimes in there, I have to pay you interest on them too. So even though you put only 11 loonies in the jar, I have to pay you interest on $12 because you left the dimes (interest) in there and they added up to another dollar. Which means, instead of giving you 10 cents in interest, the bank is going to be paying you 12 cents.

"When you have $20, I'll have to pay you 20 cents. When you get to $25, I'll have to give you 25 cents. Can you see how leaving the interest in the account lets you earn even more interest? That's compounding. When your interest earns its own interest, compounding is at work.

"Before you go off thinking that some bank is going to pay you 10 cents on a dollar every week, let me bring you back to reality. It's not. It'll pay you a lot less. But that doesn't matter. The concept is the same. When your money earns more money and you let that extra money build and earn even more, you're making the Magic of Compound Interest work for you."

So that's how you explain compounding to a child. If you're still not sure yourself, go through each step of the exercise, and the concreteness of the example will bring the magic home to you too.

RULE #85: PATIENCE IS A VIRTUE

Most people are impatient. They start to save and want those savings to grow quickly. Some even buy investments they don't understand (see Rule #74: Don't Buy What You Don't Know) to try to grow their savings faster.

Relax. Slow down. Consistent savings and time will work wonders for you. Have some patience (and see Rule #84: Know How Compounding Works).

If you allow your impatience to get the better of you, you'll get frustrated with the progress you're making in the early days. That might drive you to do stupid things. Or it might make you feel that saving is a slog, you'll never have enough anyway, so you might as well spend your money.

Don't be a dope. Saving takes time. So does investing. I know life has speeded up dramatically. We now multi-task. We want our food to be ready in 30 minutes or less. Even the number of edits per minute in a typical movie has increased in the past three decades. But some things take time. And patience is still a virtue. As Warren Buffett says, "The stock market serves as a relocation center at which money is moved from the active [read: people who trade often] to the patient."

It can be hard to practise patience in saving and investing if you don't also practise patience in the rest of your life. Slow down. Be purposeful and focus on the things that you do. Cook a slow meal. Embrace challenges and work through them slowly until you build your patience muscles. And most important, be patient with yourself. You are a work in progress.

RULE #86: THE KNOW YOUR CLIENT FORM DOES NOT GIVE YOU A GOOD RISK PROFILE

When you become an investor, your advisor is required to have you fill out the Know Your Client (KYC) form. This is touted as a way to ensure you're only investing in things appropriate to your risk profile. But if that's the only risk profiling you go through, it's a total joke. Those forms aren't intended to help you determine how you feel about investing and the risks you're willing to take. The KYC form is a "cover your butt" designed to protect institutions from reprimand and lawsuits.

To be able to stay the course with an investment plan, you must truly know your risk tolerance. So if the Know Your Client form is all the advisor or company has to offer you in terms of helping you decide what you'll be comfortable buying, run for the hills.

That said, if you invest in something that is contrary to the KYC form you filled out and your investment goes south, the company and the advisor are technically on the hook for putting you in an investment contrary to your known profile. You could sue and get some or all of your money back. That's what happened to friends of friends of friends of mine. They got caught up in the Bre-X gold scam, but their KYC forms indicated that they weren't comfortable with that level of risk. They sued their advisor and settled, recovering their lost investment savings.

RULE #87: CLEAN UP YOUR DEBT MESS

Sure, the credit card companies let you have all the rope you needed to hang yourself. And the banks wanted you to take on lines of credit as emergency funds or just in case you saw something you wanted to buy. Hey, it's the bank's job to sell you credit. It's a product, like flour or shoes or a new couch. You don't go around saying, "That darned supermarket made me buy too much flour," do you? So accept responsibility for the mess you've made by taking on too much consumer debt and get busy fixing the problem by doing the following:

1. Make a plan to get out of debt. DIY is the way to go, and *Debt-Free Forever* will show you how. Resist the urge to offload. If you go with a debt settlement company, not only will you pay a lot of money but your credit rating will go into the tank. Ditto credit counselling. If you're going to seek help, go directly to a bankruptcy trustee and talk about declaring bankruptcy or making a consumer proposal. If you want to keep your credit rating (provided it's still a good one), then you'll have to clean up your own mess.

2. Call your creditors and ask for a reduction in your interest rate. Tell them that you're on the verge of insolvency and you need their help to pay them back what you owe. Tell them that you're prepared to declare bankruptcy if they force you to, since you have to eat.

3. If you've received offers of low-interest credit, do balance transfers and get that debt paid off before the special rate ends. Once the "enticement period" wears off, the rate will likely skyrocket, so don't get caught.

4. Find a way to make more money and throw it all at the debt, making every minimum payment but using the rest to pay down the debt with the highest interest rate first. Once that debt is gone, apply the payment to the next highest interest rate. Snowball until it's all gone.

5. Do you have stuff you could sell to make a payment against the debt? Sell it. Every penny you use to pay off your debt is a penny that won't accrue interest.

6. Can moving to less expensive digs free up enough money to get that debt paid off faster? I have a very good friend who bit the bullet—she moved to an apartment that was half the size and not nearly as great as the one she had—and now she has the money to get her debt paid off. Once the debt is gone, she'll look at her budget and see if she wants to move again.

7. If you own, could you take in roommates, a border, a student . . . anyone to help bring in some extra cash?

Stop whining about being in debt. You had your fun. You made a mess. Now it's time to clean it up. Get busy.

RULE #88: CHARGE YOUR KIDS RENT

I think it's downright dumb the way some parents let their adult children live at home, do little or nothing to pull their own weight, and pay no rent.

If you have adult children living at home who are working full-time, charge them rent. How much should you charge? Collect 35% of their net income. I don't care what you do with the money. Go on vacation. Stash it away to help them with a future down payment on a home. Just collect the rent every single month. If they don't want to pay, tell them they have 60 days to find new digs. Then their stuff is going in the garage and you're changing the locks!

Adult children need to pay their way to keep their self-respect. Let them off the hook on rent and other financial responsibilities—let them spend their income any ol' way they want—and you'll be teaching them to live on a disposable income they'll never again have. That spending behaviour is damn hard to change, so when they leave home, they fill the gap by using credit and dig themselves into horrendous amounts of debt.

If you let your children live at home with no expectation of taking care of themselves, they won't. Why would they? They've got it good and they know it. YOU will have created the monsters—and they may be there to stay!

FAMILY

RULE #89: PLAN TO GRADUATE WITH LOANS OF LESS THAN ONE YEAR'S NET INCOME

The old rule was "Go get an education; damn the cost." But that's not working. Graduates come out of school with an albatross of debt around their necks and end up working for far less money than they imagined. The debt lingers. They struggle. That's no way to live a life. So Rule #89 replaces the old rule.

If you're using student loans, you better figure out how you're going to pay back those loans once you graduate, so you know how much debt you can afford to take on.

Think you'll be making about $40,000 a year net? Then you can afford about $40,000 in student loan debt. A $40,000 loan fixed for three years has a monthly payment amount of $1,286 and will cost over $6,000 in interest. Over 5 years the payment drops to just over $800 a month but will cost you more than $10,000 in interest. Over the repayment default of 9.5 years, the payment will be just under $550 a month but will cost you $21,000 in interest. So as the payment amount you can afford to work into your cash flow goes down, your overall cost goes up.

Now let's look at how that payment amount measures up against your take home pay. If you're netting $40,000, that's the equivalent of $3,333 a month in take home pay. If you're determined to get the loan paid off in five years, it'll cost you just over $800 a month—or 24% of your income. That'll leave you with $2,533 to live on: rent, transportation, cell, insurance, savings, clothes, food, fun, and everything else you want to do when you're not working.

Some experts suggest you use the "one year's gross income" rule. Let's compare. If you based your loan on gross income, you'd be a whole lot worse off. Let's say you're taking home about $2,800 a month, which is the net in Ontario if you grossed $40,000 a year. (In Manitoba, you'd only get to take home $2,666; in Nunavut, you'd get to take home $2,870.) If you have to make a loan payment of $1,286 a month, you'd be choking on your debt. If you went with the five-year term and had to pay $800, assuming you have any living expenses, that amount of debt repayment would seem completely unmanageable since it would be eating about 29% of your income, leaving you just $2,000 for everything else. That's why most people go for the longer repayment period, paying just $550 a month, upping the cost of their education by more than 50% because of the interest.

If you're planning on getting married, setting up a home, buying a car, going on vacation, or any of the other wonderful things you may want to do with your life, you better make sure that you're NOT taking on more debt than you can afford to repay.

Before you head off and borrow too much money, look at your student loan debt in relation to your earnings ability. Limit your loan total to the net amount you'll be making when you go to work. It'll still be a tight squeeze, believe me, but it won't be totally unworkable.

RULE #90: QUITCHERBITCHIN'
AND FIRE YOUR BANK

People are always whining about the fees they have to pay on their bank accounts. One of the main reasons people won't switch accounts is laziness, plain and simple. It takes work. And not a small amount of work either. If you have pre-authorized debits, trying to get them all switched over can feel like torture. But if all that's standing between you and an account that pays decent interest without exorbitant fees is laziness, you ought to give your head a shake.

Start by making a list of the things you actually need on your account. Do you even write cheques anymore? How often do you go to the banking machine? (If you're going more than once a week, you're using the ATM as a wallet. Stop!) How many swipes of your debit card do you do in a month? Do you travel a lot, requiring easy and cheap access to your money when you're on the road?

Go shopping to compare prices and features. Hit the pavement, let your fingers do the walking, or go online and narrow down the alternatives.

Ready to quitcherbitchin' and fire your current ungrateful, money-grubbing bank?

1. Open the new account. Take two pieces of ID with you when you go. And make sure you have your social insurance number, because it's a required piece of info for tax reporting purposes. If the account you're

CASH MANAGEMENT

opening is a U.S. dollar account, one piece of ID has to prove your citizenship, so take your birth certificate or passport. Get all the information you'll need to notify others, like the account number and your branch number. Order some cheques even if you aren't writing cheques regularly, since you'll need to use voided cheques to set up auto-payments and transfers between accounts.

2. List your transactions. Whether you pay your hydro bill by electronic banking, have your car insurance auto-deducted, or have your RRSP contribution transferred monthly from your chequing account, you'll have to switch 'em all over to your new account. Look over your past five or six statements and make your list. You'll want to watch for

- utility payments,
- mortgage payments,
- property taxes,
- insurance,
- credit payments (loan, cards, and lines of credit),
- other accounts that may be linked to the account you're closing,
- auto-deductions for home or life insurance, and
- all the people who give you money, such as your employer and the government—think GST, child tax credits, and tax refunds.

This will be your master list. As you transfer each item to your new account, check it off this list.

3. Reconcile your account. You have to account for every penny so you don't have any nasty surprises during the transition. Those six postdated cheques to the music teacher will bounce sky high if you close the account without replacing her cheques.

4. Switch over the deposits first. Once there's money in the account, switch over the withdrawals.

5. Leave the old account open for about two months, with some money in it to catch any missing deposits or withdrawals. Don't worry that the balance in the old account is just sitting there. It's protecting you from the aggravation caused by a poor memory. Be patient, and when there's been no activity for a month, consider yourself in the clear and close the old account.

If this all seems like too much work to you, stick with your old account. But stop whining about how unhappy you are. It'll take a little work to make things better. Or you can keep sucking up the rotten service and high fees. Your money. Your choice.

RULE #91: STAYING HOME WITH BABY IS A PRIVILEGE

Just because you may be guaranteed a year of maternity leave with job protection doesn't mean you're in a financial position to accept it. Taking a year off with a new baby is a privilege you earn only if you've planned for it and have the money to make ends meet without going into debt.

Unless you will receive a 100% top-up from your employer, you'll be relying on a combination of EI benefits and savings. EI benefits are calculated as 55% of your normal earnings up to a maximum salary of $45,900 (for 2012). The maximum works out to about $485 a week before taxes. Yes, mat leave benefits are taxable income. (See Rule #24: Calculate Your Taxes to Avoid a Tax Bill.) Check with EI to see what your benefit will be well before you have to start counting on it. In all likelihood, you'll have to live on less money. To see the implication of the mat leave income drop-off, **practise living on your mat leave income for the duration of the pregnancy.** Put the rest away for emergencies, to buy the baby stuff you'll need, or to start an education savings plan. If you can't swing it while you're preggers, you might want to consider taking less than a full year's mat leave so you don't end up mired in debt.

The other thing to think about is which partner should take the most time off. Traditionally, women do this, but when they are the primary breadwinners, then the income loss is felt doubly. Do the math to see who should take time off and how much, and how that will impact the family's financial stability.

RULE #92: PAY YOUR MORTGAGE OFF BEFORE RETIREMENT

Planning to carry your mortgage into retirement? Hey, if your income is about to go down—most people don't have much more than 65 to 70% of their pre-retirement income during retirement—shouldn't your expenses go down too? Being mortgage-free is one of the best ways to cut your living expenses in retirement. And it doesn't take a ton of money to achieve the goal.

Your home is the most expensive item you are ever likely to buy. A $300,000 home with $30,000 down means you'll end up with a $270,000 mortgage. At an average interest rate of 6.5% for 25 years, you'll spend $272,555 in interest on top of the original $270,000 principal you owe, more than doubling the cost of your home!

Increase your mortgage payment by just $100 a month and you will save over $37,000 in interest. Pretty sweet, eh? It gets better. Not only will you save buckets of money, but you will also have your home paid off three years sooner.

It doesn't take a lot of extra money to make a difference. But it does take a little foresight. And a little cutting back. And a little discipline.

So now that you know you can save over $37,000 on your mortgage, where are you going to find the extra $100 a month to increase your mortgage payment so you can retire without a mortgage?

If you think it's okay to carry your mortgage into retirement, where are you going to find the money to stay in the black if your income drops by 30 to 40% but your expenses stay the same?

RULE #93: DO *NOT* CASH IN REGISTERED SAVINGS TO PAY DOWN DEBT

The tax implications of taking money out of an RRSP are enormous. I know people who have taken money out of their RRSPs and they are NEVER prepared for the amount of tax they will have to pay on those withdrawals.

If you ask to make a withdrawal from your RRSP, the bank is required by the Tax Man to keep back a portion and send it in to cover your taxes. This is referred to as the "withholding" tax, and it increases as follows as your withdrawals increase:

- withdrawal of up to $5,000—10% withheld
- withdrawal of $5,001 to $15,000—20% withheld
- withdrawal of $15,001 or more—30% withheld

The really important point is **that may not be all the tax you owe.** Since you'll pay tax on those RRSP withdrawals at your marginal tax rate, you could end up with a whopping tax bill.

Let's say you take $4,000 out of your RRSP. The bank will withhold 10%, or $400, and send it to the Tax Man. But if you're earning $45,000 a year before taxes, you aren't paying taxes at the rate of 10%. Your marginal tax rate is actually much higher: 32% in Alberta, 36% in Nova Scotia, and 38% in Quebec. So if you're living in Alberta, you're actually going to owe $1,280 in taxes on that RRSP withdrawal. You've already paid $400, so you'll still be on the hook for $880 in taxes.

Remember, too, once you've taken the money out of the RRSP, you can't put it back. You've lost that contribution room forever, which is yet another good reason not to cash in your RRSPs to pay off your debt.

RULE #94: STOP PROCRASTINATING

Have you been meaning to do a full review of your money and how you've been doing? Planning to get a will drawn up? Thinking this might be the right time to start an education savings plan for your kids? If all you're doing is planning and thinking, you may be trapped in procrastination mode.

Hey, why do today what you can put off till tomorrow, right? Life is so busy. There are things that must get done today, and whatever you've been shoving to the back burner isn't one of them.

Answer me this: WHEN will you take that step you've been meaning to take for . . . how long has it been? When will you call the bank and renegotiate your account fees? When will you call your credit card company and get your interest rate or credit limit lowered? When will you choose the guardian for your children?

If you know you should be saving, but you just aren't, you're procrastinating. If you believe it's high time you set up a filing system, but tomorrow you'll have more time, you're procrastinating. And if you're avoiding addressing your ever-growing debt load because it's so intimidating, well . . .

Unpleasant tasks—like facing our own mortality and buying life insurance—are rarely as horrible as you think they are going to be. Bite the bullet and do the crap you're dreading the most first to get it out of the way. Make a date to get it done and then give yourself a reward when you've got it done.

If you're overwhelmed by the size of what you must do—like

creating a debt repayment plan, or rebalancing your investment portfolio—break the job down into manageable tasks. Once you've halved or quartered the job, do something to start, no matter how small, so you create some momentum.

If it is fear of failure (or is it fear of success?) that has you dragging your feet, create a clear picture of the completed project in your mind and think about how you will feel when it's over. Focus on the result, not just the process. Keep reminding yourself how good you'll feel when you're finished.

Just don't want to do whatever it is you should do? We all have to do crap we don't want to do, don't like to do, don't see the point in doing. Hey, why should I have to scrub the lime scale off the inside of the shower stall? And, by the way, who stamped "change the bed linens" on my forehead? Schedule the things you know you should be doing for a time when your energy is up.

Finally, once you're on task, don't let yourself get distracted by kids, email, or something funner. A lack of focus can make jobs that should only take an hour take all day. Then you blame the job. But it's not the job. It's the lack of focus. Create a to- do list with priorities. Block time for The Thing You're Dreading and then make a rule that you are not allowed to move out of your chair, make a call, surf the Net, pick up a book, until you've finished the must-do task.

RULE #95: FOCUS ON *BEING* MARRIED, NOT JUST ON *GETTING* MARRIED

People are willing to drop megabucks for their weddings. The average cost of a wedding in 2011 was over $23,000. But since all my weddings added together haven't come to $23,000, someone's using my share!

Hey, I don't care what you spend on your weddings as long as you've saved the money and aren't taking on debt, and you don't whine about not being able to afford a home later on.

For every hour you spend planning your wedding, be it an elaborate extravaganza or a simple soiree, you should spend at least two hours talking to your soon-to-be-mate about life, the universe, and everything including your money.

Who will manage the money? How will you share your expenses? How accountable will you be to each other?

I can't believe people hook up without ever figuring out if they have the same attitudes to money, and how they'll deal with differing perspectives. Do you know what your buddy is bringing to the relationship in terms of assets and liabilities? Have you talked about whether you have any/enough life insurance? Are you planning to have kids? Who will stay home? How will you deal with changes in income? What will your life look like in five years?

While it might be exciting to plan a wedding, planning a life together is far more important. Hey, go ahead and have a great party. Just remember, it's one day. One day! Marriage is for the rest of your life. Take the time to focus on being married, not just on getting married.

RULE #96: SELL UNREGISTERED INVESTMENTS TO PAY DOWN DEBT

People like to look at their money in separate pools. They may be carrying $2,500 on a credit card, but they're very smug because they've got $5,000 invested.

If you have unregistered investments—mutual funds, GICs, Canada Savings Bonds, and the like that are not in an RRSP—and expensive consumer debt, it makes more sense to sell those investments and pay off the debt.

The return you're earning on those investments is in before-tax dollars. If you earn $100 and your marginal tax rate is 20%, you only end up with $80 in your pocket. But the interest you're paying on your debt is in after-tax dollars. If you have to pay $100 in interest on your debt, you'd have to earn $125 so you could pay your taxes and have $100 left to pay your interest.

So your investment is producing a net $80 return, but you have to bust your butt to earn $125 to get the $100 you need to pay the interest on your debt. See the gap? You're better off selling the unregistered investments and paying down the debt to eliminate as much of the interest costs as you can.

Once you've paid down your debt, take the money you would have used monthly for debt repayment and start an automatic investment plan to rebuild your assets.

RULE #97: BE HONEST ABOUT YOUR MONEY

Money is the big secret. We're more willing to talk about our sexual preferences than our money. And some of us take the money deception so far that we actually lie to ourselves. Wow!

Imagine if you had to wear a T-shirt that disclosed on the back how much you make and how much you owe. Suppose your car's licence plates showed the accruing interest on your debt. Sure would make you think twice before you did something stupid with your money, wouldn't it?

Being honest is a great way to hold yourself accountable for what you're doing with your money. You won't have to pretend you have the money to keep up, and you won't have to go into debt trying. You'll be able to breathe because you won't have to worry about the mess catching up with you. And you won't measure yourself by arbitrary financial standards.

Are people who drive expensive cars really better than people who drive second-hand domestic cars?

Are people who own in chic neighbourhoods really better than people who own (or rent) less prestigious digs?

Does how much you make really define what kind of person you are?

"To thine own self be true." When I was a young bird, my Aunty Angie wrote that quote in my autograph book and I took it to heart. I've worked hard at knowing who I am and being me. I am honest (maybe to a fault). And I'd rather be disliked for the person I am than for the person I'm pretending to be.

If you're not being honest about your money, how's that been working for you? Not so much? Maybe it's time to figure out what's important to you, what you value, what you'll stand up for. Once you know, tell everyone.

If you're suffering from imposteritis, it's time to take a course in YOU and figure out who YOU really are. As Judy Garland said, "Always be a first-rate version of yourself instead of a second-rate version of someone else."

RULE #98: YOU CAN'T BEAT THE TAX MAN ON RRSP WITHDRAWALS

People are always looking for ways to beat the system. Getting money out of an RRSP or RRIF without paying tax may sound like a good idea, particularly if you're desperately trying to get out from under. Resist the urge to participate in any such "scheme."

If you have no idea what I'm talking about and wouldn't dream of trying to screw the Tax Man, you can skip this rule completely. This is for the folks who think they can pull a fast one. The Tax Man wants you to know he's reviewing these kinds of transactions thoroughly and has already reassessed thousands of taxpayers. He warns that you should avoid any offer of

- withdrawal of funds from an RRSP or RRIF without paying tax (promoters often promise to return part of the taxpayer's investment by offshore debit or credit cards, offshore bank accounts, or loan-back arrangements),
- immediate access to assets in "locked-in" RRSPs or RRIFs, and
- income tax deductions of three or more times the amount invested in an RRSP.

While these schemes are made to appear very professional and therefore legitimate, they are not. Even if you are provided

TAXES

192 · GAIL VAZ-OXLADE

with opinion letters from professionals that give the impression the letter writer endorses the scheme, don't bite.

The government will not be denied its pound of flesh, and if it lets even one RRSP holder off the hook for taxes, it opens the door to millions in lost taxes. You can bet your first-born it will review, challenge, and win against any attempt to not pay the taxes on RRSP withdrawals.

RULE #99: A PREAPPROVED MORTGAGE DOES *NOT* MEAN YOU'RE GUARANTEED FINANCING

Many people are under the misconception that a preapproved mortgage means guaranteed financing. That's not true. Just because you're preapproved doesn't mean you're guaranteed financing. Lenders can still say no if the home you've chosen doesn't meet their lending criteria or if you bid up the house price past your borrowing limit or their perception of its real value.

What would you do if your banker turned around and said, "Sorry, you're not approved"? Unless you have a "conditional on financing" clause, according to your offer you must close. Failure to do so would result in forgoing your deposit (and how long did you scrimp and save for that?) and opening yourself to legal action.

Conditions on an Offer to Purchase aren't popular with real estate agents since conditions are one way a sale can go south. So many agents encourage their clients to bring in a "clean" offer—one without any conditions. But if you do, you only have yourself to blame when you discover you can't close because your financing fell through.

RULE #100: DON'T CLAIM YOUR RRSP DEDUCTION RIGHT AWAY

Most people think you have to claim your RRSP deduction in the year you make your RRSP contribution. You don't. While most people do take the deduction for their RRSP contribution from the get-go, there's no rule that says you can't hold off. In fact, holding off makes sense when you'll end up getting back more money from the Tax Man by delaying your tax refund gratification. If you're just starting out and earning not so much, don't claim the deduction. Wait until you're in a higher tax bracket so you'll get a bigger bang for your buck.

Let's say you're living in British Columbia and earning $37,000 a year. Your marginal tax rate—the rate of tax you pay on the last dollar you earned—is about 20%. So if you put $1,000 in an RRSP, you'd save about $200 in taxes. But if you held your deduction for when you were earning more, you'd save more in taxes. If your income went up to $42,000 a year, your marginal tax rate would go up to 22.7%, so you'd save $227 dollars. If your income went up to $56,000, your marginal tax rate would be about 29.7%, so you'd save almost $300 in taxes.

Life changes are another reason to hold off on claiming deductions. For example, say you were to go on maternity or parental leave in the early part of the year. Since your income is dramatically reduced for that year, your marginal tax rate will also be lower.

If you were living in New Brunswick and earning $76,000,

you'd be paying a marginal tax of 34%. If your mat leave income dropped you to $35,000, your marginal tax rate would only be 24%.

Claiming the deduction for an RRSP contribution would mean frittering away a perfectly good deduction on a low-income year. Better to hold the deduction for a year when your taxable income is back up—say the year you return to work full-time. Then, even though your RRSP contribution limit might be less (based on the previous year's earned income, when you were on mat leave), giving you little room to manoeuvre when trying to minimize taxes, your un-deducted contribution from the previous year would come in handy.

Whether you're having a baby, taking a year off to get an MBA, or planning a sabbatical, knowing you can delay claiming your deduction without losing it means you can plan to make those RRSP contributions work even harder in terms of the deduction you'll eventually receive. It also eliminates the excuse "What's the point? I don't pay that much tax now anyway."

RULE #101: DEFINE RELATIVE VALUE BY YOUR DISPOSABLE INCOME

"Relative value" refers to the relationship between what an item costs and what you have to do to pay for it. If a concert ticket costs $140 and you earn $10 an hour, you might think you'd have to work for more than two days to afford that concert ticket. That would add a whole new spin on the real cost of that ticket, right? Well, sort of . . .

Just because you earn $10 an hour doesn't mean you can use all that money for Wants. First, you must pay for your needs. And this is where the pill gets tough to swallow.

Relative value is based on how hard you have to work in order to pay for something with your **disposable income**: the income you have left after you've satisfied your needs.

Let's say you earn $47,000 a year after taxes. Assuming you work 50 weeks a year and 40 hours a week, you'll work 2,000 hours a year.

Let's also say that when you add up your monthly must-pay amounts—things like rent, food, phone bills, debt repayment, savings—you're spending $3,600 a month, or $43,200 a year. That leaves you with $3,800 a year in disposable income.

To figure out your hourly disposable income, divide your disposable income—in this case $3,800—by the number of hours you work—in our example 2,000. That gives you a whopping $1.90 an hour. That's right. You've got an hourly disposable income of a buck ninety. (See why no one wants to do this? But if you want to figure out relative value, you must.)

Now take that concert ticket and divide its cost by your hourly disposable income: $140 ÷ $1.90 = 73.68. Yup, you'd have to work almost 74 hours to afford that ticket. So is the ticket worth 74 hours of your life? If your answer is "Yes," off you go to the concert. If you pause and think, good. If your answer is "No," you've just saved yourself $140 that you can put towards something that is really important to you.

Being financially responsible doesn't mean you never get to have any fun. It means you choose carefully, shop consciously, and only spend your money where it'll give you the most value for the hours you've had to work to earn it.

RULE #102: STOP USING PLASTIC

If you're one of the people who pay off their balances in full every month on time and live within their means, I'm not talking to you.

If you're carrying a balance on your credit card or you're always in overdraft, either you are as dumb as a sack of hammers or you have no self-control. If you're dumb, do you want to stay dumb forever? If you have no self-control, stop using your plastic and only shop with cash.

Studies have shown that buying decisions play out in our brains as a fight between a pleasure centre seeking the bliss of acquisition and an aversion centre seeking to avoid the pain of paying. When we pay with plastic, we subdue the "pain" and so the "pleasure" wins. But if we have to dole out cold, hard cash, we are much more likely to think twice. Studies have also shown that shopping can lead to more shopping. It seems that buying that fateful first item may open the shopping floodgates.

If you've got an impulse control problem, try this the next time you go shopping:

1. Make a list of what you're going to buy.
2. Put the money for each item in a separate envelope or wallet.

Allocating your money before you head out the door and shopping with cash are two great ways to help keep the impulse monkey off your back.

RULE #103: WORK IS WORK IS WORK

Some people are prepared to work hard at pretty much anything to make a buck. Some people are snobby and consider some jobs beneath them. Hey, if you're prepared to let pride—or is that laziness?—go before your financial fall, you'll learn the lesson of humility soon enough.

Sure, there are jobs we'd rather not do. In some countries, it is only the most disenfranchised who have to do the nasty work. But choosing not to earn enough money—by whatever means necessary—to live because you're too good for a particular job means you're as thick as pudding.

When it comes to keeping a roof over your head and food in your tummy, work is work is work. The source of the $10 you need to feed your family today is irrelevant; you need ten bucks. And you should be prepared to do whatever it takes to (legally) get your hands on that ten bucks.

Living on credit as a substitute for working to earn money is stupid beyond mention. And if you think a job is below you, but you're prepared to spend the money you haven't earned by using credit, you're a jackass.

Do you know what Warren Buffett's first job was? The guy who is richer than Croesus started life running a newspaper delivery business. George Lucas started life as a teaching assistant. Rod Stewart was a gravedigger. Michael Dell was a dishwasher in a Chinese restaurant. Demi Moore worked for a debt collection agency. Jerry Seinfeld sold light bulbs by phone. Stephen King was a janitor.

People don't always just start at the bottom and work their way up. Some people give up perfectly lucrative jobs to do something else. When I switched from corporate consultant to freelance writer, I took a significant cut in pay. But I wanted a different life. It took a few years, but I turned that freelance writing into a really good job and then a career in television, where I ended up making more than I had as a corporate consultant.

Joy Behar, who was co-host of *The View*, gave up the security of being a teacher for stand-up comedy. Andrea Bocelli gave up corporate law to be a tenor. And everyone knows Martha Stewart went from being a stockbroker (loads of money) to a domestic goddess (not much money to start).

What you do does not define who you are. What you're not prepared to do to make ends meet does.

RULE #104: A CONSOLIDATION LOAN DOES *NOT* PAY OFF DEBT

When you get a consolidation loan, you do not pay off your debt—you simply shift it from one place to another. If you take your $2,000 credit card, your $12,000 line of credit, and your $6,000 Buy Now Pay Later and consolidate them into a single $20,000 loan or line of credit, you haven't PAID OFF your debt. You've shuffled it around. Maybe for good reason (perhaps to lower your interest cost). But I won't believe that's why you did it if you use the words "paid off." And if you think you paid off your debt by consolidating, you're delusional.

Consolidating using a mortgage is one of the more time-honoured ways of pretending you've paid off debt. Lots of people consolidate using the equity in their homes and think everything is okay because now it's a mortgage payment. Isn't a mortgage good debt? Consolidation makes sense when you then work aggressively to repay the debt. But most people don't. They sit back smug in the belief that all is well because they've found a less expensive way to go broke.

Tell the truth. You've still got consumer credit; it's just been shuffled to somewhere you don't have to look at it. And believe me, it's costing you. So don't let me hear you say you "paid it off," when all you've done is moved it around. If you're dishonest with yourself, you'll never break the bad habits that got you into debt in the first place.

RULE #105: DON'T FALL PREY TO THE SUNK COST FALLACY

A "sunk cost" is money you've already spent. It's an economic term. The "Sunk Cost Fallacy" is the belief that because you perceive the money is already spent, you keep on spending it.

Mentally, you perceive your various pots of money as having different values, and react to them in different ways. The money you've already made the commitment to spend becomes a "sunk" cost; you see that money as gone, even though you're actually spending it each month.

There's the commitment you've made to your super-duper cable package; that $100 a month is "sunk" money, even though with one quick call, you could cut your costs in half and slam $50 more against your mortgage every month. The money you blow on your cell phone is "sunk" money too. You've already spent it by the time you get the bill, even though a call to revamp your plan, and a commitment to using the phone only within the parameters of that plan, could save you hundreds of dollars every month.

Sunk costs are everywhere, including

- the magazine subscription you continue to pay to renew even though you don't read the magazine anymore;
- the book- or DVD-of-the-month club that keeps sending stuff you end up paying for, even though you have copies on the shelf you have yet to enjoy;

- the auto-ship face cream that keeps coming, even though you haven't opened the last two boxes you received;
- the health club or gym you never go to;
- weekly lottery tickets you're sure will come in as soon as you stop buying;
- the renewal on the shopping club membership you haven't used enough; and
- the subscription costs on a dating site you're paying, even after you've met your mate (or is that a "just-in-case"?).

Don't just keep spending money because you've got into the habit of not thinking about those costs as money you could reallocate elsewhere. Look at where your money is going, and if it's going somewhere habitually, decide whether it's time to stop sinking your boat with sunk costs.

RULE #106: DON'T SHOP ON YOUR BALANCE TRANSFER CREDIT CARD

You got yourself a lower-cost credit card to do a balance transfer. Smart. Keep being smart. Do NOT use that card for any additional purchases.

While the balance transfer offer may seem like a gift, the new purchases interest rate can be significantly higher. All your payments will go to the "balance transfer" pot first, so your "new purchases" pot will continue to build up at that much higher interest rate.

Let's say you got a balance transfer card with a "1.5% for nine months" offer and you transferred $1,200 to the new card. If you look closely at the card paperwork, you'll see the interest rate on new purchases is very different. We'll assume for this example that the new purchase rate is 24.99%.

If you buy a DVD for $24.99, that'll go into the "new purchases" section, and you'll pay interest on it at 24.99%— assuming you're carrying any balance on the card, which we know you are! But every payment you make will be applied to the balance transfer first. Until that $1,200 balance transfer is completely paid off, every additional charge you make is racking up interest at 24.99%.

Never use a balance transfer credit card for making purchases. It's strictly a "get this debt paid off" card. And you better have the debt gone by the end of the balance transfer period or you could be facing wickedly high interest rates.

RULE #107: SAVING IS EASY— INVESTING IS COMPLICATED

"Saving" is the act of taking money out of your cash flow and setting it aside for some date in the future. "Investing" is what you have to do to make your savings grow. Often the two terms are tied together, and because a body doesn't understand "investing," it decides not to "save." Oy!

Don't fall into the trap of putting off saving because you're not sure how to invest the money. Start with investment options that are completely safe: high-interest savings accounts, term deposits, GICs. If you find you want to broaden your investments to potentially earn a higher return, then learn about bonds, holding mortgages as investments, and how the stock market works.

If you were picking up knitting needles for the first time, you wouldn't try to make socks. (Trust me on this.) You'd start with washcloths. After you'd made about a dozen, you might try a scarf. When it was time to learn to make socks, you'd ask for help: you'd get a teacher to explain the somewhat complicated (for a newbie) terminology and guide you. And you'd practise, practise, practise. You'd probably have to unravel your work two or nine times before you got it just right.

The same rules apply to learning to invest: start with the easy stuff (like GICs) and then move on to the more complex. Ask for help from someone who knows what's what . . . yup, a professional! And practise by finding an online site where you can pick investments and watch what happens. Take some courses. Once you feel confident that you know what you're doing, you're ready to put your money where your fingers have been and actually buy an investment like a bond, stock, mutual fund, or index.

Learning about investing takes time. Saving takes discipline. Do not use your ignorance about investing as your excuse not to save.

RULE #108: NEVER TRAVEL WITHOUT PRIVATE MEDICAL INSURANCE

While most holidays go smoothly, protect yourself by making sure you've got enough medical insurance. If you haven't heard a horror story from some poor sap who broke an arm or ended up sick while on vacation, you may be lulled into thinking this doesn't happen often enough to warrant the insurance costs. Don't fool yourself.

On the last trip my cousin Stone took, his assistant asked him if he wanted travel medical insurance. Since Stone had been having some odd things happen to him of late, he said, "Sure." On the day he was due to return home, he passed out in the washroom, cracking his head on the bathroom sink on the way down. He woke up with a huge gash across his eyebrow. Eight stitches, a CAT scan, and $8,000 later, he was on his way home. Thank heavens he had put the travel insurance in place.

Language barriers, sky-high costs for treatment, and the stress of dealing with a foreign medical system will only be worse if you have no insurance. And if you're banking on your provincial coverage, you're a dope. Most provinces provide very limited funding for medical services outside Canada. Breaking your leg in Florida could set you back $35,000, with only $2,000 covered by your provincial health plan.

You may even need medical coverage if you're going from one province to another. While there are arrangements in place among the provinces, if the standard fees are higher in the province you are visiting, you'll have to cough up the differ-

INSURANCE

ence. And you'll have to pay costs incurred upfront and wait (and wait and wait) to be reimbursed.

Before you buy travel insurance of any kind, find out what coverage you already have. Your credit card may offer baggage or trip cancellation insurance. Your personal property insurance may cover lost or stolen luggage. Your car insurance may provide collision and liability coverage for rented automobiles. Your employer's plan may offer coverage so check there too. And if you're buying out-of-province medical coverage, remember that many policies won't cover medical problems you already have, such as a heart condition. Read the policies carefully.

If you travel frequently, consider a multi-trip plan. These plans usually provide coverage for a year regardless of the number of times you leave the country. Check with your home- and auto-insurance companies to see if it would be cheaper to buy your travel insurance through them than through a bank or travel agency.

Keep your policy number and your insurance carrier's claim phone number in your wallet so that it is available if you need it. Contact your insurance company immediately if you must make a claim. You paid big bucks for your coverage; let the experts handle it from there.

BTW, if you have people coming to Canada to visit you, make sure they have medical insurance that covers them for their stay. If not, you can buy visitor health insurance so that if the worst does happen, you don't end up weighing whether to take visitors to the hospital against the huge costs they'll face because they're not covered by an insurance plan. Remember, provincial medical benefits do not extend to visitors from another country or even from another province.

RULE #109: PAY YOUR BILLS EARLY

You can't wait until the due date on the statement to pay your bills. While some companies have a grace period following a bill's due date, if you try to pay on the due date using online banking, telephone banking, or a bank machine, and the payment isn't posted that day, you'll be charged a late payment fee. Get in the habit of paying all your bills at least three business days before the due date.

RULE #110: ASK THESE QUESTIONS
BEFORE YOU BORROW

Borrowing money is serious business. Don't go into an agreement with your eyes tightly closed. Read the paperwork and make sure you know the answers to these questions:

1. **What will my payment be?** You need to be able to work the payment into your cash flow without buggering up your budget. If your loan repayment amounts (all of them) are over 15% of your take home pay, you should not be adding more debt.

2. **What will this loan end up costing me in the long run?** Add up what the total cost of borrowing will be so you aren't pretending the interest you're paying doesn't matter. Let's say you decide you need a new car. It costs $26,800 and comes with a 7% interest rate over five years. In the end, that car won't have cost you $26,000. It will have cost you $36,289. Are you prepared to pay almost $10,000 more for that car? If not, rethink how you're going to get into a vehicle. You could buy used. You could buy cheaper. You could go with a shorter term so you end up paying less interest. Or you could look for less expensive financing. Zero interest sounds good to me. If the lender says (in a deep, patronizing tone), "Well, since you have a variable interest rate, that will depend on what the rate is

each month," ask for a calculation assuming today's rate plus 1% for safety.

3. **Can I get a better rate if I secure the loan?** The interest rate on a secured loan—that's a loan that has assets of some kind attached as collateral to guarantee the loan—is supposed to be lower than on an unsecured loan.

4. **How long will it take to repay the loan?** Don't settle for the repayment amount you're offered by the lender without ever figuring out how long it will take to get the loan paid off or how that will affect the overall cost of the loan. Stay under the three-year limit for consolidated consumer debt. (See Rule #9: Calculate Your Own Debt Repayment Plan.)

5. **Is there a penalty or fee to repay the loan early?** Once upon a time loans were completely open and could be repaid in full whenever. Not so much anymore. More and more lenders are charging a fee if you make extra payments or decide to repay the whole loan early.

6. **If I miss a payment, how will that affect my interest rate?** Lenders have become far less flexible and far more punitive for even small slips. If you miss even one payment, you'll likely see your interest rate increase by 2% or more. If you have a variable inter-

est rate, lenders can raise your rates at any time with barely a hint so your very affordable line of credit could become an albatross in no time flat.

7. **What will I give up to get this?** Life is about choices. Choosing to work a monthly payment into your budget probably means figuring out what you're not going to spend that money on elsewhere. Will you forgo your family vacation this year so you can afford those loan payments? What are you prepared to give up to get whatever it is you're planning to finance? This is not a theoretical discussion. Look at your budget and figure out where you're going to get those loan payments. What are you really going to do without?

If you don't know the answers to these questions before you sign on the dotted line, you're going into this decision with your eyes half shut. That alone should tell you that you shouldn't be borrowing.

RULE #111: IF YOU HAVE TO LIE, DON'T BUY

Ever gone shopping, brought home a bag of something, and hidden it? Have you ripped the tags off clothes to pretend they're not new, lied about what you paid for something, or stored new purchases in your car?

If you bring home shopping bags and hide them from your mate, your mother, or your roomie, you're probably worried about what she or he will have to say about your shopping. Ditto if you rip off tags, have a credit card your partner doesn't know about, or took out a loan without telling anyone. And if you haven't told your mother, brother, best friend that you're barely making your minimum payments on all your debt, you're hiding. Time to fess up and get busy making the problem better.

Secret spending and hidden debt can destroy a relationship. Lying about what you're buying, how much debt you have, and what you really want are sure ways to end up in a big fight. It may take a while, but that's where you'll be. But you know that . . . right?

Sure you do. Folks aren't oblivious to the implications of their financial infidelity. In one survey, 38% of people were concerned the revelation of their secret spending would result in their spouses booting their butts to the curb.

If you're lying about what you're buying, it means you know you're doing something wrong. Stop doing the wrong thing so you can stop lying about it.

RULE #112: YOUR SITUATION IS UNIQUE

We're all unique. Each of us has to find the way that will work for us. However, if you're using your uniqueness to violate the basic principles of sound money management, then you're in denial.

It doesn't matter if you have a special diet, a weird job, or challenging family circumstances; if you don't obey the rules of sound money management, you're going to end up with bigger problems.

It doesn't matter what your "special" circumstances are; you can't spend more money than you make. You must also save a little something for the future. If you've got debt, you have to get that debt paid off. And if you don't have a contingency plan for when the crap hits the fan, you'll be sunk.

No situation is special enough to justify ignoring the rules of sound money management. If you do ignore the rules, don't claim uniqueness as your rationale. Tell the truth. You simply don't care whether you're a financial mess.

REALITY
BITES

RULE #113: YOU'RE NOT RESPONSIBLE FOR OTHER PEOPLE'S DEBT

You don't automatically assume your partner's level of indebtedness simply because you choose to tie the knot. The only way to be on the hook for anyone else's debt is to actually sign up for it. If you don't co-sign, co-borrow, or in some way put your John Hancock on the paperwork, nobody can collect the debt from you.

However, if you have joint assets—think matrimonial home here—a partner's share of those joint assets could be affected when the bill collectors want their money back. They can force the sale of joint assets to get their piece of the pie. That's one reason you follow Rule #2: Don't Marry a Money Moron.

You also can't inherit debt. If your parents die owing a ton of money, it's not your problem, as long as you're not signed on the debt. Their debt will be paid from the assets they had at the time of their deaths. If there weren't enough assets, the creditors have to eat the loss.

FAMILY

RULE #114: COUNT YOUR SAVINGS IN $, NOT %

Your local supermarket is having a sale on deboned chicken breast (or tofu, for you veggies). Buy four packs for $27.75 instead of $37 and save 25%.

The electronics store nearby is also having a sale. You've been planning to buy a new MP3 player, so you've been watching the sales. They're offering a $165 player for $155.75, which works out to be about 5.6% off.

Which is the better deal? Don't do any math; just go with your first reaction. Which is the better deal?

I'll bet your first thought was that the 25% off the chicken (or tofu) was a better deal. A 5.6% savings on a $165 MP3 player is nothing to jump up and down about, right?

Both deals offer the same $9.25 savings. Putting more value on the chicken deal because the $9.25 savings represents a higher percentage saving means you've fallen into the percentage comparison trap. In sweat-stained dollars, both deals are exactly the same and you should be equally willing to take them.

Stop thinking of your savings in terms of percentages; focus on the dollars you'll keep in your pocket and make your decisions based on cold, hard cash.

RULE #115: MONEY LENT IS A GIFT

I have always held the philosophy that money lent is money that has been gifted. Trying to collect has the potential to cause so much heartache. If you don't want to risk a rift in the family or losing a good friend, don't lend these people any money. If you can afford it, make it a gift. If they pay it back, it's a bonus. If they don't, you don't feel the need to make them, and you don't create a family rift or lose a friend.

FAMILY

RULE #116: PAY YOUR CREDIT CARD BALANCE IN FULL

If you don't pay in full every month, most credit cards charge interest from the day your purchase is posted to your account. So if you owe $1,000 on your card this month and you make a payment of $999, you will be charged interest on the full $1,000 because you didn't pay your balance off in full. By not paying off your balance in full, the interest rate clock clicks on back to the day you made the purchase.

CREDIT

RULE #117: NEGOTIATE—DON'T COMPROMISE

"Compromise" is the word that usually comes up when you start to talk about "evening the score." Have you noticed how much people like to keep score? Partners say things like "I've been to dozens of his boring games. It's time he compromised and came to a musical with me." Or "We've spent every single holiday with her family. It's time for her to compromise so my family gets to see the kids at Christmas."

I think that scorekeeping is a really bad idea. And I hate, Hate, HATE the word "compromise." Whenever it's been thrown at me, as in "You'll have to compromise" (said in a deep, patronizing voice), it's usually because I've done just about enough compromising and have drawn a line.

The idea behind compromise is that both couples do it evenly, so that over time it's a fifty-fifty wash. Not in my experience. Usually, one partner is much "better" at compromising, and turns into a doormat for the sake of peace. The other claims to compromise, but it's on very small things. Then the scorekeeping starts.

The problem with scorekeeping is that sometimes it takes a long time before the other person gets his or her way, and the score builds and builds on one side of the scoreboard, making the person who is doing all the compromising feel like a fool. Eventually, if you're in a real partnership, it comes out in the wash. But what about all those feelings of resentment and being taken advantage of in the meantime?

Consider the word "negotiate." I like the idea of negotiation.

Here's how it works:

"Honey, I want us to go to my parents' for the holidays."

"Okay, sweetie, I know that, but I hate your parents. Your mother always acts like I was the worst possible choice in a mate. She looks right through me. So there's no way I want to spend $500 of my vacation fund travelling there and back."

"But she hasn't seen the kids in five years. And she's sick. This is really important to me."

HERE'S WHERE THE NEGOTIATION COMES IN . . .

"How important on a scale of 1 to 10?"

"It's a 9.5."

"Well, on my scale it's an 8.5 for me NOT to go, so you get this one."

What if the other person makes his or her score a 10 all the time? That's where my brand of negotiation is so great: For every three in a row one person gets, the other gets an auto-default to what he or she wants. So if you play the 10 card three times in a row to get your way, you better be prepared for what comes next, because it's my way all the way, baby!

For most couples this kind of negotiation works because on a case-by-case basis, you're determining just how important it is to each person. If something is a 5 to me and a 7 to you, clearly you get what you want. If it's a 9 to me and a 3 to you, I get my way. If it's a close call, which it can often be, then you'll have to negotiate on a finer point.

"Not going to your mother's house is a 9 for me, baby. Sorry."

"Going is a 9 for me, so what now?"

"Well, how long do we have to stay?"

"I'd like to stay five days."

"Okay, I'm prepared to give this to you if we stay two days."

"TWO DAYS! How about three?"

"How about two and we call it three? Hey, man, the fact that you're getting me to go to your mom's house is a frickin' miracle. Cut me some slack. And think of all the money we won't have to spend on wine while I'm trying to get through the visit."

"All right, we'll go late on Friday and leave early on Sunday. That'll seem like three days."

"No, buddy, it'll seem like a month. But I'll buy that."

Try it. See if you can make it work for you. It doesn't matter how small the negotiation is, remember the three-in-a-row rule. It's bad for the relationship dynamic for one person to get his or her own way all the time, no matter how right he or she may be.

RULE #118: OPEN A LINE OF CREDIT BEFORE YOU RETIRE

If you think you might need access to credit during retirement (and who doesn't), then the time to open a line of credit is while you're still working. Plan to do it about two years before you retire. Get everything set up and in place so that you aren't turned down on the grounds of having "too little income."

This isn't about frivolous spending and wanton waste. A line of credit may give you the flexibility to deal with immediate costs as you leave investments in place until they naturally mature or the time is better to sell them, at which point you would pay off the debt.

Don't make the line too high. Twice your monthly retirement income should be enough. And set some parameters for what you'll use the credit for: no wants, only needs. Also decide ahead of time how long you're prepared to keep the balance on the line. Carry the balance too long and you'll increase your costs substantially. A six-month rule should work, but you'll be the best judge.

Now, when an unexpected expense comes up—your furnace breaks or your transmission blows—you won't have to cash in that investment at just the wrong time to get at the money you need to take care of the problem. You can use your line and pay it off from cash flow or from an investment when the right time comes to sell.

RULE #119: DON'T ACCELERATE YOUR HOME BUYERS' PLAN REPAYMENT

When you took money out of your RRSP through the Home Buyers' Plan (HBP) to make a down payment on a home, you weren't really using your RRSP as a retirement savings plan; you were using it as a home-buying savings plan.

In the rush to get to debt-free, don't accelerate your repayment of the Home Buyers' Plan loan at the cost of not making a regular RRSP contribution and claiming the deduction to which you may be entitled.

You are required by law to repay one-fifteenth of your HBP loan each year. But that loan is interest-free, so it's not costing you a penny (except for the lost return in your RRSP). If you speed up the repayment at the cost of not making a regular RRSP contribution, you could be letting the Tax Man have more of your hard-earned income than you should.

Plan to repay the one-fifteenth you owe each year. Take any other money you have allocated for your RRSP and use it as a contribution, for which you'll receive a deduction.

Hey, if you can max out your RRSP contribution and pay more on your HBP loan, go for it. But don't sacrifice the tax benefit in a mad dash to be debt-free. That's being penny wise, pound foolish.

RULE #120: DON'T BE A SUCKER

Gullibility can strike at any time, in any socio-economic group. If you've ever taken out a loan you couldn't easily afford to repay, fallen for a "sure thing" in terms of an investment, or bought something you didn't really understand, you've been a sucker.

Financial scams would not exist but for the gullible. And people wouldn't wring their hands and whine about their losses if they weren't ignorant (or is that self-deceiving?) about their investment choices.

Whether you're being sold a product warranty based on a fear of loss, an investment based on your desire to grow rich quickly, or the idea that credit can be a substitute for cash in the bank, you're a sucker.

Don't be.

Recognize that when things seem too good to be true, they probably are.

Know that the only way you're going to make lots of money is to bust your ass; there's no easy way to get wealthy.

Think about why you want to take action. If you're responding from a place of fear or sense of loss, someone's pulling your chain. Walk away and reflect about it.

Foreign lotteries, requests for help moving money from one country to another, even pleas for loved ones, might all be hooks to reel you in.

When Gemma contacted me, it was because her grandmother had been scammed and she wasn't sure what to do.

"She thought she was talking to my cousin Paul," said Gemma. "The man phoned up and called her 'Grams,' and she just assumed it was him."

Paul wasn't Paul. He was a telephone scam artist who wanted Grams to send a money transfer, but not tell the rest of the family because he was so embarrassed to be asking for money from her. She complied.

"What can we do to get her money back?"

Sadly, not a thing. But I suggested that Gemma contact the Canadian Anti-Fraud Centre (PhoneBusters) at 1.888.495.8501, or by email at info@antifraudcentre.ca.

"Trust, but verify" is the antidote to gullibility. Take some time before you respond or react. Do some research. And don't act from a place of fear or respond to a plea for help.

RULE #121: DON'T SKIP PAYMENTS

If you skip a payment on your credit card, loan, mortgage, or phone bill, don't be surprised if the following month your interest rates have skyrocketed. A missed payment sends the message "Trouble! Alert!" and creditors compensate by charging more interest. Lots more interest.

    If you're in danger of not being able to make a payment, don't just arbitrarily skip. Call your creditors and negotiate a payment amount and a plan for catching up. Perhaps your creditor will agree to take half the regular payment as long as you don't miss one during the time you've agreed to. Or perhaps you can negotiate to have the interest clock turned off, as long as you give postdated cheques for repayment of the principal. Call and ask how your creditors will help you make good on your repayment by giving a little so they can get back what they are owed. Be proactive. Acting like an ostrich means you'll end up with a butt full of buckshot.

CREDIT

RULE #122: ASK FOR A CASH DISCOUNT

This replaces the rule "You have to pay the price on the ticket."

When you pay with cash, you should negotiate for a discount with your shopkeeper. (And shopkeepers, you should be offering a discount for cash purchases.) This replaces the rule "Everyone pays the same at the store."

When retailers accept payment from you in the form of a credit card, there's a cost associated for them. They pay somewhere between 2% and 4% of the sale price in any transaction for which they accept a credit card.

Let's say you go into a store and buy an item for $50 on your credit card. You'll owe your credit card company $50. But the merchant won't get $50. She may get somewhere between $46 and $48. The rest is shared (not necessarily evenly) between the brand (VISA or MasterCard, for example, which processes the transaction) and the bank that issued you the credit card.

The kind of card you use affects how much the retailer gets dinged. Premium cards carry higher fees. So if your bank is offering a premium card with big cash-back options, know that every retailer you use that card with is eating a bigger service fee for accepting payment on that card. That's how The Bank can afford to offer you so much "cash back." No, it's not out of the goodness of The Bank's heart.

According to a Bank of Canada survey, on an average $36.50 transaction, the cost to the retailer for taking a credit card is 82 cents, or 2.25%. Bigger stores pay less, since the cost of an electronic transaction falls as the volume increases. That means smaller retailers pay a disproportionately higher cost for accepting your credit card.

Retailers aren't allowed to not accept a premium card even if it costs them more. If a shopkeeper accepts VISA, he must accept all VISA cards, regardless of how much he'll end up having to pay in processing fees. Nor can retailers offer a discount for certain cards to encourage people to use those cards. However, **retailers do have the right to discount for cash**. Canadian retailers haven't picked up on this. Nor have Canadian consumers. But it's an idea whose time has come, so if you buy with cash, you should ask for a discount. And if the retailer tells you she can't give it to you because it's against the rules, then tell her the rules:

"You may not be able to discount between cards, but there is nothing in your agreement with VISA or MasterCard that stops you from giving me a cash discount. So you can give me 1% off for cash, or I'll use my credit card and you can pay 2% to 4% for processing this transaction."

As consumers, we should encourage small retailers to discount for cash by offering to pay with cash in order to save them the outrageous fees they have to pay. I want to see a flurry of signs in stores: "We give a 1% discount for cash purchases." If retailers don't twig to this, then they've got to stop whining about how much credit card fees are costing them. They can't expect consumers to switch to cash with no incentive.

If you think a 1% incentive isn't worth it, how would you feel if I offered to pay you 1% more on your savings account? You wouldn't turn that down, would you?

RULE #123: A SUPPLEMENTAL CREDIT CARD DOESN'T BUILD A CREDIT HISTORY

Being added on a mate's credit card won't do a thing for your credit history, since everything will still be reported in your mate's name. Get your own card. If you've been declined for a regular credit card, start with a secured credit card, use the card regularly, and pay it off right away. It'll take a year or two, but you'll build your credit identity.

RULE #124: DON'T GAMBLE

If you buy a lottery ticket, it's gambling. If you go to a casino, it's gambling. If you play the ponies, it's gambling. If you buy an investment you don't understand, it's gambling.

Why do people gamble? Makes me scratch my head. About 5% of Canadians—that's over a million dopes—plan to use a lottery windfall to finance retirement. You're more likely to be struck by lightning TWICE than win the big prize. Despite that, Canadians spend about $8 billion a year with the five regional lottery associations. More than half of us play the lotto regularly, often buying multiple tickets to try to increase our odds.

The odds of winning a big lottery can run as high as one in 85 million, close enough to zero as to be indistinguishable.

As for the folks who think the casino is anything other than an evening's entertainment—oy! The problem with going "just once" is that there's no telling when the gambling bug will bite. Take the case of Joanna.

Joanna is in her late thirties, a single mom. She works hard. She struggles to pay down the debt she's built up while raising her son, Sammy. A casual gambler, Joanna walked into a casino one night, pulled the arm on a slot machine, and won $25,000.

"It was so easy," she said. "And I thought I could do it again." So Joanna kept going back. And back. And back. Eventually, she gave the casino her house. "It was so embarrassing. I'd worked so hard to get a home for my son and me."

Joanna told me all this only because she's a friend. (So

clearly, I've changed her name.) She could not admit it to her family. And she wouldn't go for help, because she felt like such an idiot. But Joanna learned her lesson and stayed out of the casinos.

Stayed out until she was feeling a little squeezed by life and remembered that easy $25,000 windfall. She grabbed her vacation money and headed out to double it. Not so much. More self-loathing. More recriminations.

Who knows why some people can walk away after a night of fun, while others get stung by the gambling bug. The only way to avoid the potential downside is to stay away from gambling completely. Com' on, folks, what's it gonna cost you to NOT gamble? And how can you possibly justify Not Saving, when you're blowing money on the ponies, the slots, or on lottery tickets?

RULE #125: BUSY PEOPLE SPEND LESS MONEY

Idleness can kill a budget faster than green grass runs through a goose. People who don't have enough to do end up shopping. If you want to spend less money on nonsense, become a really busy person.

- Have a job that eats up gobs of your life.
- Get a second job.
- Have family and friends who demand your company.
- Belong to groups and associations.
- Volunteer your time to help others.
- Become involved with a religious or spiritual group.
- Take up a new hobby (and do it; don't shop for it).

People who shop for entertainment, to kill time, or to socialize with friends need to find useful things to do with their time. Retail therapy is for ninnies.

Get busy and stay busy. Busyness means less time to think about what's missing in your life. The missing boyfriend or girlfriend, the missing fabulous kitchen or marble floors, the missing sassy wardrobe or perfectly coiffed hair will be far less noticeable if you're racing from one satisfying and personally expanding experience to another. Busyness means less browsing. Busyness means you're actively having a life.

When you're focused on accomplishing, the shopping gremlins can't get a foothold in your consciousness. You're so busy doing that shopping becomes a chore best accomplished quickly and efficiently.

RULE #126: LAZY PEOPLE SPEND MORE MONEY

Some people are too lazy for words. People buy prepared food because they can't find the energy to cook a meal from scratch. They throw away clothes because they won't make time to stitch on a new button or fix a seam. They let their houses fall to rack and ruin because they can't be bothered changing furnace filters, cleaning eaves, or caulking windows.

Some lazy people spend money on interest because they can't be bothered to work hard enough to be able to pay for the things they want. If you can't afford to pay for something, you shouldn't be putting it on credit. **You're not entitled to what you can't pay for.** If you really want it, get your lazy ass in gear and earn the money to pay for it.

Hey, I'm all for buying the services of other people when

a) I've got the money (so I have NO debt and I'm saving what I should be), and

b) I can spend more time making money or am doing something else that adds value to my life.

But I can't believe the number of lazy people who won't clean their own houses, wash their own clothes, or cut their own grass, even as they whine about the debt they're carrying or how impossible it is to find money to save.

Our society has become one that values convenience over sustainability. Water in bottles is more convenient than filling your own reusable bottles at home. Takeout is more convenient than making a balanced, home-cooked meal. Driving to the corner store for milk or bread is more convenient than walking. "Convenience oriented" could be the new synonym for "lazy."

If you're spending hours in front of the television when just an hour a week could have your money mess cleaned up, you're lazy. If you have a pile of debt growing larger by the day because you "just don't wanna get a second job," you're lazy. If you've thought to yourself, "I really must . . ." but you've done sweet-diddly-squat, you're lazy.

Cut it out! Get off your rump and do what needs to be done.

RULE #127: DO *NOT* HAVE JOINT CONSUMER CREDIT

Joint credit is a terrible idea. If you can't borrow on your own, you should not be borrowing at all. If your mate can't qualify, that says it all. Using two signatures to squeeze into a loan is a very, very bad idea.

I don't care how much you love your honey; relationships go south, and if you're on the hook for the debt, it'll mess up your ability to start fresh. So no joint credit cards. Nope, not even for joint expenses. No joint instalment loans: car loans, investment loans, Buy Now Pay Later loans. And if you must have a joint line of credit, make sure it takes both signatures to access the money, so you always know when the line is being used.

For all you people who want to spout "trust" and "love" at me, I'd like to introduce you to all the other people who felt exactly the way you do until they got screwed over by a departing mate who left them holding the bag! Pay attention. No joint credit!

RULE #128: PLAN YOUR FUNERAL

I'm not a fan of funerals . . . I avoid them whenever possible. I've left instructions to give away all the parts of my body that can be reused; the kids can then sell me to some pharmaceutical company if they're resourceful. Or they can cremate me and use the ashes to keep the bugs off the tomato plants. But for all of you who, for religious or personal reasons, plan to be planted, do your family a favour and start thinking about what their lives will be like the week you kick the bucket.

The average cost of a funeral ranges from $5,000 to $7,000 and usually includes

- the transfer of remains,
- embalming and preparation,
- use of facilities for viewing and service,
- a solid wood casket with velvet interior,
- a hearse and a limousine, and
- professional service charges.

One of the biggest advantages of planning a funeral is that you're making what can end up being very expensive decisions at a time when stress levels aren't a factor. Many are the stories of spouses and children who have overridden their partner's or parents' desire for simplicity because they were pressured— be it by a smooth-talking salesperson, by family, or by their perception of societal demands—into going with something far more elaborate . . . and expensive.

When you plan and pay for your funeral in advance, the job's done and that's that. Isn't it better to look at all the options available and decide which is right for you in the rational light of day so your family won't end up spending more than they can afford? Having made all the decisions ahead of D-day, you've eliminated your family's struggle with the decision making at a time when they least need the added stress.

RULE #129: DON'T PASS UP FREE MONEY

People kill me. They whine about how expensive life is, how much everything costs, how little money they have to save, and then they totally ignore free money. I scratch my head.

If your company has a pension plan and offers you a savings match on your contributions, that's free money. It's like getting a raise. Why would you pass that up? (See if there's a deferred profit sharing plan, and check that box too!)

If you're a parent, when you put money into a Registered Education Savings Plan, the government gives you money to help with your child's education. If you put $2,500 in the plan for Little Susie, the feds will add $500. That's an immediate 20% return. Why would you pass that up?

If you're a student, the money you get in the form of scholarships, bursaries, and fellowships is tax-free money. Do you know that almost $7 million in scholarship money goes unclaimed each year? Why would you pass that up?

If you collect points, redeem them and put the cash you would have spent into your savings account. There. You've turned all that swiping into free money. If you don't belong to the rewards programs your retail stores offer, you're missing out on free money. Why would you pass that up?

Don't shop with coupons? Really? Coz it's too much work? I bet you work hard to make sure you get the cheapest gas available in your area. If you'd work to save 2 cents a litre on gas, why wouldn't you work to save 20 cents on a loaf of bread or 50 cents on a bottle of detergent?

Every penny counts. Stop walking away from the free money people are trying to give you and start taking advantage of every way to put more money into your pocket now and in the future.

RULE #130: NEVER BUY WHAT YOU CAN BORROW

We all have a lot of stuff. It piles up in our cupboards, in our basements, in our garages. Every time we "need" something, we go out and buy it. Often, we put it on credit, where every day the balance accrues interest even as the whatchamacalit sits idly on a shelf.

I'm out of the "buy it" business. I haven't stopped shopping completely, but I won't buy anything anymore that I'll use only once or twice a year. When I needed a power washer to clean off my deck, I posted on Facebook, "Who has a power washer to lend for the weekend?" Three people said, "Me!" I bought my girlfriend Pammie a lovely tin of tea for the loan. I can hit Annie up next year and Sylv the year after. I don't need to waste my money on a power washer. I've got three sitting in other people's garages.

I'll bet you're wasting gobs of money, when your friends and family would be happy to share their stuff with you. Imagine if four or five friends or neighbours bought the lawn mower that you each use once a week in the summer, or the snow blower, or the ladder, the nail gun, the steam carpet cleaner, the sewing machine . . . I could go on and on and on.

We'd all have a lot less stuff in our houses. And all that stuff would have to work harder for the good money we paid for it.

I'm sure you have stuff you can share with friends, neighbours, or family. Or maybe you can do a service in exchange. As long as you reciprocate, borrowing is a fine idea, and one that can save you money. And if it means that the things we are buying are being put to use more often, that's good too.

SAVING

RULE #131: CREDIT IS SMART—
DEBT IS STUPID

You'll no doubt need to use credit at some point in your life: to go to school, to buy a car, to buy a home. I'm a fan of credit cards, particularly for people who are trying to establish a credit history. But if you want credit to work for you, as opposed to you working to pay off debt, then you must stay on the right side of the balance sheet when it comes to using those credit cards.

You're making credit work for you if you use your cards and pay your bill in full every month. If you carry a balance, you're in debt. As long as you're using credit to establish a credit history and for convenience, you're fine. The minute you start carrying a balance, it means you're spending money you have not yet earned. Never mind what some moron lender tells you about paying just the minimum to have a better credit score . . . that advice is designed to make you pay interest. And paying interest is dumb. Don't do it.

If you don't have the self-discipline to pay your credit card balance off in full and on time every single month, then don't use a credit card. It's that simple. Denying your nature will get you in a lot of debt and a heap of misery. Tell yourself the truth and stay away from temptation.

RULE #132: CRAP HAPPENS

Crap doesn't happen to YOU. Crap just happens.

It doesn't matter how carefully you plan, how diligent you are, how good a person you are; crap happens. It happens to everyone. And just because you can't see it happening in someone else's life doesn't mean it isn't.

When you look at other people's lives, you never know what caca they're dealing with. It may look all rosy from where you're standing, but everybody—absolutely all of us—has crap in our lives. It's how you deal with your crap that makes all the difference in the world.

Life is like the weather: some days are sunny; others, partly cloudy. You'll go spells when it doesn't rain for days or weeks or months, and just when you think it'll never rain again, BAM! Thunder, lightning, and a torrential downpour.

Since life, like the weather, is unpredictable, having all the pieces in place helps to offset whatever rolls your way. If storm clouds roll in (you lose your job or become ill) having an umbrella—an emergency fund—can help to keep you dry. Without money in the bank, it's hard to handle the crap you're dealt and stay afloat too. Money in the bank means options. If you don't want to end up drowning in your personal monsoon, get yourself the biggest umbrella you can.

If you've hit a wall, if your life feels like unadulterated hell, if you can't imagine ever finding your feet again, breathe. You must KNOW that this, too, will pass, and you must BELIEVE that you can have the life you want. It may take some time. It

REALITY BITES

may require that you bear down and do the day-to-day for a while. Remember, where you are today is not where you're going to be tomorrow. So suck it up and push forward.

If you've been lucky enough to get off scot-free thus far, count your blessings and make sure you're ready for when it's your turn. To think that crap will never happen because you have carefully thought out your plans is delusional. Crap always happens. If you don't have a backup plan, your lack of preparedness could drive you down the wrong path. But if you accept that even the best-laid plans can be sent awry by things beyond your control, and have a plan—and an emergency fund—for dealing with a setback, you're far less likely to dig your misery hole even deeper.

If you've been having a great life, say, "Thank you," and use the good weather to make hay. It won't always be sunshine and buttercups, so enjoy it now and store up the energy for when things aren't so great.

RULE #133: DON'T OVERPAY YOUR WITHHOLDING TAX

People think it's exciting to fill out a tax return and find that the Tax Man is going to send them back money. And the more money they're getting back, the bigger the little dance they do. Wow! You've just given the government an interest-free loan and you're celebrating?

If you're getting a tax refund, it means YOU PAID TOO MUCH TAX.

I've actually had people tell me that they like getting a refund because it's "forced savings." Are you kidding me? Savings on which you earn nothing for the year while you struggle to come up with the money to achieve the goals you've set with yourself?

Here's a form that is remarkably useful for keeping money out of the government's hands: Form T1213. It lets you request permission to have your employer reduce the amount of income tax taken off your paycheque every month.

If you can demonstrate that you're eligible for certain recurring deductions that will reduce your tax bill at the end of the year, you can trade in your tax refund for more take home pay. Do you make monthly RRSP contributions by way of pre-authorized withdrawal? You're eligible. Do you have child-care expenses? They're deductible. Do you tithe monthly? Hey, those charitable donations will get you a tax reduction. If you have rental losses, interest expenses on investment loans, or carrying charges, those are eligible too.

Fill out Form T1213 instead of paying extra tax and getting refunded; you'll pay less tax so you'll have more cash to use to pay down debt, build an emergency fund, save for your kids' education, contribute to an RRSP, save for a down payment on a home, whatever it is you want to achieve.

Complete the form and send it to the Tax Man each year. While you can do it at any time, the best time is in October or November for the following year. Once you're approved, the Tax Man will provide instructions by letter to you, which you then give to your employer, who will adjust your pay for the remainder of the year.

Stop feeling good about getting a tax refund. If the government has been using your money without paying a red cent in interest, you should feel like a dope. Get the form, fill it out, and keep your money!

RULE #134: REVIEW YOUR CREDIT CARD STATEMENT EVERY MONTH

Make sure you review your credit card statement every month. It's not enough just to pay the bill. You need to compare the charges that have come through on your statement with those you noted in your spending journal. This is the only way you'll know if you've been overcharged, if your account has been fraudulently used, or if you've been charged interest in error.

If you think that because you're paying your balance off in full every month there won't be any surprises, think again. I've never carried a balance on my credit card, so I was surprised when I used my card one day and it was declined. The reason: the credit card company had decided to lower my limit. The lowered limit was on my last statement, but I'd missed it.

Credit card companies lower limits for all sorts of reasons. Sometimes the "money markets" are tight and they're looking to reduce their exposure to losses. But sometimes they use a limit reduction to push you closer to your limit, or even over your limit, so they can charge you higher interest and more fees. And don't think they won't just because that's lowdown and dirty. Hey, it's a dog-eat-dog world, and you better pay attention if you don't want to become lunch meat.

Take the time to review your credit card statement so you don't end up overpaying in interest or for fraudulent or mistaken charges.

RULE #135: ASK YOUR INSURANCE BROKER TO PROVE HIS INDEPENDENCE

Insurance brokers pride themselves on providing the best product to their customers. In fact, that's their claim to fame: they search out the best product at the best price and you benefit. Maybe not.

Many insurance brokers steer all their business to just a couple of insurance companies. Usually, they choose the companies that offer them the most generous commissions and the biggest bonuses. Some do it for the perks: trips away and other special incentives. And ya gotta know that the cost of those incentives is built right into your premiums.

If your broker is unwilling to disclose how much he makes off your policy, why would you be willing to open up all your financial information for him to look at? If your broker can't show you that she deals with a number of different companies, and how she matches products to needs, why would you be willing to trust her to find you the best deal?

When choosing a broker, ask:

- How much will you make off the sale of this insurance contract?
- What other incentives will you receive?
- How many different insurance companies do you regularly deal with?

INSURANCE

- What percentage of your business do you book with each of those companies?

Options exist for you to do your own comparison shopping before you hit a broker up for numbers. Google "comparison shopping online insurance" and check out the comparison sites that pop up. Make sure that if you're in Canada, you're using a Canadian comparison site. Armed with information, you can then challenge your broker to beat your numbers—after you've sucked his or her brain dry for all the info you need to know to make a fair comparison!

RULE #136: THINK ABOUT THE FUTURE

Everything in life is about making a choice. You can marry or not. You can have children or not. You can go into debt or not. You can save or not. You can buy a house or not.

When it comes to making choices, if you're only thinking about how you feel right now, you're not going to make the best decision. (See Rule #62: Understand Opportunity Cost.) You must weigh present wants and needs against those of the future to make a good decision. It's the "would you rather" game.

Would you rather have a snappy new purse to go with your outfit, or be able to buy another week's groceries for your family should you lose your job? (consumption versus emergency fund)

Would you rather have a hefty car payment on a snappy luxury car, or own your early-model domestic outright so you can save the difference? (status versus retirement)

Would you rather knock a year off your amortization, or take that vacation to the sunny south? (debt freedom versus holiday gratification)

I'm not judging your answers. You're the person for that job. But playing the "would you rather" game can help to set things in perspective.

If you've never thought about your decisions in the context of present versus future, you're among the majority. But that doesn't mean you should stay there.

Grab a piece of paper. Draw a big box and divide the box into four equal smaller ones by putting a vertical line down the middle and a horizontal line across it.

Label the top-left box "Need Now."

Label the top-right box "Need in the Future."

Label the bottom-left box "Want Now."

Label the bottom-right box "Want in the Future."

Now write in the various boxes the things you want to do with your money. Paying the mortgage would be Need and Now. If you don't pay that sucker on time, thems gonna take your house away. Ditto making the minimum payments on your debt and having enough money for food. Where does getting to debt-free fall? How about your emergency fund? Saving for a vacation may fall under Want and Future. These are the things you really want to do or accomplish. But they aren't "make it or break it" costs you must deal with in the here and now. Satisfying the things in this quadrant means managing the next two really carefully.

Your satellite bill, cell phone bill, and gym membership all fall under the category Want Now. You've made the commitment to spend the money, so you must keep it or risk losing your good credit. But these are prime areas where trimming could leave you more room for Need and Future: retirement savings, educational savings, a new (to you) car.

Buying new shoes, unless they are your only pair or specific in purpose, would fall into one of the Want boxes. So would magazine subscriptions, another drill, or buying something at your sister-in-law's home shopping party.

Analyze how you're currently using your money based on these quadrants. Are you really achieving what you want? Or would you rather be doing something else with your money?

RULE #137: GET OFF THE HEDONIC TREADMILL

Ah, pleasure. The "mmmmmm" that comes from a fabulous massage. The "wonderful" that comes from having someone else clean your house. A facial. A glass of wine. Having someone else cook you a fabulous meal. Flying off to someplace warm in the winter for a weekend. Tearing through the country on a new motorcycle.

The more money you make, the more you have to spend on the things that bring you pleasure. But does spending more money always result in increased happiness? You might be surprised to learn that happy is happy, and while you can spike your happiness, you can't sustain it through consumption.

The hedonic treadmill, also called "hedonic adaptation," describes people's return to a stable level of happiness regardless of the negatives or positives in their lives. So while you might think that getting a massage every week would make you happier, in reality, after a few massages your level of happiness returns to your happiness set-point.

The desire to achieve those pleasure spikes is what drives people to spend more and more money with decreasing satisfaction. It's why that forty-seventh pair of shoes has virtually no impact on your happiness past the moment you bought them. And yet, it is that desire to achieve a pleasure spike that pushes people to continue consuming even after the pleasure of consumption wanes.

Ironically, even as we have more stuff than generations before us—bigger houses, nicer cars, more toys—we're no happier. In fact, we're experiencing a lot more stress as we strive to keep up with the Joneses and get our record levels of debt paid off.

Since we tend to base our "needs" on habitual consumption and on the consumption of our peers (including those we identify with on television), things that would have been "extras" have become "essentials," and folks have lost perspective. Living in a nice house leaves us wanting more as we tour the homes of the rich and famous on TV. Our normal bathrooms are so plain beside those in-home spas, our bedrooms so drab in comparison to those fabulous made-over sanctuaries. And so our desire to keep up drives us to higher levels of dissatisfaction with what we have, tethering us forever to the hedonic treadmill.

What's the solution?

Context.

If you're comparing your crappy eight-year-old van to the snappy new sedan your friend is driving, you also have to compare the number of hours you both work, along with your family lives, your health, and every other factor that influences you both. You can't just compare on one vector.

Yes, she may have a nicer car, but I bet her children are a mess, her husband is a jerk, or her job is killing her.

All of us have good stuff and bad stuff in our lives. In the best of cases, the crap and the pleasure balance out. But comparing your crap with someone else's pleasure and then feeling bad about your circumstances is ridiculous.

Knowing what you want is key. If you don't know what you want, it's easy to look around and want what other people have. (This is exactly the problem with Princesses. Not knowing what they really want, they focus on the superficial.) But if you know what you want, it helps you to take pleasure from what you've got as opposed to whining about what's missing.

You can't have it all at the same time. So when you're falling into the Poor Me bog because something isn't just right (or is downright awful), it helps to be able to focus on what you DO have that you actually want. That's called "counting your blessings."

Focusing on creating a sustainable life is a good way to get off the hedonic treadmill. Looking outward (volunteering, serving others) also helps. So does swapping acquisition of "stuff" for "experiences."

You get to choose the life you lead. If you choose to feel dissatisfied with what you have, to feel pressured to keep up with those around you or resentful about your circumstances, you're making your own misery. If you choose, instead, to figure out what's really important to you, to focus on achieving your goals and taking the time to reflect on your blessings, you'll have swapped the hedonic treadmill for sustainable happiness.

RULE #138: PROTECT YOURSELF FROM A MONEY MORON

If you are living with a partner who is irresponsible with money, you have three choices:

1. You can stay, living life on the rollercoaster and hoping for the best.
2. You can leave, uprooting everyone and bearing the cost of the breakup both financially and emotionally—so you better be dead sure this is the right choice.
3. You can accept that you can't change your mate, stop your whining, and create a protective wall that isolates your partner's aberrant behaviour and keeps your family safe.

Here's how to go about that third choice:

- Make sure you are not on the hook for any of your mate's borrowing, including overdraft protection. (See Rule #127: Do NOT Have Joint Consumer Credit.) No sharing of bank accounts either. Keep your cards and your PINs to yourself. If you've shared them with your mate, change them NOW!

- If you own a home together, accept that your home may not be around forever. Any joint assets will be at risk if your partner ends up in bankruptcy, because those assets will be part of the proceedings. Paying down your mortgage may be an exercise in frustration: whatever assets you build up may be affected by your partner's wanton spending and rampant debt.

- Keep all the important must-pay bills in your name. Put all extraneous bills—cable, telephone, sports fees, and so on—in your partner's name. If your buddy blows at getting the bills paid on time, you don't want it to affect the really important things or your credit history.

- Make sure you have a big fat emergency fund. While the general rule of thumb is six months' worth of essential expenses, if you're married to a money moron, you'll need to have nine months' to a year's worth of expenses socked away. Your partner is an emergency waiting to happen. Be prepared.

- Save/invest separately. Ha! Who are we kidding? Your partner isn't saving. Just make sure she doesn't know where the money is or have any access to it. It doesn't exist as far as she's concerned.

- Come up with a plan for the expenses. He has to give you a specific amount every week to meet the family's needs. If he doesn't, then you're stuck with a free-loader. If he does, that money goes into an account that you use to make sure the essential bills are paid.

The other stuff he can pay from his own account. Remember, you've got separate accounts!

- Keep your hand out of your pocket. This is the toughest thing you'll have to do. You cannot save your partner. You should not attempt to rescue her when the tears start. It's part of the condition. You have to grit your teeth and NOT bite the hook. If you fail at this part, you'll fail altogether!

This isn't about punishing your partner; it's about protecting yourself. And if you have children, they need your protection. Just because one member of your team can't see beyond his or her own nose doesn't mean the whole family should suffer. If you've got a partner who just doesn't get it, you've got a rough road to walk.

As for all the other people in your life who are digging a hole to Debt Hell, go read Rule #46: Don't Put Yourself at Risk to Help Others.

RULE #139: DON'T SEEK HELP
FROM CREDIT COUNSELLING

This replaces the rule that says "If you're in debt, head to your local not-for-profit credit counselling agency for help."

Ever wonder where credit counselling gets its money? Not from you. The service is usually free or offered at a minimum cost. But nothing in life is free, and credit counselling is no different.

When you go to credit counselling, it's usually with the intention of getting your debt paid off as quickly as possible and at minimal cost. The sell from the credit counselling agency is that it can negotiate with your creditors and get the interest clock turned off. That's true. And that's because it's to the well-being of the credit card companies to get you to pay back as much of what you owe as they can. That's why **credit card companies are the primary financial supporters of most not-for-profit credit counselling agencies.**

But if you're paying less interest, that's a win, right? Wrong.

The minute you negotiate a settlement using a credit counselling agency, you take a hit on your credit record. Seeking credit counselling (or going through a consumer proposal) puts an "R7" on your credit history. Having a bill go to collections or going bankrupt puts an "R9" on your credit history. Thing is, as far as lenders are concerned, there's no diff between an R7 and an R9; they both indicate you're a crappy credit risk. So all that blah, blah, blah by credit counsellors about bankruptcy making you a bad credit risk is hypocritical, since credit counselling is just as bad for your credit reputation.

It gets worse. While a first bankruptcy will sit on your credit history for seven long years, credit counselling might sit there even longer. That's because the R7 will stay on your history for six years from your last payment against your debt. So if you choose a three-year repayment plan, the R7 will remain a part of your history for nine years: the three you were making repayments plus an additional six. That's right—you'd be worse off than if you'd gone bankrupt.

Bankruptcy is no walk in the park. But credit counselling isn't the solution everyone seems to think it is. The best option is to scrape by and get your bills current, even if you have to eat noodles. Cut out all other expenses for however long it takes and get your debt paid off. If you don't have the money to put a roof over your family's head and keep food in their bellies, go talk to a trustee about bankruptcy. Skip credit counselling. It's not really set up to help you. Just look who's paying the bills!

RULE #140: CHANGE YOUR BILLING DATES

If you've ever wished you could move a bill so that you could pay it with your next paycheque, you can. Too many bills coming in at the same time of the month can squeeze your cash flow something awful. It might even send you into overdraft. Blech!

Make a list of what you have to pay by date. If your rent or mortgage comes out on the third, and that's the first bill of the month, it goes at the top of your list.

Then plot when those bills and the amounts you must pay on a "month at a glance" calendar.

Next, put in your paydays. That's when the money is coming in. Actually write on the calendar the amount that is being deposited to your account.

If you get paid on the thirtieth of the month, that money will be used at the beginning of the next month. If you get paid biweekly, there will be some months when you get paid three times instead of twice. Figure out how many months of the year this happens so you can allocate the "extra" paycheque appropriately. You may decide to live as if you only get two pays a month, and use the "extra" for boosting things like home maintenance or your vacation fund.

If you have more bills to pay than money to pay within a given period, it's time to call some of the companies you deal with and change your billing dates. It's a pain, but a little effort now will make managing your cash flow a whole lot easier over the long term.

Keep in mind that you may have to pay a pro-rated bill

when you change your billing date. If, for example, you change your billing date from the fourteenth to the twenty-second, you will have eight days more service on your bill, so it may be higher. After one month, it'll smooth out.

Remember to allocate your income to bills so that you not only cover everything that must be paid, but also have the money you need for things like groceries, transportation, entertainment, and whatever else you pay on a day-to-day basis.

RULE #141: FIGURE OUT YOUR MOTIVATION

People are generally motivated by one of two fundamental needs:

1. the need to do things that will help them achieve their hopes and dreams, or
2. the need to do things that will help them feel safe and secure.

In other words, some of us want to win and some of us want to avoid losing. Your job is to figure out which of these two motivators turns your crank, and then design your approach to managing your money accordingly.

If you're **achievement oriented**,

- You'll want your money management strategies to answer the question "What are some things I can do to make sure everything goes right?"
- You'll work towards a target of achievement: Look—I have my first $5,000 saved.
- You'll want to get to debt-free to beat your lender at his game.
- You'll research your shopping purchases to make sure you get the best deal.
- You'll track your spending so that you know how much you have to spend.

If you're **safety oriented,**

- You'll want your strategies to answer the question "What are some of the things I can do to avoid anything that could go wrong?"
- You'll track your spending to avoid having your bank account overdrawn.
- You'll research your shopping purchases to make sure you don't get ripped off.
- You'll want to move from *debt-ridden* to *debt-free* so you can experience a sense of security.
- You'll work towards a target of avoidance: I have $5,000 saved, so I don't have to worry about the next emergency that crops up.

If you don't understand how to frame what you're trying to achieve, don't be surprised if you keep falling off the rails. Find the context that works for you and you'll find your motivation and your self-control.

RULE #142: KNOW THE RULES FOR WRITING OFF A HOME OFFICE

Simply having a home office isn't enough to get a break from the Tax Man; the tax deduction depends on what you use your home office for, along with the nature of your work status. Employees can't deduct home office expenses unless they are required to maintain a home office by their employer.

If you're self-employed, to be allowed to deduct home-office expenses, your home office must be your principal place of business, which means you must spend more than 50% of your time there. The Tax Man also wants to be assured that the space is used "exclusively for the purpose of earning income from business and used on a regular and continuous basis for meeting clients, customers, or patients of the individual in respect of the business." In other words, it can't be a sometimes office, sometimes den, sometimes extra bedroom.

You can write off a portion of your costs for

- heating
- lighting
- water
- maintenance
- cleaning materials
- telephone
- Internet connection

Keep your invoices so you can demonstrate the costs and

the percentage you wrote off. And see a tax expert, who can guide you through which receipts to keep and how to calculate what you're allowed to write off.

You can't use your home expense deduction to create a loss for tax purposes. So if your home-based business made a profit of $6,000 (before home expenses), even if you have $6,500 in home expenses, you can't report the $500 because you can't deduct more in expenses than you made. You can, however, carry forward that $500 to the next tax year, assuming your biz is still going.

RULE #143: DESIGNATE BENEFICIARIES ON EVERYTHING

Want an easy way to avoid probate costs and pass assets directly to those you want to have them? Make sure you designate a beneficiary or three right on the plans themselves.

On your RRSP, if you designate your spouse, the money rolls directly to him or her with no tax consequence. If you designate a minor child, or a child dependent for mental or physical reasons, there is a formula for the payout to the child that reduces the tax payable on the plan. For everyone else, the plan gets cashed in, added to your income for the year you croaked, tax is paid, and the remaining money is distributed to your designated beneficiaries. But since the money didn't go through your estate, no probate fees have to be paid.

Probate fees vary by province and by size of the estate. Do a Google search on "probate fees" and "Canada" to find what applies to your region of the country. As an example of what you can save: if you're in Ontario and your $47,000 RRSP has to be probated, you'll pay $235, and if your $147,000 RRSP has to be probated, you'll pay $1,705, all of which could have been saved by simply naming a beneficiary on your plan.

RRIFs work the same as RRSPs. However, when you convert from RRSPs to RRIFs, you have to make the beneficiary designations again, since the previous designations won't carry over.

On your tax-free savings account, you may make a beneficiary designation in every province and territory except

Quebec. When you die, the TFSA is closed and the money distributed without tax consequences.

On life insurance policies, the designation means the money passes directly to your heirs with no tax consequences. Since insurance policies have two forms of designations, you must be careful which you choose. If you choose an "irrevocable" designation (people do this to guarantee support payments after a divorce, among other things), you won't be able to change the policy coverage or beneficiaries without the consent of those beneficiaries. Stick with a "revocable" designation wherever possible to keep your options open.

If your financial institution's representative tries to tell you that you can only designate your estate, or that you can only name one beneficiary—so you'd have to choose between your children, for example—(yes, I've been told this), tell them to bugger off. It's your money and you can leave it to whomever you wish.

Whenever you make a beneficiary designation, make sure you back it up with your will, just in case. And make sure they say the same thing. If a beneficiary designation on a policy or plan differs from the will, usually the last document signed becomes relevant in determining which designation takes priority. However, since each beneficiary would likely bring forward a claim, a legal war might be the result.

RULE #144: STOP DOING MENTAL MATH

If you're tracking your spending in your head, you're not tracking your money. I don't care how much of a math wizard you think you are, if you're practising mental math, you're deluding yourself.

All sorts of psychological factors come into play when you do mental accounting. Never mind the little mental tricks we play that end up costing us substantial amounts of money every year. Some people round down as a matter of course: $17.62 becomes $17. Others underestimate their expenses while overstating their incomes: just look at all the folks who think of their incomes in gross dollars and their expenses in net dollars, immediately creating a gap they end up filling with credit.

The only way to know what you're doing with your money—really KNOW—is to track your spending against your income. If that's too much work (lazybones!), then your lack of attention to detail will have a cost. Don't whine about not knowing where you're money is going, or not having anything to save, or not being able to get out of debt, or not being able to get your house paid off faster, or any of the other things that are "wrong" with your money. Your mental math is the problem. Fix that and you'll be surprised at what you learn about how you're spending your money.

RULE #145: CHOOSE YOUR WORDS CAREFULLY TO GET ON THE SAME PAGE FINANCIALLY

If you find yourself dealing with money differently from your significant other, that should not be the end of the discussion. While it may be tempting for one or both of you to stick your heads in the sand and ignore your differences, that's not going to work over the long term. Getting on the same page sometimes has as much to do with how you talk about the changes you need to make as the changes themselves.

If one person has to bully the other to keep the balance in the balance sheet, it'll never work. And if one person is doing all the compromising, it'll never work. It truly does take a team effort to ensure that the needs of both people—and the needs of the family—are met.

The first thing you have to realize is that you aren't really fighting about money. You're fighting about having different priorities. It's a struggle for power—and the money is the tug-of-war rope.

Words matter when broaching money concerns with your partner. Instead of saying, "You're spending us into a hole," try "I'm concerned about having enough money saved to buy the home we've talked about." Instead of "It's time for you to grow up," try "I'm really concerned about what'll happen if an emergency comes up and we have no money saved."

It's not just what you say—it's how you say it. Put it in the context of your concerns or fears instead of trying to beat the poor sod into submission and you may find you're more successful.

Better yet, put it in the context of what he or she wants and you're far more likely to see a change.

RULE #146: CASH FLOW IS KING

Most business owners already know this rule—well, they do if they're managing their businesses properly. But the idea that "cash flow rules" is just as important to folks managing their money at home.

"Cash flow" refers to how your money flows in and out of your bank account. When you get paid, in comes some money: income. When you pay for something, buh-bye money: expenses. How you match the two is a big determinant of whether you sleep soundly or feel you're always running to catch up.

If you've bounced a cheque or auto-debit, if you've ever had to "run to the bank" to transfer money (literally or figuratively), if you carry a balance on your credit card, use overdraft protection, or spent money on fees because you hit some other bank's ATM, you've got a problem with cash flow.

Here what you need to do:

1. Match when the money is coming in with when it's flowing out, using a calendar, and then change some of your billing dates so the flow is even. (Didn't know you could do this? See Rule #140: Change Your Billing Dates.)

2. Cut all unnecessary recurring expenses until your cash flow is smoothed out: cable, subscriptions, auto-billings that are not must-haves.

3. Chop back spending until you're ahead of the cash flow wave.

4. Aim to be a month ahead of your expenses. So your June income would actually be paying your July expenses. You want to always have a minimum balance of your next month's worth of expenses in your account. You can use one month's worth of your emergency fund to accomplish this. Now when you're planning your spending in July, you know exactly how much money you have to work with because you put it in the bank in June. No guessing. No surprises. And if in a month you're a little short of money, you'll know so you can make the adjustments to your spending. No more credit card balances. No more overdraft protection needed. No more running to cover your butt.

RULE #147: LIVING TOGETHER IS *NOT* THE SAME AS MARRIED

Because so much of our legislation recognizes common-law relationships as the equivalent to married, people are under the misconception that as long as you've lived together for a set period (one to three years, depending on the province) or had a kid together, you're as good as hitched. Maybe in your hearts and in your minds, but not in your wallets. And the real tell is when it comes time to get un-hitched.

Married people have rights under the law that common-law couples do not (except in B. C., where married and common-law are the same). The matrimonial home, for example, is the place where two married people live together. It doesn't really matter who put what into the home, or whose name is on title; as long as you've lived in the house together and you're married, it's considered a joint asset. Not so for common-law couples. If you don't officially tie the knot, property rights cannot be assumed. In fact, property that you bring into the relationship continues to belong to you alone, so the end of the relationship does not automatically mean a fifty-fifty split.

If you've contributed to the upkeep of the home, if you've had a hand financially in improving the property, or if you've made payments against the mortgage, you can try to get that money back by going to court. But it'll take a trial to settle any dispute that can't be handled amicably. That'll cost big money—perhaps even more than you're trying to recapture. And the only way you stand a snowball's chance is if you have

FAMILY

loads of evidence of your contribution: receipts, cancelled cheques, bank statements showing auto-debits to pay the mortgage, and the like, all from your own account.

While cohabitation agreements may seem like a cynical CYA, they're a better idea than leaving yourself exposed. Your cohab agreement can describe what you'll contribute and how your assets will be divided in the event the relationship doesn't cross the finish line. Cohab agreements are particularly important where there's a significant difference in what each person is bringing into the relationship and/or will be earning during the relationship. And while not everyone is keen on the idea— as many aren't on pre-nups—having the discussion is better than playing the "well, let's just see how this turns out" game.

For the cohab agreement to have any teeth, you need to both enter into it willingly and with separate legal counsel. You'd be wise to identify which property you want to have treated as separate property and how joint property will be split. Will it be fifty-fifty, sixty-forty, or some other ratio that seems fair to both? Make sure you also identify which debts will be shared. Better yet, share no credit (except for the mortgage) and keep this aspect of your money completely separate.

If there are children from a previous relationship, child support is covered under the law should you split with a common-law partner, but you should talk about how ongoing support will be handled. And if one partner will stop working, even though spousal support is also covered under the law, support should be negotiated as part of the agreement so that everyone knows exactly where things stand.

To save money on the legal execution of your cohabitation

agreement, do your homework upfront, have the things you need to include written out, and then see a lawyer to talk about anything you may have missed. You can initially do this together, but then each of you will have to seek independent legal advice to make sure the agreement meets the test of not being coerced or one-sided.

RULE #148: INCREASE YOUR
INSURANCE DEDUCTIBLES

The deductible on your insurance policy is the amount that you must pay out of pocket when you make a claim. If you have a $500 deductible on your home policy and there's a fire in your kitchen, you would pay the first $500 for repairs and the insurance company would cover the rest

Every time you file a claim on your insurance, your premiums go up about 10% for three years or more. To avoid those bumps in premiums, most people choose to cover smaller costs on their own. If you're going to pay for small expenses yourself, then you might as well raise your deductible and save some money.

Homeowners' insurance deductibles typically start at $500. Increase your deductible to $1,000 and you could save up to 20% on your insurance costs. (And if you beef up your home security—a smoke detector, burglar alarm, or deadbolt locks—you could get a 5% discount.)

With insurance companies just looking for an excuse to raise your premiums—your first at fault accident will push your premiums up by 15% for six years or more and your second will double your premiums—you wouldn't make an insurance claim for less than $1,000, so raise your deductible.

Boost your emergency fund to cover the higher deductibles. Bundle your home insurance with your auto insurance and throw your premium savings into your emergency fund.

INSURANCE

RULE #149: DON'T WASTE MONEY ON YOUR CAR

If your car isn't super or turbocharged, run it on regular gasoline. If the engine doesn't knock or ping, it's fine. For most engines, all premium gasoline does is cost you more money.

Make sure your tires arc inflated properly. When it gets cold outside, the air pressure inside your tires shrinks. (Look at the label on the doorpost of your car to find what it should be.) Proper tire pressure will not only increase your gas mileage, it'll also make your car handle better.

Are you still "warming up" your car? Stop! You're burning gas, going nowhere! You don't think your mileage is crappy enough?

Don't haul crap in your car. For every extra 45 kilograms (100 lbs.) you carry, your fuel efficiency can drop by 1 to 2%. If you're not using your roof rack, take it off—it affects your car's aerodynamic efficiency, reducing your fuel economy by as much as 5%.

Turn on your air conditioning. Since driving at higher speeds with the windows down greatly increases drag, using your A/C is the more efficient choice. While A/C makes extra work for the engine, increasing the amount of gas you burn, most air conditioners are very efficient, so driving around town using the A/C only reduces fuel economy by about a mile per gallon (1 km/2.4 L), not enough to really matter.

Keep your engine tuned. According to Natural Resources Canada Office of Energy Efficiency Auto$mart Thinking program, a well-tuned engine can improve fuel economy by up to 4%, while a poorly maintained vehicle can increase fuel consumption by up to 50%.

RULE #150: LOSE YOUR BAD HABITS

Bad habits aren't just bad for you—they're hard on your budget. Smoke a pack a day and you're blowing about $3,000 a year. Drink two bottles of wine a week and that's another $1,600. Eat out three times a week and watch $4,000 a year go down the toilet. See how easy it is to blow $8,600 on crap?

So many of the things we do, we do because we have always done them. They've become habits, and we unconsciously carry on without considering the cost. Time to figure out what that bad habit is costing you so you can find the motivation to quit.

1. Add up how much you spend in a day on your habit. If, for example, you drink two cups of tea at $1.25 each, you're spending $2.50 a day.

2. Add up how much you spend a year satisfying this habit. If you do it daily, multiply the cost by 365. If you do it only on workdays, multiply by 250. If you do it once a week, multiply it by 52.

3. Add up how much you've spent satisfying this habit so far in your life. So if you've been smoking a pack a day at $9 a pack, and you've been smoking for 7 years, it would be $9 × 365 × 7 = $22,995. (Holy crap! How can you claim to not have any money to save?)

4. Identify how much you would save if you gave up this bad habit. So if you buy a magazine every week at the supermarket, spending $7 a pop, and you've got 30 years left before you kick the bucket, it would be $7 × 52 × 30 = $10,920.

You can spend your money any way you want. But wasting good money on bad habits is dumb! Figure out what your bad habit is costing you. Quit. Put the money to use on something that is good for you.

RULE #151: MONEY ISN'T YOURS UNTIL IT'S IN THE BANK REDUX

This rule is so important that I'm giving it to you again.

The delusion that some future source of money is already ours is at the crux of many of our financial woes: you don't save because you believe you'll be making more later on and can save then; you use credit because you believe you'll be able to pay it off at some future date (when exactly?); you don't watch your pennies because there will always be more money. Perhaps the most pathetic examples of this delusion are the folks who believe their parents' money is their money: eventually, those people will die and you'll be in the money. Yuck!

The most naive examples of this delusion are people who, having gotten a new job, immediately start spending money on credit because they know they have a "steady paycheque." Whether you're a recent grad moving into your first full-time job, or you've just landed the job of your dreams, hold your horses. **The money isn't your money until the cheque has cleared the bank**. Have you heard the old saying "There's many a slip twixt the cup and the lip"? All kinds of things can happen to money you think you're going to get. And even if you have a cheque in your hot little hands, until that cheque clears and the money is in your account, it's not your money.

My young friend Bobby got a great job right out of university. He and his girl, Pam, decided they could finally afford to get married. It was a lovely wedding, which Bob and Pam put on his newly acquired line of credit. Bob was six months into

CASH MANAGEMENT

his new job when they started house hunting. They got preapproved for a whopper of a mortgage. They found a nice little house and stayed well below their preapproval limit. But Pammie wanted new appliances. So they did a Buy Now Pay Later with the intention of paying off the appliances—and a new TV Bobby just had to have—before the due date. Eight months in, Bob's boss called him into his office and apologized. The company wasn't doing well. They were going to have to let him go. Bobby was stunned. There he was with a $1,300 a month mortgage, a line of credit with a $20,000 balance, and $12,000 worth of BNPL coming due in mere months. Pammie's $2,200 a month take home pay wasn't going to come close to bailing them out.

Spending money you anticipate getting is putting the cart before the horse, and if you do it, you're setting yourself up for a big fall. It's dumb to get stuck with stupid debt all because you have the patience of a two-year-old.

As for all the folks who think they can bank on money from their elder relatives, get a life. Are you seriously telling me that you're waiting for Aunt Doris to die and leave you her fortune? Or your mom? Or your grandfather? What if Aunt Doris decides to leave all the money to her cats? That'd teach ya, wouldn't it?

The only money you can count on is the money you bust your butt for. And only after the cheque has cleared the bank. So don't count your chickens before they hatch.

There. I'm done beating this horse now.

RULE #152: HIDE MONEY FROM SPENDTHRIFTS

If you have a partner who is a spendthrift, separate your savings so your buddy doesn't feel so rich so quickly. This isn't about keeping secrets. Partnership requires honesty. This is about taking the cookie jar off the counter and putting it in the cupboard, where it'll be less tempting. (This also applies if you're the one who can't keep your hand out of the cookie jar!)

If you have one account for savings, one for emergencies, one for the vacation fund, one for present buying, one for accumulating money for the house insurance—you're getting my drift, right?—then the love of your life will have to work to add them together to feel rich. (Read Rule #40: Figure Out Your Money Set Point.) Also keep your savings separate from your pal's so you don't suffer when your buddy goes spending.

Partnership means respecting both people's issues. One guy doesn't have the right to ignore the other's needs. If your honey just won't stop spending, you may have to take more drastic measures—like withdrawing all services until the message gets through.

RULE #153: MAKE CHOICES, NOT DEBT

Stop whining about the way your expenses have gone up. Yes, you pay more for bread than your great-grandmother did. (Actually, she made her bread, and if you did too, you might save some money.) Your grandmother also didn't have to think about how to work cable, cell phones, and high-speed Internet into her budget. Life changes. You add new things to your must-have lists. Expenses go up.

If you're of a certain age, you probably never had a cell phone as a child (they weren't around back then, eh?), and you're scratching your head at why a teenager needs a data plan. If you're younger than that, it's only a matter of time before the words "When I was growing up, we never . . ." come rolling out of your mouth. Whatever your history, remember that we each choose to spend our money to meet our own unique and very individual needs.

As a working mom with children who were often apart from me, I armed my kids with cell phones at an early age so I could get them any time I wanted to. If Malcolm was waiting for me to pick him up somewhere and I was running late, the money I was spending on his cell was worth every penny because I could call him and didn't have to worry about him panicking when I didn't show up on time.

I chose to put cell phones on my priority list. Other stuff fell off to accommodate the cost I was adding to my budget. That's the key. If you're going to add costs to your life, then you've got to be willing to cut costs elsewhere. Money is a finite resource. When it's done, it's done. Using credit to make it feel like you have more money is a stupid game that will cost you big-time. Make choices, not debt.

Some cost increases take from the money we'd like to spend on pleasures, or even on other needs. When electricity costs jump and you're forking out money to light and heat your home that you'd normally spend on food, it can be a tough pill to swallow. Your options are to get smarter about how you're using electricity, or trim elsewhere in your budget by getting smarter about how you use your other resources.

You are in control of how you spend your money. But you can't have it all at the same time. You must decide what's important to you right now, and spend your money on those things, leaving the less important things for another day.

RULE #154: EMBRACE ANTICIPATION

We've lost the desire to anticipate. No longer do we want something, dream about it, imagine it. In our "get it right now" society, we see, we want, we buy. We've traded anticipation for instant gratification, and we're not happy with the results.

Ever had the experience of really looking forward to buying something, only to find yourself wondering what the big deal was once you actually own it? While wanting stuff is very exciting, the thrill of buying is often short-lived. Once the hunt is over and you've bagged your treasure, it seems that not very much time passes before your excitement fades, even turning to disappointment as you see a new, snappier version.

I love anticipation. In my world, **it's not the getting—it's the wanting.** That's why I always have something that I'm working towards having without rushing the getting. When I bought my home, I knew I'd need new floors. The existing flooring was a mishmash of 15-year-old carpet, vinyl, and laminate. But I know the pleasure of anticipation, and so I set about imagining my new floors as I saved the money to buy them. Sure, I could have come up with the money and done the floors lickety-split. Or I could have put the floors on credit and then paid them off over time. But I know that 80% of the fun is in anticipating the having, so I played it out.

Over the next two and a half years, I walked around my house anticipating the hardwood: no more stains on the carpet, no more musty smells. As the money piled up in my "hardwood floors" account, I dreamed of them. I thought about bamboo floors. I thought about dark floors with high baseboards. I looked at the floors in all the houses I went into. I asked about floors and listened to what other people thought. And I bounced my ideas off folks whenever given half a chance.

When I finally did the floors, I'd been thinking and talking about them for a long, long time. I knew exactly what I wanted. It was wonderful to see the dream take form. My floors are beau-ti-ful! And boy, did I get my money's worth: two and a half years of dreaming, plus new floors. (Hey, isn't that why some people buy lottery tickets?)

Even as I was installing the floors, I set my sights on my next project: the back deck and garden. With a two- to three-year time frame, I've got some serious anticipation ahead of me. I'll gather ideas, cut out pictures, buy the odd piece of garden art, plan, salivate, anticipate. All the while I'll be piling up money in my "garden" account, so when the time comes, I can make the backyard exactly as I want it to be.

Learning to anticipate makes your money go way further. Instead of being frustrated because you can't have something RIGHT NOW, turn that frustration into anticipation and enjoy the waiting by using the time to dream, to relish, to plan.

If you've never anticipated, this may be a really big leap. Start small. Put off buying the next thing you want by just two months. While you wait, imagine what it'll feel like when you finally do get it. Think about the having. Dream about the getting. Can't you practically taste it?

For the next thing, wait four months. Then six. Now you're anticipating.

RULE #155: IF YOU SPLIT UP, TAKE YOUR NAME OFF THE CREDIT

One of the biggest mistakes people make when they separate or divorce is to assume that the divorce takes care of each person's liability for the other. Not so. If you are personally signed onto debt your partner had—you co-signed for a car loan, for example, or you have joint credit like a line of credit or a credit card—the only way to protect yourself is to have your name removed from documentation.

All creditors—from banks to mortgage lenders, from credit card companies to the Tax Man—have one thing in common: they want to be paid. Since lenders aren't bound by divorce decrees or separation agreements, they will go after you if you have joint credit and your ex doesn't pay.

In the best of all worlds, you'll pay off all your joint debt with the proceeds from your joint assets before you go your separate ways. But don't forget that line of credit you've never used on which you are both still signed. If Buddy decides to run it to the hilt and then declare bankruptcy, you'll be left holding the poop.

Individually signed credit won't affect you. If Buddy owes the Tax Man or has outstanding student loans—or any other kinds of credit—on which you have not jointly signed, it's not your problem. And if you are the auxiliary user of a credit card—so it's not your card, but you've been able to use it—the debt isn't yours either.

The one exception to this rule is debt incurred for the

"necessities of life." Each province in Canada has a provision permitting spouses to incur debt in the name of the other to keep body and soul together. So, in anticipation of separation, if your partner were to go out and sign a new rental agreement, use a credit card to stock up on food, or buy clothes or medical supplies for the kids, both parties would be equally liable for this debt, regardless of who actually made the purchases.

Of course, in order to close joint accounts, you'll have to pay them off. Lenders will be loath to remove your name if there are balances outstanding, and they think of you as a potential source of repayment. If your partner insists on keeping the family car on which you are signed, make sure before you agree that you have documentation that shows you are no longer liable on the paperwork. Otherwise, insist on the sale of the car—or any asset for which there is a joint loan—so the loan can be paid off or significantly reduced.

BTW, if you think you can pull a fast one by transferring all the debt to one person and all the assets to the other so the first can go bankrupt, think again. Creditors will go back through your credit history to see if transactions were made with the intention of avoiding repayment and they'll get ya!

RULE #156: MONEY BEGETS MONEY

We're all in a mad dash to spend everything we make and then some. But money is a little like chickens. If you eat all your chicks, there won't be any to have more chicks. Save a few chicks, and watch those chicks have more chicks, and in time you'll have more chickens than you'll know what to do with.

It's the same with money. If you take some of your money and set it aside to earn more money, over time your flock of money will grow. While at first it may be just one or two chicks, compounding will kick in. (See Rule #84: Know How Compounding Works.)

Once you're in the money breeding business, you'll be surprised at how quickly it can grow. Just remember, if you spend all your money, you'll have no money for breeding purposes. So set aside a little of what you earn to build up your breeding stock.

RULE #157: FIGURE OUT WHAT YOU WANT MONEY FOR

We all want money for different reasons. Sometimes it's as simple as having a dream—like owning a home or being able to go back to school to finish a degree—and needing money to make that dream come true. But sometimes the "dream" is a little less concrete: to be financially independent, to be able to share with others, to help the kids get a leg up, to feel safe.

If you can't articulate what you want money for, you'll likely end up using it for a bunch of stuff you later regret. Ever had the sense that you've been working hard for a long time with little to show for it? Perhaps it's because you haven't yet figured out what you want money for.

This isn't something you'll do in one sitting. You'll need to noodle on the idea of what it is that money—or more money—will do for you.

- What would you do differently if you had more money?
- How would you know when you had enough?
- What was the last thing you bought that you wish you hadn't?
- How does having money (or not having money) make you feel?
- What do you really, really want to do with your money?

- What are you willing to give up to make your dream a reality?

I was having a conversation with a girlfriend one night. We were talking about the things we've collected over our lives. I've collected hippos. I have a huge number of books. I love my indoor garden. But I also collect money.

She laughed when I said I collected money. "I've never thought of it that way," she said. "I guess that's what savings are."

I know what I want money for. I want to ensure that I can take care of my family no matter what. I want to feel safe and not have to take anyone's crap. And I want to enjoy my life.

I prioritize savings so I have money in the bank to take care of my kids and to be able to tell dick-wads to peeze off. And I focus the money I spend on the things that give me the most pleasure . . . not on every little thing that grabs my fancy.

If you really want to own a home, knowing that will help you focus on piling up a down payment. If your down payment money ends up in your travel fund it may be because seeing the world is more important to you than owning a home. Hey, if that's what you want, that's fine. Just know it. Remember, you can't have it all at the same time. You need to choose. And once you've chosen, don't go beating yourself up.

There's nothing wrong with prioritizing travel over a home. Don't let anyone tell you there is. It's your money and you get to use it any way you like. But you have to be prepared to accept that if you travel, you likely can't also own a home. Are you prepared to give up one for the other? If not, how will you balance the two?

If you want to feel good about how you're using your money, figure out what you want that money for. Knowing what you really want will help you stay focused on using your money in ways that will give you the most satisfaction.

See, also, Rule #154: Embrace Anticipation.

RULE #158: ESCHEW ENVY

Ever wish you had someone else's life? If you're bitter about the gorgeous house your sister lives in, what kind of car your best friend drives (that you can't afford), or how great your brother-in-law is compared with your slug of a husband, you've got an Envy Problem. People create this problem for themselves. They imagine that others' lives are so much better, and then they look for evidence to support their supposition. Fact is, every life has good stuff and every life has crap.

The big joke is that while you're busy envying Jane, Jane's envying Michael, who in turn is envying you. It's human nature to think that what other people have is better . . . that's the Grass Is Greener syndrome. But if you can change what you're thinking about—stop focusing on the other and focus instead on yourself—you can change the feelings. As with every emotion, envy is born of thought. Since you thought your way into feeling this very negative emotion, you can think your way out of it. Change your perspective from what is missing in your life to what you have—take some time to count your blessings—and watch your envy dissipate.

Sure, your cousin Sue eats out three times a week, has a cleaning lady, and sends her kids to private school, but you have enough food and a clean and cozy place to sleep. (Besides, do you know how much debt Sue is carrying on her line of credit? It'd make you cringe!)

RULE #159: NEGATIVE EQUITY IS AN OXYMORON

The car industry has come up with a great ploy to keep people buying new (or new to them) cars without thinking about the last loan they took out. Dealers simply take whatever is still outstanding and roll it into the loan for the next vehicle, calling it "negative equity."

"Negative equity" is an oxymoron. An oxymoron is a figure of speech that combines contradictory terms. "Adult children" is an oxymoron. So is Charlie Brown's "Good grief!" Then there's "non-working mother," which can only ever be said by someone who doesn't have children. Comedians like to use oxymorons to make fun of things: like "postal service" and "city workers." Some oxymorons will get you in trouble: "rolling stops" will cost you money. So will "negative equity."

See the *moron* in "oxymoron"? That's what you are if you let some car salesman talk you into rolling the debt in the vehicle you haven't yet paid off into a new vehicle, simply because you can't stick with the plan long enough to get the debt gone. What are you even doing on a car lot if you still owe money on the car you're driving? Are you a sucker for torture? A new car will always be appealing to people who love cars. If you let yourself get drawn in and you buy the "negative equity" sell, you're an idiot! (Oh, I said that already.)

RULE #160: REALLOCATE DEBT REPAYMENT SMARTLY

Okay, so you've paid off the consumer debt you rolled into your mortgage. Or you're finally debt-free after throwing scads of money at the problem for the past three years. Congratulations! Now that you don't have to repay consumer debt, what are you going to do with the money you had allocated to debt repayment?

While your first instinct might be to throw a party and then incorporate all that money back into your cash flow, take a deep breath. You've been living without spending that money for quite some time. If you cut your budget to the bone, you'll no doubt want to ease back. But before you just dump your whole debt repayment amount back into your budget, think. Wouldn't it make sense to use at least a portion of that money to bulk up your savings? And if you've still got a mortgage, how about ratcheting up your mortgage payment so you get to mortgage-free a little faster?

Take an even-handed approach and you'll end up accomplishing a lot more than just blowing scads of money on dumb stuff.

Assign one-third of your old debt repayment amount to savings: boosting your retirement savings, building up your emergency savings, or establishing a school savings program for the kids.

Use another third of your old debt repayment amount to achieve a specific goal: get to mortgage-free faster, renovate the bathroom, or set aside some money for your next maternity leave.

Incorporate the final third of your old debt repayment amount back into your budget to give you some more breathing room in areas like clothing and food, and to have some fun!

Getting to debt-free forever feels fabulous. No doubt you'll want to celebrate. Go ahead. Then make a plan for how you're going to use your money to make the best life you can.

RULE #161: WEIGH MERS AGAINST RETURNS

Every time someone starts in on a conversation about MERs I want to stuff my fingers in my ears and sing "Lalalalalalalala" at the top of my voice.

What is a MER? It's the acronym for a management expense ratio. What's a "management expense ratio"? It's financeeze for "fee." Why the hell we have to use three words instead of one and then shorten those three words to an acronym is beyond me. Except that keeps the investment chatter going, doesn't it?

I wasn't going to write about MERs. When I hear people talking about MERs and how you should do everything possible to minimize them, I know I'm looking at folks who don't really understand what's going on and are just blathering on because they enjoy the sound of their own voices.

So Gail, doesn't it make sense to pay less in fees, no matter what they're called?

Maybe. Maybe not.

If you buy a mutual fund that has a MER of 2.5% because it's actively managed (yes, that costs more) and it gives you a return of 9%, and you buy another mutual fund with a MER of only 1.5% and it gives you a return of 7%, which one did you do better on?

Here's the math:

9% return − 2.5% MER = 6.5% return
7% return − 1.5% MER = 5.5% return

See, it isn't about the MER. It's about the MER relative to the return you're earning on the investment. If you're paying 20% in fees and earning a 40% return, you're still up 20%. Did you really think a 20% return would come without a hefty price tag?

Don't get caught up in the blah-blah-blah about MERs without understanding that the fee is only relevant in the context of the return being earned. Subtract the fees you're paying from the percentage return earned to see if you're happy with the money you're making on your investment. And when people start in on why high MERs are such a rip-off, know that you're listening to folks who want to look smart—but maybe aren't. (See Rule #200: Mutual Fund Averages Don't Mean Diddly.)

RULE #162: YOUR FINANCIAL NEEDS WILL CHANGE

At different points in your life your needs will be different. Sounds obvious. And yet so many people do very little to reassess where they are, how their goals may have changed, and how to adjust their money usage to reflect their changing lives.

The old "graduate, get married, have children, empty your nest, and retire" paradigm isn't true for everyone anymore. Some of us get married later. Some of us go to school later. Some of us empty our nests, only to find them filling up again. There is no longer a set pattern to our lives. But there is still the need to deal with the fact that as our financial needs change over time, the lifestyle choices we make must also change.

This rule is about figuring out where you are right now and deciding how you will use your financial resources to achieve what you want RIGHT NOW, and in the future as you see it from here. Recognizing that you can't have it all at the same time, what do you really, really want, and what are you prepared to do or give up to get it?

Whether you've bought a home and now have to forgo vacations because your housing costs have gone up, or you've decided to go back to school and now have to take a pass on all that clubbing you used to do, every choice comes with its pros and cons. Being willing to accept the cons along with the pros is part of being a grown-up.

So is thinking about the choices you're making. People assume that they should buy a home, and never spend much time considering what they may no longer be able to do to afford it. Ditto having kids: people find themselves in the family way without having given much thought to how they will deal with the reduction in their income and the additional expenses and time commitment. They swap their disposable income for disposable diapers, but want to keep doing all the things they did when they had more money (and time).

With each decision you make, as you enter and leave each stage of your life, you'll gain and you'll lose. You may gain stability, but lose freedom. You may gain joy, but lose disposable income. You may gain a buddy to share your life, but lose the independence to make all the decisions.

Today, look at where you are in your life. What do you really want at this stage of your life? Make your pro and con list for each "I want," and then figure out if you're prepared to take the steps to make this stage what you really want it to be.

RULE #163: DON'T TREAT YOUR HOME EQUITY LIKE A PIGGY BANK

Your home may be your single biggest asset. And it's great that you bought a home if you did it to have a place you like to live. But it's also a huge investment. You'll pay thousands of dollars in interest over the life of your mortgage—anywhere from twice to three times the original cost of the home. Hey, that's part of the process. As long as you continue to build equity in your home, you're more than likely to come out ahead. With a plan to be mortgage-free by retirement, you can look forward to living for less, or selling and using the proceeds to help you through retirement.

All this is predicated on building equity. Far too often, people see the equity in their home as "free money" or an easy way to dig themselves out of consumer debt. If you're running up your credit cards or lines of credit, all the while eyeing the appreciation in your home as your solution, you're using your equity like a piggy bank.

Each time you refinance to pull cash out of your home, you're extending the time it'll take to get to mortgage-free. You're also paying thousands more in interest. If you're smart, you want to build equity. If you're growing the debt on your home because you can't stop scratching your consumer itch with credit—well, you're like a dog that has to pee on every hydrant.

I do recommend that people who have seen the light and want to reduce their interest costs do a consolidation to their mortgage. But I also tell those people to continue making the debt repayment they would have made on their outstanding consumer debt to their mortgages until that debt is gone. (See Rule #104: A Consolidation Loan Does NOT Pay Off Debt.)

So, if you had $40,000 in consumer debt on which you were paying 12%, and you could transfer that to your mortgage and pay only 6%, I'd say go ahead. But y' know that $897 you were paying towards the consumer debt? You have to keep putting that towards the mortgage payment, in addition to your regular mortgage payment, so you get that $40,000 paid off lickety-split.

You can do it in a couple of ways:

- you can increase your mortgage payments; or
- you can save that money and take advantage of the annual prepayment option to whack it against your mortgage.

The important thing is to NOT treat your mortgage like a Get Out of Jail Free card. Debt consolidation comes with a cost. Being responsible and getting the debt paid off as fast as you can is the only way to minimize that cost.

RULE #164: KNOW WHAT YOU'RE SPENDING ON YOUR KIDS

Some people see kids as way to spend money they don't have to account for. As long as they can say, "It's for the children," they're fine with whatever they're spending. Some people believe they owe their kids everything those little mites desire. (Or is that guilt making you spend money you don't have?) Most people don't have a clue what they're spending on their progeny because they don't keep track.

If you have children, they should have their own spot on your budget for all the stuff you're spending on them. Don't just lump it under "kids" and leave it at that. Break it out into categories like

- child care
- allowances
- clothing
- toys
- sports
- lessons
- activities
- tuition
- gifts
- educational savings

Add these up. How much of your income are you spending on your children? Did you have any idea? Are you happy with what you're spending? If not, what are you going to change?

One of the biggest problems I've seen is the total denial of parents about what they are spending and how that sets a kid's expectations for his or her later life. If kids always get every toy, every dress, every video game they ask for, when will they learn they have to make choices? Kids need to learn that they can't always get what they want. Your children shouldn't be so comfortable at home that they never want to leave. If life after you sucks more than putting up with your nosy, bossy-socks parenting, they won't ever leave. That's not healthy for them or for you.

I can't tell you how much money you should be spending on your children. And it's natural to want to give our Mini-Me's everything their hearts desire. But if you're shopping up a storm and providing your children with a lifestyle they'll never be able to afford for themselves, are you really helping them come to terms with their future lives? Or are you setting them up for disappointment?

As for all you people who don't think twice about what you're spending—or how you're paying for stuff—just because it's "for the children," you're playing a game with yourselves. If you've been using your children as an excuse to scratch your shopping itch, it's time to stop. Your children are for loving, not for shopping.

RULE #165: DON'T SKIP FILING A TAX RETURN

Even if you have no income, or you don't think you make enough to have to pay tax, you should always file a tax return. Why?

- It's the easiest way to establish your TFSA contribution room. Yah, I know, you're not getting a deduction for the contribution, but the Tax Man doesn't care.
- You may have had deductions for tax withheld by your employer and you can claim those back.
- There are provincial and federal refundable tax credits that you can benefit from even if you have no earnings or have paid no tax. Why turn your back on free money?
- If you want to get the GST/HST credit, the only way to apply is by filing a tax return. Ditto the Canada Child Tax Benefit.
- Even if you don't have to pay tax, if you have "earned income," you will build up RRSP contribution room by filing a return.
- It's the only way to get the Guaranteed Income Supplement.
- It'll let you split pension income with your partner so you end up paying less tax as a family.
- If you are in school or have a child in school, you may be able to transfer unused tuition, education, and textbooks amounts to a parent, or carry them forward to deduct in future years.

TAXES

- If you have a student loan, you'll be able to claim the interest paid.

A tax return should even be filed on behalf of young children who do not have to pay tax but have taxable income should file a tax return to establish their retirement savings contribution room . . . no, you don't have to be over 18!

RULE #166: PAY YOUR TAXES

Some people are under the impression that paying taxes is optional. It's not. If you don't give the government its share of your money, it can take some pretty heavy-handed steps to get what it thinks it should have.

There are stories of the Tax Man emptying bank accounts (uh-oh, there goes your mortgage payment), shoving people into overdraft to the max, and grabbing money off a body's open line of credit. The Tax Man will also garnish your wages, leaving you with far less money to make it to the end of each month.

If Canada Revenue Agency determines that you're **deliberately falsifying** information, it can penalize you up to 200% of the taxes evaded and send you to jail.

Unfiled tax returns normally lead to penalties and interest charges but can also result in prosecution.

If you've filed late, you'll pay a penalty of 10% of the taxes owing unless you're a repeat offender, in which case you'll pay more. You'll also have to pay interest.

If you've filed on time but have outstanding taxes, you'll be hit with interest, but there are no penalties or prosecution.

Okay, so you fill out your tax return and you realize you owe money, but you just don't have it. Here's what you should do:

First, and foremost, file your return by the due date so you avoid the late-filing penalty.

Next, call the tax department and explain that you're coming up a little short. The Tax Man will happily work with you on a payment arrangement, all the while charging you interest on your outstanding balance.

Get another job, sell something, but find a way to pay The Man his money. The last thing you want is for him to get impatient and go take it himself, maxing out your credit or garnishing your wages.

If, after you've filed your return, you realize you've made a mistake or missed claiming a deduction or credit, you can file an adjustment request using CRA's website (the My Account service) or Form T1-ADJ, which you can download from www.cra.gc.ca. For heaven's sake, don't make a change on your existing tax return and try to refile it. You'll just confuse the hell out of the Tax Man.

It doesn't matter how long it's been since you filed your taxes, you need to come clean with the Tax Man. Putting it off for yet one more year is only going to make the problem worse. And if this is the first year you're working, don't procrastinate because you're not sure what you should do. Get some help from a tax specialist or buy yourself a software program that will lead you through the process.

RULE #167: DON'T RETIRE TOO EARLY

I know you were sold the idea of Freedom 55. Hey, it was a good sales pitch. Witness all the people who have come to believe that 55 is the new 65. But early retirement has some significant drawbacks. You won't have as much time to pile up the money you'll need. You'll have to live on your savings for longer. And you might die of boredom!

If you're contemplating early retirement because you're just sick to death of what you've been doing, consider a shift, a restyling of your life. If you believe you have enough money saved, take a sabbatical. Do some travelling. Go back to school. But be prepared to go back to work—perhaps different work—full- or part-time once you've had your breather.

If you're planning to work during your retirement, don't draw your CPP early. If you're under age 65 and you're working, you'll have to make CPP contributions, so you'd be taking and giving at the same time. Wow! Dumb system. Don't let it bite you.

The earlier you take CPP, the less you'll get. You'll lose 0.6% per month. So starting your CPP at age 60 would mean you'd lose 36% of your CPP. For every month you delay taking your CPP past age 65, you'll see an increase of 0.7%. So if you wait until you're 70, your benefits will go up by 42%, which can really help with inflation protection.

Since CPP income is taxable, if you take your CPP when you're still earning an income, the government will just tax it back. What a waste. Wait to draw your CPP and you could actually qualify for more income.

RULE #168: PLAN BEFORE GIVING

I don't know about you, but I am bombarded with requests to give. From the kid selling chocolates at the door, to the constant calls from every charity under the sun, to the mailings asking for donations, the stream of requests is endless. And saying no can feel mean, cheap, or selfish.

Your good heart shouldn't have to come into conflict with your budget. If you are of a sharing mind, the best thing to do is to plan to help, as opposed to just doing it reactively.

Start a "sharing jar" or put a category in your budget for helping people out. Allocate a specific amount you want to be able to share and then stick with that amount. You know that if you go over that limit, you aren't sharing consciously— you're just reacting, which is no different from impulse shopping. If, in a particular month, you don't spend all the money, you can accumulate it until you do need to spend it, like you would the money for your car maintenance or property taxes.

Rather than responding to a wide range of requests with $20 here and $30 there, focus your giving on a few charities. If you're responding to telephone solicitations, at-the-door requests, or mailers, giving $20 a year to 15 different organizations, you may not be doing much good. Small donations don't make much of an impact, since they barely cover the administrative costs of putting you on regular contact lists. Find charities that are truly important to you and support them with larger donations or by volunteering.

Now you have a plan. You know how much you can share

without putting your own financial stability at risk. And you know you're no longer going to give on a whim, because you're more conscious about your plan. When the little beggars show up at the door, smile and say, "Not today, m' love. I plan my sharing and I've already fulfilled my gifting this month."

RULE #169: MAINTAIN YOUR HOME

There is always something to be done on a home. There are gardens to be weeded, walls to be painted, lawns to be cut, plumbing to be fixed, curtains to be replaced, roofs to be repaired, snow to be shovelled, carpets to be cleaned, furnaces to be maintained . . . the list goes on and on and on.

Home maintenance can be expensive. One rule of thumb is to estimate about 3% of the value of your home every year to keep it in tip-top shape. So on a $200,000 house you'd need to include about $500 a month in your budget for maintenance.

The recent run-up in home values means people are bucking the 3% rule because so much of the increase is in the land itself. If you're living in a very expensive area, you can use 3% of the value of the house or condo sans land costs. Just look at your home insurance policy for the breakout of your "building" coverage. But even that can be high for places like Vancouver, where the average house now costs over $800,000.

Ultimately, like all the guidelines I offer, you have to do what makes sense for you. Putting aside $2,000 a month for home maintenance is obviously ludicrous. If you can't use the rule of thumb, then you have to do the following legwork:

1. Make a list of all the things you need to maintain in your home: roof, floor coverings, driveway, furnace, inside and outside painting, air-exchange, garden, air conditioner, fridge, stove (you get my drift).

312 · GAIL VAZ-OXLADE

2. Identify the age of the items and the likely date for replacement.
3. Estimate costs.
4. Save to the estimates. If your roof will need replacing in seven years and will cost you $12,000, you must save $1,714 a year, or $143 a month, to afford the new roof.

Yes, this is much more work. But you'll get a more realistic idea of how much you have to set aside each month. Or you can use the 3% rule of thumb. It's your choice.

RULE #170: DON'T MIX BUSINESS INCOME AND PERSONAL INCOME

Perhaps the biggest mistake the self-employed or small-biz person makes is mixing business and personal income.

If you're self-employed or have a small business, you must keep your business income separate from your personal income. That means having separate bank accounts. It means having separate credit cards or lines of credit. And it means keeping meticulous records of the money flowing in and out of the business.

To take money for yourself, you transfer money from the business account to your personal account. There must be a trail the Tax Man can follow. You can spend personal money any way you want. But there are rules about what qualifies as a business expense. Learn the rules so you don't break them.

First, you need to set your salary and live on it. If your work efforts bring in $2,000 one month and $6,000 the next, and you think of all that money as spendable, you're going to run into trouble; it's only a matter of time.

Smooth out your cash flow by deciding what your minimum monthly personal income needs to be. This is your salary. No matter how much money you bring in through the business, you'll only transfer this amount into your personal account. The rest stays in your business account and piles up. Then, in months when billings are low, you'll still have a whack of cash so you can transfer salary to your personal account.

A couple of times a year, look at your business account and

decide that if you have enough money, you can take more money personally. You'll know this is the case if you have at least six months' worth of salary and business expenses covered before you pull an extra cent. Once you do have the "float" in the business account, you can relax a little, take more salary, or give yourself a bonus to pay for that special something you've been wanting.

If this is bewildering for you, go speak with your accountant and spend the money to set your business account up right.

RULE #171: WORK HARDER TO PAY MORE TAXES

Okay, the rule is a bit of a tease. I'll admit it—I'm trying to get your attention.

When I tell people that they should Make More Money, very often the response I get back is "It's not worth it to have another job because I'll end up paying the whole thing in taxes."

Good lord! So the reason you're not prepared to make more money is that you don't want to pay more taxes? You'd rather stay broke, poor, or in debt than earn more money because you want to screw the Tax Man? Really?

It's true that as you earn more money, you move up the tax scale and end up paying more in tax. But a sound tax management strategy—like using an RRSP to save for retirement—can help to minimize the Tax Man's bite.

BTW, the highest marginal tax rate in Canada in 2011 was 48.22%. That means if you earned an extra $100, the most you'd pay in taxes would be $48.22, leaving $51.78 in your pocket. That's a far cry from not being worth it. And you'd have to make a crap-load of money—over $130,000 a year—to hit that rate.

More important, the "pay it all in tax" ruse is an excuse to not have to work harder. You don't have to make excuses. You can say, "I'm quite happy with my life the way it is, and have no intention of working harder to make more money." It's your life. You get to do that.

In making your choice, you also have to live with the consequences. Less money means you can't have all the things your best friend has, busting her ass and paying more in tax. No, you can't have her new car, her fabulous fridge, or the vacation with the family. You're making the choice to work less, and that means buying less stuff.

It's your choice whether you work harder. You choose. But don't use more taxes as your rationale for why it makes no sense. It just makes you look stupid.

RULE #172: IT'S NEVER TOO LATE

GOALS

I like this rule so much I made it the title of one of my books. I can't tell you the number of people I've met who are quick to claim that they're out of time. What they're really out of is hope. They've given up.

If you have a mind to change your life, it's never too late. Dancer Kazuo Ohno didn't take his first dance lesson until his late twenties. Leonard Cohen didn't release his first album until he was 32. Colonel Sanders didn't open his first Kentucky Fried Chicken store until he was 40. Rodney Dangerfield didn't get no respect till he was 42. Laura Ingalls Wilder didn't publish her first Little House book until she was 65. And if you don't know the story of Susan Boyle, have you been living under a rock? At 48 she got discovered and her life changed completely.

It doesn't matter where you are now. It's where you want to go and how hard you're prepared to work to get there that really counts. You'll have to take some chances. You'll have to bust your butt. But you can have what you want if you want it badly enough.

Don't let a big paycheque get in the way of following your bliss. Money is money. But doing stuff you love to do is the bestest feeling in the world.

And don't think that because right now you're mired in debt, struggling in a crappy marriage, or working for a jerk that you have to stay where you are. Think of one thing you've decided it's too late for and make a plan to make a change. You're the maker of your life. Make it what you want it to be.

RULE #173: YOUR BANK WILL GIVE YOU ALL THE ROPE YOU NEED TO HANG YOURSELF

This replaces the old rule "They wouldn't give me credit if they didn't think I could pay it back."

Yes, they would. Banks are in the business of selling money. If they think you're a higher risk, they simply charge you more interest to make up for that risk. But they're more than happy to help you borrow your way into Debt Hell. Counting on the bank to lend you only as much as you can afford to borrow is like counting on the fox to take care of the chickens.

I've seen a lot of people's finances over my life, and yet even I am surprised when I come upon a 21-year-old making $24,000 a year to whom a bank has given a credit card with a $15,000 limit. Not in any normal world would that young person ever be able to pay back that high a balance. And if good credit adjudication rules were being followed, that young 'un would never have qualified. But banks don't care about your ability to repay the balance in a timely fashion anymore. Now they're most interested in keeping you on the minimum payment hook for a long as possible because you're a cash cow!

YOU have to know how much you can afford to borrow. Work out your monthly payment using calculators online and make sure it fits into your cash flow without making it squeak. If you're spending more than 15% of your net income repaying consumer debt, you've got too much debt, so don't borrow any more money. You should also only borrow for good reasons. Save the money before you spend the money.

RULE #174: LIFE ISN'T FAIR

I get letters every week from people who admonish me for giving selfish, egotistical, and ungrateful show participants money when there are hard-working people who could use that money for good. They tell me, "It's not fair." (You do know we're making a TV show, right?)

Hey, life's not fair. Anyone who told you different was lyin' to ya. The reality is we are all dealt very different cards. Learning to play the hand we're dealt is the key to making a life we love.

You can bitch and whine about other people being "luckier," or you can set about making your own luck. You can look enviously at the new coat, the snappy truck, the shiny hardwood floors, and bemoan your sorry existence, or you can figure out what you really want and go get it.

Fair doesn't come into it.

Some people get better looks. Some people get more brains. Some people have more money. Some are funnier. Some are kinder. There's no point in weighing one person's bounty against another's since it's not going to make a lick of difference to either's circumstances.

If you want to have a great life, first figure out what your version of a great life looks like. If it looks like someone else's great life, you've got an envy problem (See Rule #158: Eschew Envy.) Once you know what you really, really want, go get it.

RULE #175: TELEVISION IS *NOT* REAL LIFE

People want to grow up to be Carrie Bradshaw from *Sex and the City*. They want to wear the clothes she wears. They want to mirror her famous shoe collection. They think it'd be great to live in New York City and write a column for *The New York Times*. It would be great. But it isn't real. Carrie Bradshaw is a fantasy. It's kind of like wanting to be Cinderella after the ball.

Kim Kardashian is real, but she comes from a family with a b'zillion dollars. And if you think the inane conversations recorded for television are her life, think again. The woman is an industry. She busts her cute not-so-little patootie to bring home the big bucks.

You can't have the things Carrie has, because she's a fictional character. You can't have the things Kim has, because you don't make the money she does. If you try to emulate the people you see on television, you will always be dissatisfied with your life. And you'll always be broke. Have you ever heard Carrie fart? Have you seen Kim tweezing the hairs on her chin, or popping a zit? (I guess that all happens in the commercial breaks, eh?)

Television is meant to entertain. It's not meant to set a standard you should emulate. If you try, you'll fail. And you won't have much more than a pile of debt and some very uncomfortable shoes to show for all your effort.

REALITY
BITES

RULE #176: IF YOU'RE CARRYING A BALANCE ON YOUR CREDIT CARD, CUT UP THE CARD

Continuing to use your credit card as you attempt to pay off your debt is like pouring water onto a beach: The payments you make just get absorbed by the new spending you're doing. If you've got a credit card with a balance and you're serious about getting out of debt, cut up the card (don't cancel it) so you can't use it. Then get busy paying it off. You can request a replacement for your cut-up card only after your balance is zero.

RULE #177: CONSUMABLES ARE *NOT* INVESTMENTS

If I had a dime for every time people tried to convince me that something they wanted to buy was a good investment, I'd have my own private island.

Investments increase in value over time (usually). Consumables do not. A handbag is not an investment. A pair of designer shoes is not an investment. A TV isn't an investment. Neither is that $35,000 kitchen you're putting into your house. Hang on now. Surely the kitchen increases the value of my home. Well, how long are you planning to stay in that home? Five years? 10 years? Longer? If you put in a $35,000 kitchen and stay in your home for 5 years or more, when you go to sell your house your kitchen will be OLD! While it may be better than the crappy kitchen you replaced, no buyer is going to look at your kitchen and pay you $35,000 more for your home. Nope, your kitchen was a consumable and you consumed it.

Home maintenance IS an investment, and yet people are loath to spend money on infrastructure that doesn't look all bright and shiny. Ever heard anyone say, "Hey, come over and look at my new roof! It's fabulous!" Didn't think so. Go read Rule #66: Take Care of Your Stuff.

Just because you plan to keep whatever you're buying for a long time does not mean it's an investment. It's still a consumable. And the value is still going to go down. You can buy whatever you want with your money. You don't have to justify a purchase by calling it "an investment."

FINDING BALANCE

MONEY RULES · 323

RULE #178: EXPERTS DIFFER

One of the biggest frustrations for folks for whom money is not an easy subject is the conflicting information experts deliver. One guy says all you need for an emergency fund is $1,000. Another goes from declaring six months' worth of income as enough to raising the bar to eight months. One guy says pay off the smallest debt first so you get a motivational push to keep going. Another (me!) says pay off the debt with the highest interest rate.

Who to believe?

I remember the frustration I used to feel when I watched The Spurts (my term for Spouting Experts) delivering information I thought was wrong. I imagined them undoing all the hard work I had done trying to convince people to do it The Gail Way—which is, of course, the right way.

I got over it. You should too.

Experts have opinions. Our opinions are shaped not only by our knowledge, but also by our experiences. Here's a case in point.

A well-known expert in the U.S. says categorically that it's wrong to give kids an allowance without tying it to chores. When I first heard her say this, I just about blew a gasket. But this woman doesn't have children. She doesn't know the piles and piles of money we shell out every year to keep our children clothed, help them learn, or show them a good time. Based on her experiences looking in, giving kids an allowance is teaching them they don't have to work for money.

Fact is, kids don't have to work for much until they come of a certain age. We buy their running shoes, shorts, and T-shirts in the summer, and their coats and boots in the winter. We wouldn't dream of not buying these things. If we go to the store and it's hot outside, we buy them a Popsicle. If there is a book fair at school, we buy them books. We buy toys, shampoo, computers, cell phones, cars, educations, dental care, movies, vacations . . . we spend a lot of money on our kids.

When I talk about giving kids an allowance, **I'm talking about putting some of that money we're already spending in their hands so they can learn how to manage it.** If we wait until kids are old enough to get jobs to teach them about money, we'll have missed years and years of opportunity. And if we insist that they work for their money at home, who pays you to make dinner or walk the dog? Isn't that part of being a family?

I've raised my children with allowances. From the time they were six, I started to teach them about saving, sharing, planned spending, and enjoying how they spend their money. I helped them see that they had to make choices. I impressed upon them the need to put off buying yet one more set of Pokémon cards if they wanted to have the money to go to the movies with their friends. As they grew older, I gave them more of the money I was spending on them, so they'd have to learn how to manage it.

All this is to say that when you are listening to experts, keep in mind that they are not only delivering facts and processes you can use, but also their own experiences and biases. If you identify with the person and want to follow his way, that's your choice. If you don't like what she says, or don't agree, you can choose to walk your own path, taking only as much information from The Spurt as you need to achieve your goals.

Above all, before you take any expert's advice, make sure it's applicable to YOU. If you try to force-fit yourself to some Spurt's idea of what is right, appropriate, or smart and it's not really a good fit, you'll chaff at the process.

There is no such thing as one right way. Well, there is: it's the way that makes a difference in your life, which may mean piecing together the system or strategy that will get you to where you want to be. I tell you what I think will be the best way, as do dozens of other Spurts. You are the only person who can decide what will work for you.

RULE #179: ATMS ARE *NOT* WALLETS

Some people can't plan their way to the bathroom. And nowhere does it show more than on their bank statements, where every other transaction is a cash withdrawal that comes with a $1.50 + fee. For heaven's sake, if you're paying ATM withdrawal fees, stop. It's a total waste of your money.

To avoid ATM fees:

Choose the right account. Some folks pay more than they need to because they insist on sticking with a bank account they've had since Betty White was in diapers. Shop around and find the account that gives you the most of what you need for the lowest possible cost.

Only use your own bank's ATM. Using another bank's ATM or, worse, those cash machines that are popping up like so many pimples, can double or triple your withdrawal fees. Don't do it. EVER! If you're dealing with a bank that has no ATMs where you are, change your bank.

Stop making small withdrawals. Indiscriminately pulling money from whichever ATM is at hand, and paying $1.50 to $3 on a $20 withdrawal is dumb, Dumb, DUMB! Only make withdrawals twice a month and make those withdrawals last.

Go over your budget to see how much money you usually need to have every two weeks (or monthly). Look at your spending journal (you do have a spending journal by now, right? If not, go read Rule #19: Write Down What You're Spending) to see what you usually pay for in cash. Withdraw as much as you'll need. You don't have to keep it all in your wallet. Hollow out a book on your bookshelf that you can use as a safe and store the extra money there.

Make sure your "safe" is also stocked with a little extra money . . . maybe an extra $50 to $100 for those unexpected cash expenses that sometimes crop up: the kids' school field trips, the supermarket special that's a really good deal, the extra gas for that trip to Cousin Susan's shotgun wedding.

Once you've made your cash withdrawal, stay away from the bank machines. If you run out of cash, too bad! You'll have to shuffle through your pockets and the couch cushions until your next scheduled withdrawal. Eventually, you'll get tired of having no cash, and you'll learn to manage it more efficiently.

RULE #180: PRACTISE, PRACTISE, PRACTISE

I'm a little impatient—I'll admit it. I was the girl who didn't put in the heat shield when I was building my first barbecue because I skipped that instruction. And I've scooted ahead on a few things I would have done better had I taken a little more time. But I'm learning patience. Along with it, I'm learning the value of practice.

One of my many husbands (okay, I'm done practising being married) once said to me, "I'm not going to wallpaper that room. If I've wallpapered just three times in my life, how can I be any good at it?" He had a point. The things we are best at are the things we do over and over, developing skills and a rhythm. The first time you drove a car, you were probably obsessed with all the little things you had to do: check your mirrors, anticipate the traffic, watch for pedestrians. Over time, with practice, those things became second nature.

Much of what's involved in sound money management we could stand to practise before we dive into the deep end. There are folks who buy a home and have no idea what the costs involved will be, or how they'll cope. There are people who jump into investing without so much as a nod to the shallow end of the pool.

Slow down. Take your time. Put some practice into the mix before you make a big financial commitment. The objective is to make some of the mistakes beginners inevitably make—through ignorance, excitement, or fear—while you're still pretending. Get those first 5, 10, or 20 mistakes out of your system and learn from them.

There are dozens of sites on the Web that will let you create an imaginary investment portfolio, track and trade your investments, and develop some skills and experience as an investor. If you're planning on buying a home, figure out what your carrying costs will be on that new property. Subtract your current rent from the new costs you'll have and put the difference in the bank. Now you're a) saving more for when you do buy, and b) practising living on the disposable income you'll have when you become a homeowner.

If you're determined to become educated so you can take control of your money, you must be willing to commit the time and effort necessary to practise and become good at what you want to do. And keep learning. The money world is constantly changing. New offerings come to market. New tricks are used to separate you from your money. Practise vigilance, so you don't end up perfecting regret.

RULE #181: NEVER BUY CREDITOR INSURANCE

Creditor insurance is one of the most expensive forms of insurance going. Lenders like to offer it as protection against unforeseen events that can affect your ability to make your payments, such as disability or death. Don't buy it. While you might be strongly encouraged, resist. Nobody can force you to buy insurance. Some do try adding it to your account to see if you resist. And you should. This is one of the biggest rip-offs in financial services today because it's overpriced and it's sold on fear.

If you are charged for a service that you did not agree to buy, make use of your financial institution's complaint-handling process, or contact the Financial Consumer Agency of Canada, which will investigate to see if your lender has gone offside.

INSURANCE

RULE #182: EXAMINE YOUR LIFE

I gave a copy of an early draft of *Money Rules* to several people to read. I was over for dinner with friends to whom I'd given a copy, when Casey asked, "What do you do with the information you collect in the spending journal?" I just about fell off my chair. I realized for the first time that I had never explained how the info in the spending journal is used along with the budget to monitor where you are and where you're going. Duh!

When I told my friend Victoria this story, she laughed. "We like to analyze everything," she said. Not everyone does this?

A spending journal allows you to

- track your spending so you're doing it consciously, and
- use the information you've gathered to see how you're doing on your budget.

To examine your spending, you enter all the info you've gathered in your spending journal into your budget to see if you're over or under in categories, and if you're on track to achieve your goals. Tracking your spending and analyzing it in your budget also lets you examine your life to see if your money is doing for you what you want it to. Running a little high on household maintenance this month? Next month you can decide to trim back on coffee or on eating out to put things to rights. Had an unusually high food month because your sister and her family came to stay for two weeks? Next month you can put a moratorium on shopping until you're back to even. Had to fork out a ton of money for new school clothes because the kids went through a growth spurt? You can reallocate some of the money from your vacation fund to cover your immediate costs; next month (and perhaps for a few months depending on what you spent), send the clothing money back to the vacation fund to even up.

It takes discipline to use a spending journal and a budget to watch where your money is going. It takes determination to have the life you want. Examine your life and see what you need to change.

RULE #183: FIND SOME BALANCE

I try to live my life in balance. It doesn't always come easy, contrary to what some people think. It actually takes work. Balancing career with family means saying no to some opportunities to make money so that I have time with my children. Flying hither and yon to make a buck means being able to take the kids on that trip that will open up their world and expand their horizons. I'm always balancing what I'll do for money with what I want to accomplish elsewhere in my life. And I weigh carefully what I have against what I need and what I want so that I don't end up unbalancing my life in a way that'll takes heaps of energy to correct.

We all face times when our lives fall out of balance. There will be times when you run short of money, have to scrounge to come up with rent, or must work three jobs because the caca has hit the fan. And there will be times when you feel as if you're rolling in clover. If you remember that the point is to keep things flowing as smoothly as possible, then you'll sock away some money in the good times so you have some flexibility in the not-so-good times.

If you've been shopping up a storm, racking up debt, and not saving anything for the future, you're unbalanced and you'll be miserable. You might not be miserable now as you relish the heat of acquisition and pleasure, but it's only a matter of time before you feel the chill of bill collectors and not being able to keep a roof over your head.

Balance is the ability to deal with a variety of things at once, giving each just as much attention as it deserves. You can't do any one thing to the exclusion of all the others. That means saving some money, even as you are working your butt off to pay down your debt. It means looking for small ways to cut costs, even as you spend to keep a roof over your head and to enjoy your life.

When you're assessing how you're doing financially, look at both sides of the balance sheet to make sure you're moving along to where you want to be next. Is the debt going down? Are the assets going up? It doesn't matter where you are right now; if you want to be somewhere else—in a better place— you need to look at the whole and create some balance.

RULE #184: KNOW HOW CREDIT CARDS CALCULATE INTEREST

If you're like me and you always pay the amount owing on your credit card by the payment due date, you never have to pay interest, so you may not much care what your interest rate is or how it's calculated. But if you carry a balance, or if you ever take cash advances, read on.

Interest on a credit card is charged differently, depending on the type of transaction on the card. Maybe you made a new purchase. Maybe you're carrying a balance from last month, which would be a "previous purchase." Perhaps you took a cash advance. Or maybe, in an attempt to get your interest costs down, you did a balance transfer.

New purchases usually don't rack up interest unless there's a previous balance on the card or you pay after the due date. At that point, the interest clock clicks on back to the date of the purchase, so there's no "grace" period. If you carry so much as a penny as a balance, instead of getting a free ride from the date of purchase through to the date owed the following month, the interest clock clicks on back to the minute you did the transaction. The interest-free—or "grace"—period never applies to cash advances. The minute you pull that money off your card, the clock clicks on and you start paying interest, usually on your entire balance. Ditto most balance transfers.

The interest you'll pay is calculated in one of two ways:

1. using the "average daily balance method," or
2. using the "daily balance method."

While these calculations are different, they often yield much the same results.

Credit card companies use one of two methods to decide whether the interest-free period applies to your new purchases. On some cards, the interest-free period applies to your new purchases if you pay your current month's balance in full by the due date. This can be called "method one," or "one cycle billing." But some credit cards want to penalize you when you carry a balance even for one month, creating "method two," or "two cycle" billing. With this method, the interest-free period applies to your new purchases only if you pay your current month's balance in full, by the due date, AND you are not carrying a balance from the previous month.

While it may feel like torture to read your credit card agreement, if you don't, you're walking blind into something that may bite you in the butt down the road. And whenever your credit card company sends out a notification that your terms and conditions have changed, pay attention.

A lack of attention allowed method two, or two cycle billing, to take hold in Canada (it was born in the U.S., where credit card companies regularly stick it to their customers). If more people had had their heads up and rebelled, our lenders would never have kept this option. Now that it has a strong foothold, it would take a tsunami of customer cancellations to have it reversed. That's lost ground consumers will never regain.

RULE #185: SET CONCRETE GOALS

GOALS

People are always awishin' and awantin.' Hey, you can spend loads of time daydreaming about what you could have, or you can make your dream into a goal, nail down the specifics, and get busy achieving your dream.

The dream I hear most often is "I wish I could own a house of my own," so I'm going to demonstrate the process using that as the example.

STEP 1: MAKE THE GOALS SPECIFIC.

"I want to buy a house" is not a clear picture. You have to make the goal specific. Do you plan to buy a fixer-upper, or a house that's in perfect live-in shape? Is it a starter home, or your "live in forever" house? To rent out, or as a stepping stone to your next house? Is it a fully detached house, a condo, or a cabin in the woods? Is it a bungalow, a three-storey Monster Home, or something in between? Will you pay $75,000, $500,000, or $2.1 million? The more detail you include—the more clearly you paint the picture of your goal—the easier it is to achieve.

Buying a house is a big deal. There are a lot of steps in the process, and you have to figure out all the steps and set deadlines for when you'll take those steps. You'll have to:

- Figure out how much house you can afford.
- Decide where you want to live.
- Decide when you want to move in to your new home.
- Decide how much down payment you want to have.

- Save the down payment.
- Save the closing costs.
- Shine up your credit history.
- Get preapproved for a mortgage.

STEP 2: SET DEADLINES.

A goal without a deadline is just a dream. So for each of the steps you identify, you must set a date. By when do you want to buy your new house? Six months, three years, five years?

Take your steps and add a timeline to each one to set milestones, as in . . .

- I will figure out how much house I can afford by the end of next week.
- I will calculate how much of a down payment I'll need to avoid mortgage insurance by the end of the month.
- I will create a plan for accumulating the down payment by the end of the month.

A good test of your "steps" is to hand them to someone else and ask if the steps make sense, are clear, and are complete. Ask others to help you see the holes in your plan.

STEP 3: MAKE SURE THE GOAL IS ACHIEVABLE.

It's easy to dream. And sometimes our grasp exceeds our reach. If you want to achieve your goal, you need to be sure it's realistic. If you make $35,000 a year, how are you going to come up with a $60,000 down payment on the $300,000 house of your dreams in a year? Will you be able to afford to carry the house? Will you ever get preapproved for a mortgage?

This is an important step. It's not meant to rain on your parade. It's meant to help you see just how pie-in-the-sky or realistic your dream is. If you can't ever achieve what you think you want, wouldn't you rather know so you can get on finding something you can achieve to work towards? Wouldn't that be better than beating your head against a wall of frustration?

STEP 4: FIGURE OUT WHO CAN HELP.

It may simply be that you need some help to achieve your dream. Figure out who will help you with your house buying. You may have a partner (mate, sibling, parent) who will help you save up a down payment. Maybe your sister will live with you and pay rent to help you with the carrying costs. Perhaps you can ask your friends and family to contribute to your house-buying fund for birthdays and special occasions, as opposed to buying you dumb stuff you really don't want.

There may be experts or specialists that you'll have to recruit. You'll likely need a lender, a real estate agent, a home inspector, a lawyer. How about your cousin Tony and his van to help you move, and your best friend to clean the place before you move in?

Achieving any goal can be complicated in light of what else is going on in your life. How do you dovetail what you want with your limited resources and time? Will extending some of the deadlines help? Will bringing in more people make the process easier? In the big scheme of things, how much do you really want to achieve this goal, and what are you prepared to give up to get it?

RULE #186: NEVER TAKE A PAYMENT HOLIDAY

One of the niftiest tricks the credit card companies and banks like to pull on their customers is to offer them a "payment holiday." It goes something like this:

"You're a fabulous customer and we value your business, so we're offering you a payment holiday this month. You don't have to pay us a thing."

Wow! This is special. One payment you can skip. That'll leave you enough money to go out for dinner on Friday AND Saturday. But can that be right?

When you look at your minimum payment box, you'll see a zero. Sure. No payment. That's great! You might assume this payment holiday comes with a suspension of interest charges. You'd be the only ass in the equation.

Just because you don't have to make a payment doesn't mean that interest isn't being calculated on your balance. In fact, by not making a payment, you're leaving more money on which the greedy bank can charge interest. So what looks like a gift is really a wolf in sheep's clothing.

RULE #187: HIRE GOOD HELP

One of the questions I am asked most often is "Where should I go to get help with my money?" It's a "sad but true" reality that many people have little or no faith in the folks who purport to be the experts.

If you've yet to form any alliance with a helper, or if you're looking for a new advisor, choosing may feel like an impossible task. Take a deep breath. This isn't the easiest thing you'll ever do. But it also isn't the hardest. And having an advisor you feel comfortable working with is priceless when it comes to peace of mind.

Ask family, friends, and co-workers for the names of people they like and trust. This is the least random way of choosing an advisor. Whether you're shopping for insurance, trying to find a lawyer to make a will, or looking for someone to help you with investing, start with the people you know.

Remember that you'll get what you pay for. Choose to go with a banker for free advice and know that she'll offer you only what's available through her company. Ditto salespeople who are affiliated with a specific insurance or mutual fund company. If you want unbiased information, consider a fee-only advisor. You'll pay for time and expertise, but there's less chance he'll have anyone else's agenda top-of-mind. Google "fee-only financial planner" plus whatever region you're in for a list.

Narrow your list to two or three candidates. Check their credentials and their references. (Use the website www.kyfa .com as your starting point for this.) Also check with regional licensing bodies like the Securities Commission or Insurance Commission to see if complaints have been registered against any of the bodies you are considering.

Time to meet the bodies. A face-to-face will help you get a sense of the person. Do you like his manner? Do you like her communication style? Expect your candidates to ask you questions too. They'll want to know your priorities in terms of the financial goals you're want to accomplish, along with your expectations, and how you'd like to work with them.

Questions to ask advisors include the following:

- How will you help me establish my goals and determine my best course of action?
- How long have you worked with your most long-lived client?
- Do you only provide direction—or can you also hel me with implementation?
- What are your areas of expertise?
- What are your greatest strengths?
- What are your greatest weaknesses?
- What ongoing training and education have you received?
- Tell me about the team you work with for things such as estate planning, tax counselling, and investment
- management.
- Do you have a team of professionals such as lawyers, accountants, and insurance specialists with whom you work?
- What financial products are you licensed to sell?

- Are you limited to selling the products of certain companies?
- How are you paid?
- What is YOUR investment philosophy?
- What information will you provide to me to support your recommendations?
- How often will you contact me, and how?

Once you've identified your top two or three candidates, it's time to check their references. When you're asking for references, say, "I'd like one of the three references you give me to be someone very much like me." Here are some questions to ask references:

- How long have you worked with this advisor?
- Are you happy with the services you've been receiving?
- What are this advisor's strong points?
- What are this advisor's weak points?
- What have you been disappointed or surprised by in your relationship?
- How often do you hear from your advisor?
- Who normally initiates the calls, and for what reason?
- How quickly are your calls returned?
- What is it that you really value about your relationship with your advisor?

Whomever you choose to work with should be willing and able to refer you to specialists in a variety of arenas, not all of whom work for his organization. If you need help with tax issues, if you want to write a will or if you need insurance, your advisor should have experts with whom he works regularly and to whom he can refer you. If your financial planner can't provide you with a list of resources without "checking" first, it probably means she doesn't have people to whom she refers regularly. That may be a sign she doesn't have a broad base of experts to help you achieve your goals. Run for the hills.

RULE #188: KEEP A SEPARATE CREDIT CARD FOR ONLINE SHOPPING

I have three credit cards. One is for personal shopping. One is for my business. And one I keep at home in a drawer for online shopping. That card only has a small credit limit, the better to reduce my online exposure. If I have to cancel the card because it's been compromised, I don't also have to re-jig all my automatic bill payments.

Credit cards are a much better choice for online shopping than debit cards because credit cards offer you more protection against fraudulent charges. And since your debit card gives a crook access to your bank account and up to your daily withdrawals limit, you could be without money for days. Fraudulent credit card purchases don't take anything from your pocket.

While you're at it. . .

- Don't make online purchases from a public computer.
- Make sure the site you're giving your number to is secure. The browser address should start with https:// and there should be a lock in the lower right-hand corner.
- Print your online receipt so you can compare it with the amount that comes through on your statement.

CASH MANAGEMENT

RULE #189: STUFF ACCUMULATES. USE IT UP.

Have you ever noticed how stuff piles up? How many lipsticks do you have? Bottles of nail polish? Screwdrivers? Drill bits? Shoes? Winter jackets? Fall jackets? Spring jackets? Do you see where I'm going with this?

We have a phenomenal ability to accumulate stuff. From wrapping paper and gift bags to cards, from stem wear and dishes to tablecloths, most people have more stuff than their parents did. They certainly have more than their grandparents did, who made do with two work outfits and a good suit for church. Yet we can always buy more.

How many bottles of hand lotion do you have? How many bottles of shampoo? Bottles of cologne? How many packages of soup, bags of rice, boxes of pasta? How many scarves, watches, hats, pairs of earrings, panties, socks?

Some people have so much stuff they forget what they have and go buy it again!

If you truly want to appreciate what you have, you need to remember the value of the stuff you've already got, using it up, wearing it out, and making do until you MUST buy more. Sure, you were in love with the smell of that lotion when you first bought it, and now have grown a little tired of it. Use it up anyway.

Want to appreciate what you do have? Take an inventory. Make a list of every shirt, every DVD, everything in your freezer. Then make a commitment not to buy another whatever until you're down to your last smidgen. No more eye shadow, no more pens, no more books. If you're done with it and it still has value, you've got to sell it to buy another. If you can't sell it, you've got to give it away and wait until you're without a single extra before you go shopping again.

We take our abundance for granted. Periodically putting a hold on buying anything new until we have used up what we have is a great way to reduce our expectations and increase our gratitude. It's also a great way to not spend money so you can achieve your savings or debt-repayment goals.

RULE #190: PRACTISE NOT BUYING

Some people can't walk into a store without buying SOMETHING. It is almost as if their purpose is to consume. Sometimes they're called shopaholics. Sometimes other—less forgiving—names.

If you think you might be one of those people, you can do one of two things:

- never go into stores, or
- practise not buying until you get good at it.

The first is practical only some of the time. There will be occasions when you have to go shopping for something you need. Or even something you want. Learning how to not buy is a good life skill to develop. Here's how to do it:

1. Leave your money and your credit/debit cards at home.

2. Go into a store and pick up all the things you would love to buy. Try on a new dress. Add a belt. Look for the shoes and purse that would go with them. Wander the aisles. Touch the stuff you'd love to take home. Keep a running total of what you would be spending if you had money available.

3. Think about what you have at home that is like what you're contemplating buying. Leave the stuff and walk

out of the store. Calculate how much money you did not spend.

4. Get a notebook in which you write down how you feel when you buy and don't buy. Also note when you want to buy something, and what's going on in your life at the time, so you can figure out what your triggers are. Do you go shopping when you're sad? Does boredom drive you out to the stores?

5. Every time you don't spend money, reward yourself by transferring $10, $20, $50 to your "I didn't spend this money" savings account. You're working on getting satisfaction from money saved. While you're at it, practise reverse snobbery. Say it out loud. "Damn, that woman's a fool for spending $230 on a pair of shoes." "Gosh, I'd rather have $137 in the bank than spend it on yet one more spring coat." "Five bucks for coffee . . . that's just nuts." Express contempt (quietly to yourself) for people who shop unconsciously, mindlessly buying stuff they don't need. You'd be amazed how your brain will respond to what it hears you say.

6. Look for barter opportunities. If you want something new, find a way to use what you already have to get it. At the core of bartering is using what you already have to get what you want or need. If you can't do a straight

trade, take stuff you own to a consignment store, and use the money you receive to shop second-hand. Initiate Buy Nothing Days. These are days when you don't spend any money. You'll have to plan carefully so you have milk and bread in the house. How long can you go without buying anything?

Not buying comes naturally to some folks. For others it is like torture. But the harder it is to buy nothing, the more you need to learn how to do it. A shopping addiction is a hard thing to break. But you can do it with a lot of determination and loads of practice.

RULE #191: CHOOSE YOUR EVIL

This rule came out of a conversation I had with my friend Victoria. We were talking about all the things I hate to do, and why I do some, but don't do others.

I hate vacuuming, so I hire someone to do it for me. I despise the HST return. In fact, I hate all the government paperwork I have to fill out. I'm not so much against the taxes I have to pay; it's the hours I have to spend reporting that drive me wild. I could hire someone to do it for me, but here's a case of not wanting to spend money on stuff I don't think is worth it. It seems house vacuuming is more evil than government paperwork. And the penalties I'd have to pay for not doing the paperwork are more evil than doing the paperwork, so I choose my evil, buckle down, and get 'er done.

There are some things that, no matter how much you hate them, you can't avoid. Then it becomes a matter of choosing your evil.

Here's something that may come as a surprise: I don't like posting the numbers from my spending journal into the budget every month. Many people think I relish the numbers game. Some parts I enjoy, like the analysis. Many parts I do simply because I know I should. The evils of not doing—the not knowing, the lack of control, the potential missteps—are worse than the doing.

Only you can decide what's more evil for you. (This is where the rubber meets the road in all those motivational programs.)

If the evil of tracking your spending is greater than the evil of being broke all the time, you'll never be a tracker.

Can you change your evil? If you want something badly enough, then you will do whatever it takes to get it. That's human nature. If you're not moving towards the goal you've set, then it is simply because you don't want it badly enough. Stop wasting your energy beating yourself up or whining about not getting to where you want to be. Just say, for example, "I don't really want to own my own home," and be done with it.

RULE #192: DON'T BE TOO SMART
FOR YOUR OWN GOOD

Being smart about money is the way to make money work for you. Being too smart for your own good means you're looking for shortcuts, for ways to stick it to The Man, for tricks to get rich, get out of debt, get out of working hard.

While I was on book tour for *It's Your Money*, I met a woman who said, "I've been trying to find ways to make more money, so I've been signing up for courses and buying programs that promise to help me earn a higher income."

"How's that been working for you?" I asked.

"Not so good. I've racked up $30,000 in debt doing it."

I have to admit my mouth dropped open. She clearly saw the look of disbelief (or was it the look of abject horror?) on my face, because she said, "I'm just trying to make my life better."

Each of the following scenarios comes from someone I've actually met. They aren't theoretical "too smart for your own good" stories. They are real. Do you see yourself in here?

- **You buy an investment you don't understand.** Stop pretending. Get smarter and then you'll do yourself some good.

- **You've cashed in your RRSPs** to convert to a non-registered portfolio to avoid tax at retirement, and you

FINDING BALANCE

did so while you were still working. Yes, holding RRSPs until retirement may mean you pay some tax. But you didn't pay any on the money going into the plan. And you didn't pay any on the income earned over all those years. And whenever you cash in your RRSPs, you'll pay tax; doing so while you're still working full-time guarantees you'll pay more tax.

- **You've taken out a huge investment loan** against your home in order to make your mortgage interest tax-deductible. Leveraging is one way to grow your investments. (See Rule #56: Leveraging Isn't for Everybody.) But if you're justifying this move on the basis of your mortgage interest being tax-deductible, you're doing it for the wrong reason.

- **You consider the upside of an investment** without ever considering the potential regret you may experience at a loss. One side of the equation never tells the whole story.

- **You buy an investment when everyone is talking** about how well it's doing. You've already missed the growth; you're in for the downturn now.

- **You buy a stock on a tip** because your brother-in-law recommended it or because some pundit just labelled it a "Star." Smart investors do their own research before they buy; they don't buy on a whim.

- **You buy an investment and then sell it** in a panic because the market takes a tumble. Either you don't have the stomach for investing, or you didn't understand what you were getting into.

- **Your entire asset base is made up of property.** Yes, your home will appreciate. So will your cottage. And that rental property you have may do very well too. But real estate is just one asset class, and if it's all you've got, your portfolio isn't diversified and you're breaking Rule #206: Diversify Your Portfolio, which you should go and read right now.

There is such a thing as being too smart for your own good. If you're among this lot, stop it.

RULE #193: BUY AND STAY PUT

I can't believe the number of people who change their home as often as they change their underwear. Unless you have to move because of circumstances beyond your control, stay put for at least five years, or until you break even on your costs, whichever comes first.

To calculate if you have broken even, do the following:

1. Add up the profit you'll make on the sale of your existing home. (See Rule #83: Calculate the Real Profit on Your Home.)

2. Add up the costs associated with moving to a new home:
    - legal fees
    - moving
    - service hookups
    - land transfer tax and/or GST, if applicable
    - new mortgage costs such as appraisal fee, interest penalty, and title insurance
    - new furniture/appliances

3. Subtract your costs from your profit.

If you're in the black, moving may be a financially sound move. If your costs have totally eroded your profit, or if you're actually in the negative, why are you moving?

If the decision to buy was a rotten one—you hadn't thought it through—or your circumstances have changed dramatically, you may have no option but to sell. But if you're just in an upgrade mood, bored with your home, looking for a new project, or trying to fancy-up yourself, and you're losing money doing it, rethink what it is you're trying to accomplish.

RULE #194: IF YOU FREEZE, REBOOT

Everyone falls off the rails. A family crisis may distract you from the day-to-day things you do to manage your money. Maybe you get busy having a great time—going on holiday, partying with friends, immersing yourself in a really interesting project—and the money management slides. Perhaps you just hate it so much you HAD to take a break.

It is so easy to freeze. Computers do it all the time. We hardly ever turn 'em off, walk away, and say, "Oh well, I guess that's that." Nope. We turn 'em off, wait 30 seconds, and reboot. Then we get busy again.

You have to do the same thing with your finances if you freeze. There's no shame in freezing. Everyone does it. I do it. But then I kick myself in the ass, reboot, catch up, and get back in balance. You can too.

The next time you freeze, take 30 seconds (or a couple of days) to let your system settle. Make a date for your reboot: Say, "I'm catching up on Monday evening between 7 p.m. and 9 p.m." Then DO IT!

Nobody else can switch you back on.

RULE #195: BORROW CONSCIOUSLY

If you decide to borrow money to buy something—anything from a car to a new sofa—ask yourself the following questions before you make your financial decision.

Do I really need it? You should not be financing wants. That's just dumb. There are times, however, when you must finance a need. If your shingles blow off, not repairing the roof is more of an evil than going into debt to get the roof fixed.

What's the total cost? When you borrow money, you pay more for whatever it is you're buying than if you paid cash. Let's say you decide you need a new car. It cost $26,000 and comes with a 7% interest rate over four years. In the end, that car won't have cost you $26,000—it will have cost you $34,069. Are you prepared to pay $8,069 more for that car? If not, rethink how you're going to get into a vehicle. You could buy used. You could buy cheaper. You could go with a shorter term so you end up paying less interest. Or you could look for less expensive financing. Zero interest sounds good to me. Whatever it is, know what the real hit to your bottom line will be.

What will I give up to get this? Life is about choices. Choosing to work a monthly payment into your budget probably means figuring out what you're *not* going to spend that money on. Will you forgo your vacation so you can afford those loan payments? What are you prepared to give up to get whatever it is you're planning to finance? Look at your budget and figure out where you're going to get those loan payments. What are you really going to do without?

RULE #196: YOU *CAN* BUY LIFE INSURANCE ON YOUR PARTNER

Can't get your better half to spring for the premiums on a life insurance policy? Lots of people have life partners who think insurance is a waste of money. If you think otherwise, you can take out a policy on your spouse, as long as your buddy is aware and agrees, and name yourself the beneficiary. No, you can't kill him and run to Argentina! But you can protect yourself and your family if you're prepared to pay the premiums.

INSURANCE

RULE #197: USE AN RDSP TO PROTECT YOUR DISABLED CHILD

Have a child who is disabled? Wondering how to shelter some money so your child has a stash of cash available later? Get familiar with the Registered Disability Savings Plan. The RDSP lets you grow money tax-free until you need it. There's a $200,000 lifetime contribution limit but no annual limits, and anyone can contribute to the plan. There are also no restrictions on when or how the funds are used.

To sweeten the deal, the government offers a Disability Savings Grant up to a maximum of $3,500 a year and $70,000 over the beneficiary's lifetime. If your annual net income is $83,088* or less you can get $3 for every $1 contributed on the first $500 you put into a plan, to a maximum grant of $1,500; and $2 for every $1 contributed on the next $1,000, to a maximum grant of $2,000. If your net income is more than $83,088, the grant is $1 for every $1 contributed, to a maximum grant of $1,000.

There is also a Disability Savings Bond, which provides low-income (under $24,183) families with $1,000 per year without any contributions required, so that's 100% free money for low-income families.

Starting in 2011, the feds let you carry forward unused grant and bond entitlements for up to 10 years, and you can go back to 2008 to claim them.

*These were the numbers at the time of writing, but they will change, so check the information for the year of your contribution.

Note that for individuals under 18, family income would be the combined income of the parents. However, for a person over 18, family income would be the individual's income (plus their spouse's income if they are married), even if they live with their parents.

To be eligible for the RDSP, the disabled person must

- be eligible for the disability tax credit;
- have a social insurance number;
- have filed a tax return; and
- be under the age of 50.

Any payments made to the beneficiary (or his/her estate) come in the form of a disability assistance payment, or DAP, and can only be made to the beneficiary or the beneficiary's legal representative on his or her behalf. You should consult with an expert who can help you work through the formula for calculating the DAP, because it's complicated.

For more information, go to www.rdsp.ca or www.plan.ca.

RULE #198: PRACTISE
FINANCIAL CONSERVATION

We all know that we should do our utmost to conserve our resources. Whether we're talking water or electricity, looking for ways to make what we have go further—embracing Reduce, Reuse, Recycle—is the new norm. Well, for socially conscious folks it is.

Money, too, is a resource. Like any other resource, it is finite. We may have been deluded into thinking money is an infinite resource because we've had unprecedented access to credit, but that doesn't make it so.

Since we only have a set amount of time during which to make money, and we hope to last well past our working lives, it only makes sense that we figure out what the balance should be between consuming our financial resources and conserving them.

Ordering in a couple of nights a week makes the week go a little smoother when you're rushing home late and just can't think of what to cook or you're just too tired to bother. But if you've got an $80-a-week takeout habit, that's costing you over $4,000 a year. Cut it in half and you've got an extra $2,000 for the future. Invest that $2,000 for 30 years at 7% and your conservation means you'll have an extra $9,000 to eat later on. Do it every year and you'll have almost $139,000. Food . . . check!

It's much the same when it comes to choosing where you will live. We think it's normal to have every conceivable convenience. Not willing to settle for a bathroom, we want a spa. The result: our homes cost us so much money we can't afford to save for the next chapter of our lives, when a more modest existence with money left over for simple pleasures like heat will really matter.

Conservation isn't as hard as most people think. It does take a little thought and some planning. And maybe a little less itch scratching. If you aren't of a mind to conserve, what are you planning to eat when retirement finally does roll around and you're left with a lot of stuff but not much money?

RULE #199: DON'T TAKE THE TAX MAN'S ADVICE AS GOSPEL

You'd think that if you took the time to call the tax department to find out if you could do something (or how to do something), you could bank on the advice you're given. You'd be wrong.

Just because you get advice from the horse's mouth doesn't mean that you can go ahead and follow that advice, secure in the knowledge that you're safe from prosecution or penalties. Believe it or not, tax department representatives can't be held accountable for the information they provide. There is a long-established principle of law that disallows taxpayers from seeking refuge from a negative assessment simply because they were guided by representatives at the tax department. Stupid but true.

If you want to be absolutely sure where you stand, check with someone who really knows the answer and who will be accountable to you for it: an accountant or a well-experienced tax lawyer.

TAXES

RULE #200: MUTUAL FUND AVERAGES
DON'T MEAN DIDDLY

Mutual fund rates of return are the subject of thousands of articles and almost as many books. More than one expert has made a name analyzing the performance of mutual funds, as if past performance is any predictor of future performance. It's not. Even the mutual fund marketing material says so.

Perhaps the biggest red herring used to grab newbie investors' attention is the averages quoted. You'll see them in newspapers, magazines, and brochures: 3-year averages, 5-year averages, 10-year averages. The problem is those averages can be misleading because they're designed to smooth out the ups and downs in the funds and make them look far more consistent than they may be.

Let's say XYZ mutual fund had the following returns over 5 years:

- +13%
- +18%
- +16%
- −17%
- +12%

Hey, that looks like a pretty decent track record, doesn't it? Four out of five positive years looks pretty good. And that averages out to an annual return of 8.4%. That means on a $1000 investment, you should end up with $1,497. Pretty cool.

Now let's do the real math:

$$\$1,000 \text{ (investment)} \times 13 \text{ (\% return)} \div 100 = \$130 \text{ (gain)}$$
$$+ \$1,000 \text{ (investment)} = \$1,130 \text{ (investment's new value)}$$

Start of Year	% Return	End of Year
$1,000	13	$1,130
$1,130	18	$1,333
$1,333	16	$1,547
$1,547	- 17	$1,284
$1,284	12	**$1,438**

Hey, where did the $59 go? You should have had $1,497 based on the average, but in real life, you ended up with only $1,438, for a difference of $59.

That's because when an investment has a bad year and hits negative territory, the negative return affects the value of your total investment.

Some more math:

$$\$1,547 \text{ (investment)} \times -17 \text{ (\% return)} \div 100 = \$263 \text{ (loss)}$$
$$+ \$1,547 \text{ (investment)} = \$1,284 \text{ (investment's new value)}$$

Because you had a negative return one year, you lost money . . . not just earnings, but also some of the money you started out with at the beginning of the year. So average returns don't mean diddly-squat!

If you want to assess how a mutual fund has been performing, you can't just look at averages. You have to look at year-over-year returns. That's how the mutual fund has done each year for the past 5 or 10 years (depending on how long a track record it has). If there are steady returns, the averages might tell a good story. But if there are wide swings in return, the averages won't accurately reflect the actual performance of the mutual fund. Do the math!

RULE #201: KNOW THE BEST TIME TO USE A VARIABLE MORTGAGE

Most people choose to use a variable mortgage on the strength of the difference in cost to a fixed mortgage. Let's face it, if you can get a variable mortgage at 2.5% and the five-year fixed mortgage is 5.9%, you'd be stupid to go fixed.

Maybe not.

Variable mortgages aren't for everyone. While the rate may be lower, in times of rising interest rates that lower rate may not be the bargain you first thought it would be. If you're uncomfortable with the idea that your rate can go up, and Up and UP, a variable mortgage isn't for you.

Fixed mortgages mean you have a specific payment amount you can budget for the term of the mortgage. It makes it easier to plan your life, particularly when cash flow is tight and even a small upward movement in rates could cause you a problem.

But Gail, if rates tick up, I can always lock in then.

True. But you'll be locking in at a higher rate. If the variable rate rises from 2.5% to 3%, the fixed rate will also rise. Will you have the flexibility in your cash flow to cope with that increase?

Some people cannot stand the stomach churning that accompanies living with a variable interest rate. If you aren't prepared to keep a close eye on the market, go with a fixed term.

The best time to use a variable rate mortgage is when interest rates are coming down. When interest rates are rising, locking in your low rate for a long term may suit your needs if it means you'll be able to sleep at night.

RULE #202: NOT EVERYONE SHOULD HAVE AN RRSP

This replaces the old rule "An RRSP is the best way to save for retirement."

Some people might be better off focusing on a tax-free savings account (TFSA) instead of using an RRSP to save for retirement. Do you fall into one of the following groups?

- **You have low income.** If it's taking all your money just to make ends meet, you might want to skip the whole guilt thing over not contributing to an RRSP. Look ahead a bit. If you'll be able to make do with the income CPP and OAS provide, then squirrelling away whatever you can manage in a TFSA would make more sense. And if you're going to have an income that lets you qualify for the Guaranteed Income Supplement ($17,088 in 2015, not including OAS), then using a TFSA will also work better for you.

- **You have a low tax rate.** Claiming a deduction for an RRSP contribution at a low tax rate, piling up a stash of cash, then paying more in tax when you cash out at retirement, makes no sense. If you think you'll likely always be at the lowest tax rates, go with the TFSA.

- **You are old or pretty close to retirement.** If you'll be tapping your savings within 10 years, you haven't made any RRSP contributions thus far and you're only going to be saving a small amount ($5,000 or less), and you're not in the highest income tax bracket, go with a TFSA.

- **You have a great pension plan at work.** Having a great pension plan at work means you may find yourself already paying more tax than you want to. Having a whack of taxable income in an RRSP will be less than optimal. If you're concerned about losing your OAS to the clawback that starts when your net income is $71,592 (in 2014 dollars), go with a TFSA instead of an RRSP.

You'll notice I didn't include "Young and not earning much" as a category. I'm still a big believer in RRSPs. Unless you think you'll always make very little money, even if you're young and not in a high tax bracket you can benefit from the long-term compounding in an RRSP. You don't have to claim the deduction right away. In fact, you'd be better off not to. (See Rule #100: Don't Claim Your RRSP Deduction Right Away.) But you must save!

RULE #203: ACCELERATE YOUR MORTGAGE REPAYMENT

Most mortgage calculators automatically default to a monthly payment frequency. If you want to trim years off your mortgage and save loads of interest, instead of a monthly payment choose an accelerated weekly or biweekly payment, whichever best matches your cash flow.

You'll end up making one extra payment a year, but you'll do so in such small amounts that you'll hardly notice. And since that extra payment goes directly to your principal, you'll save big-time on interest. On a $200,000 mortgage amortized for 25 years at 5.5%, using an accelerated weekly payment will save you $30,000 in interest and knock 4 years off your mortgage. And it'll only cost you $23.48 more a week. Hey, you can find $23.48 a week to save over $30,000 in interest, can't you?

Most banks will let you change your payment frequency, so if you're paying monthly, call and get it changed today. There may be an interest adjustment from your current payment due date to the revised date, so ask about that.

RULE #204: HELP CHILDREN WITH EARNED INCOME MAKE RRSP CONTRIBUTIONS

People are under the misconception that you have to be over 19 to contribute to an RRSP. Anyone in Canada who has earned income and has filed a tax return, regardless of age, has RRSP contribution room. That includes kids with a paper route, those who babysit, and children who have promising modelling or television careers. (Minors may not open TFSAs, so here's one place an RRSP has the upper hand.)

Don't claim the RRSP deduction, but make the contribution. (See Rule #100: Don't Claim Your RRSP Deduction Right Away.) One RRSP contribution of $500 (he'd need an income of about $2,800) at age 10 compounding at an average return of 5% will grow to more than $7,300 by 65. If your young 'un continues to contribute that $500 every year, he'll have more than $258,000 at 65.

Since Baby Boy's RRSP tax deduction can be carried forward indefinitely, when he does start working full-time, he'll have deductions he can use to offset the tax on his income so he has more money to pay back those whopping student loans!

But Gail, if I put that money into an RESP to start, I can avoid those student loans altogether.

Maybe. And if you're trying to decide between an RRSP and an RESP, go with the RESP first. But if you have extra money or if your kids are too old to benefit from the RESP and the CESG (Canada Education Savings Grant), get them started on an RRSP.

SAVING

RULE #205: YOU DON'T OWN YOUR COMPANY INSURANCE

One of the critical differences between having life insurance coverage through your group benefits at work and having an individually owned plan is that with a group plan you don't own the plan—your company does. Even though you're paying a taxable benefit on that policy, you can't take it with you (most of the time) when you leave. While you're covered for as long as you remain with the company, if you're wholly dependent on your group policy, you may find yourself out in the cold if you change jobs and at that point are considered "uninsurable," or are an old dog and can't afford the high premiums.

Even if you have a small individual policy that guarantees your future insurability should you need more insurance later, you'll have more options than if you choose to stick with just your company group life insurance.

RULE #206: DIVERSIFY YOUR PORTFOLIO

Don't put all your eggs in one basket—it's a proverb done to death in the investment community. Despite its repetition, many investors still don't really get what the eggs-and-baskets thing is all about: diversification. Well, that's the official term.

The idea behind diversification is that if you spread your money around, you won't have to worry about losing it all at the same time. If investment A goes into the crapper, you'll have investments B, C, D to make up the difference.

Unfortunately, some people think diversification means splitting your dollars between 10 mutual fund companies, on the assumption that if one company's investment strategy doesn't work, another's might. Sadly, what this produces is not diversification, but deworsification: a splintered portfolio that does little to reduce your exposure to risk.

The misconception that if you buy different funds or stocks of different companies you'll automatically be well diversified is just that: a misconception. To diversify effectively, not only must you buy stocks in different companies, but you must also invest within different industries and across different regions. So if your Fund A and Fund B portfolios look remarkably similar (you did read the prospectus, right?), you're not diversified; if you're holding shares of eight different financial services companies, you're not diversified; if you're investing all your money in Canada, you're not diversified.

Grab your last statement and see how many of the following points you hit.

Types of investments. The idea is to invest in some stock, some bonds, some mutual funds, deposit products, real estate, mortgages . . . you get the picture. This is referred to as "mixing your assets," or "asset mix" (sometimes it's called "asset allocation"), and it recognizes that plowing your every dollar into a single asset category is unwise because sometimes one asset category goes south and you don't want to have all your money go with it.

Industry. Since the markets are un-figure-outable (*no one knows!*), it makes sense to spread your money across several industries, so that a lacklustre performance in one industry doesn't have too big an impact on your entire portfolio. How many of these industries does your portfolio cover: manufacturing, finance, food services, technology, transportation, pharmaceuticals, retail, energy? Or you could pick a conglomerate like GE or Colgate that has its fingers in a dozen pies.

Quality of investments. Bonds are rated according to their default factor, and the higher that factor, the higher the interest you'll earn. That's why "junk bonds"—bonds with a huge default factor—pay such high rates of return. Stocks, too, have their own quality rating: blue chips are the most stable; penny stocks are the riskiest. And there's something for everyone in between.

Region. Canada represents only a small percentage of the global investment marketplace, so keeping all your money in Canadian stocks means you're limiting your portfolio. Different countries' economies do not move in lockstep, unless, of course, there's a frickin' global meltdown, in which case everyone is screwed! Back to the idea. While North America may be sliding, South America, Europe, or Asia may be rising. Having some money in different regions means you'll even out the performance of your portfolio.

Currency. If you're planning a trip to the U.S. or Europe, you'll be saying, "Yay!" as you watch the loonie rise. If you're bringing assets back to Canada from some other region of the world, a depressed dollar may increase your return. Foreign investing isn't just about how some other country's economy is doing; it's about how strongly our dollar is performing in comparison to that country's currency too. A mediocre return can be made stellar if we also make money on the exchange rate. 'Course, the opposite is true too.

Levels of liquidity. Holding some long-term investments such as stripped bonds or equity funds along with some shorter-term alternatives such as income funds or treasury bills means you can take advantage of changes in economic conditions because you're exposed to different investment time horizons. Since predicting interest rates is a tough call, diversifying your bond holdings with a variety of maturity dates means you won't have to worry about all your money coming due just when interest rates are at a low.

Deworsification isn't something that people do purposely. It can happen over time as we adjust our portfolios, adding new investments and selling off our winners (and losers). Review your portfolio annually to make sure that the strategy you're implementing is keeping you diversified in a good way.

RULE #207: WRITE YOUR OWN MORTGAGE

If you have loads of cash in your RRSP, you can write your own mortgage and pay yourself the interest. A self-directed mortgage (SDM) is a mortgage just like any other mortgage, except your RRSP is the mortgagor instead of the bank, and you make the payments back to the plan instead of lining the pockets of some third-party lender. You are borrowing cash from your RRSP, which takes title to any Canadian real estate you own, or that's owned by your immediate family, as security.

So how complicated is it? It's about a 6 on a scale of 1 to 10. Here's how to do it:

STEP 1: FIGURE OUT IF YOU'RE ELIGIBLE

You need to have a whack of cash in a self-directed RRSP for this to work. Some experts say at least $50,000 to offset the fees. I'd say no less than $100,000 in periods of higher interest rates (over 6%) and $200,000 in periods of lower interest rates (5% and under), coz those fees ain't chicken feed.

One-Time Fees
Mortgage Set-Up: $200
Appraisal Fee: $200
Legal Fees: $500 to 1,000
Mortgage Insurance Premiums: 0.5% to 2.5%
of the total mortgage

Ongoing Fees

Self-Directed Administration Fee: $100 to $250/year

Mortgage Administration Fee: $150 to $500/year

While these fees are negotiable, particularly the ones at your bank, know that since lenders are not making any money off you on mortgage interest, they'll be less likely to want to negotiate. You'll have to have some serious weight to throw around to get them to lower their fees.

Don't have enough cash in your own RRSP? You and your mate can write a "shared mortgage," where you and your partner each kick in money from your individual RRSPs and split the fees accordingly. So if Jack has $100,000 and Jill has $200,000 and they are writing a mortgage for $300,000 from their RRSPs, Jack would pay one-third of the fees and Jill would pay two-thirds.

You have to be writing a brand new mortgage, or your existing mortgage must be coming up for renewal, since you'll defeat the purpose completely if you pay your existing lender a whack of money to break an existing mortgage.

STEP 2: DECIDE IF YOU WANT TO DO THIS

This strategy is not for the faint of heart. While it isn't a horrendously complex investment strategy, it does require you to step out of the box. It means some careful planning. And you'll have to have the persistence of Sisyphus. Not all lenders or RRSP administrators will let you do this, so you may end up having to move your RRSP if you're committed to the strategy.

Just because you're writing the mortgage from your own RRSP doesn't mean you can make up the rules. The Tax Man has specific guidelines:

- You set the interest rate, but the interest you pay has to be comparable with current rates. You can use the highest rate, the lowest rate, or anything in between that you can find in the marketplace when you write the SDM.
- The mortgage must be insured, so you'll pay a pretty penny in premiums (0.5% to 2.5%) even if you have more than 20% equity in your home.
- You must qualify for the mortgage, just as you would if you had gone to a financial institution.
- Payments must be made on time or your RRSP will be forced to foreclose.

If your SDM doesn't meet the guidelines, there's a big ouch! The mortgage would be classified as a "non-qualifying investment," its fair market value at the acquisition date would be included in your income, and any interest earned by the RRSP would be taxable to the RRSP (and you'd lose the RRSP contribution room forever).

The Upsides of a Self-Directed Mortgage

- As long as you stay within the rules, you have some flexibility in terms of choosing your interest rate. Choose a higher rate and you'll be giving your RRSP return a boost. Choose a lower rate and you'll be saving on your mortgage costs.

- If you're determined to have a safe investment that pays you a fixed rate of return, a SDM will likely earn you more than you could get anywhere else, such as on bonds or GICs.
- You're moving your interest costs from your left pocket to your right pocket . . . no lender is profiting from your mortgage.

The Downsides of a Self-Directed Mortgage

- It's expensive. Estimate that you'll lose about 2% of your return to fees in the first year. Ongoing fees are smaller.
- You'll be tying up a significant portion of your RRSP portfolio in fixed income investments, which means less diversification. But if you were going to do this anyway . . .

I've done the SDM thing myself. Because I'm a very conservative investor, it made perfect sense to me. My then husband queried cautiously, "Remind me why we're doing this?" He had been playing the market quite successfully and was a little wistful at the potential lost opportunity. I responded, "We need a little more balance than we have right now in our portfolios." I was referring to the fact that his RRSP was 100% equities. He would never settle for a GIC ("What, are you kidding!"), and I had a knot in my stomach the size of Algeria at the thought of a market meltdown and what it would do to our retirement savings, so we compromised on using the self-directed mortgage. Since mortgages rates are typically about 3% above GIC rates, our SDM would earn a decent return—about 8%—without the slightest bit more risk. After all, if you can't trust yourself to repay the loan, who can you trust? (BTW, I turned out to be right about the change in market direction and he thanked me . . . a lot.)

STEP 3: EXECUTE YOUR SDM STRATEGY

Move a sufficient amount of your RRSP portfolio to cash to cover the mortgage you plan to write so that you have the money readily available. Time the move to cash to coincide with your mortgage renewal, or with the purchase of your home.

Find a bank, investment dealer, or trust company that offers this service. Again, this may mean moving your RRSP portfolio, since not all RRSP providers will let you write the SDM. Your financial institution may even tell you it can't be done under the Tax Man's guidelines. Don't listen to the idiots, and don't waste your time trying to explain the rules. Find someone who will help you execute your strategy.

Research the going rates and terms in the marketplace. Decide if you want to minimize your interest costs (so you'll choose the lowest rate available) or maximize your RRSP's return (so you'll choose a higher rate). Remember, different types of mortgages come with different rates. Leave your mortgage open and you will justify a higher interest cost. If you eliminate the prepayment option, then when you make a prepayment you'll have to pay your RRSP a penalty, thereby boosting your RRSP's return.

Add up fees and choose an interest rate for your mortgage that ensures your RRSP is making some profit. You don't want your RRSP to do worse than you could do with a GIC.

STEP 4: REINVEST YOUR MORTGAGE PAYMENTS

One of the things you may grapple with when you consider an SDM is what you're going to do with the mortgage payments trickling into the RRSP every month. If that money sits idle, your RRSP's return will suffer. There's also the issue of diversification. With a large portion of your portfolio in an SDM, you may be too heavily weighted on the fixed income side.

You can build growth into your SDM strategy by dollar cost averaging your monthly mortgage payments into an aggressive mutual fund or buying an index. Voila: security, diversification, and the elimination of the market-timing question. Should the market fall, you will be continually buying back in at the fire-sale prices.

RULE #208: ALWAYS REVIEW YOUR NOTICE OF ASSESSMENT

You know that letter you get from the tax department that tells you how much tax you owe or how much your refund will be? That's your Notice of Assessment. Read it carefully. Sometimes the guy processing your file makes a mistake. Don't let it go unchecked. If you seem to owe money you shouldn't, or you're given a big fat refund you weren't expecting, take it to an accountant and have her check the file over so you're sure everything is as it needs to be. Just because the Tax Man makes a mistake doesn't mean you will profit. His mistake will come back to haunt you.

TAXES

RULE #209: WATCH OUT FOR
LIFESTYLE INFLATION

Very often the shift from "poor student" to "working full-time" brings with it an increase in spending. Ditto the shift from just making ends meet to having more than enough. Or the shift from a houseful of kids to empty nester. Extra disposable income makes you feel "rich," so you spend more money.

You used to consider a burger and fries a "night on the town." Now you want a restaurant with ambience. You were happy to hunt through Value Village for that $10 pair of jeans. Now you think spending $160 on a name brand is just fine. You figure that because you're earning a steady or substantially higher income, you can now afford a snazzy car, better duds, and an annual vacation. If you've been given a little credit along the way, you no doubt believe that whatever you spend now you can pay off later because you make so much money.

This is called "lifestyle inflation" and it is the proof that it doesn't matter how much you make, you can find a way to spend it . . . and more. Take the people who have just bought their first home as an example. Happy to have done with second-hand everything in their apartments, they now believe that a houseful of new is their due. Or the people who have just been promoted and can't imagine how they'll spend all the extra money they are earning, so they set out to try.

Lifestyle inflation happens naturally. If you move into a nice neighbourhood and everyone is driving a new-model car, you feel the pressure to upgrade. If you start work in a cool new office where all the folks look like they just stepped off the pages of a fashion rag, you feel the pressure to drop some money on new threads. And if you've just had a baby and all your mommy friends are sipping Starbucks while they jiggle baby on their laps, you want to sip Starbucks too.

It's fine to want a car that isn't held together with chewing gum. And looking stylish can be an image builder at work. But when everyone rushes out to get the newest cell phone because "the very cool He" has one, lifestyle inflation has gotten ugly. (And you're chastising your kids for bowing to peer pressure?)

Perhaps the biggest problem with lifestyle inflation is that you develop a spending momentum that's tough to reverse. If you go on holiday every year for three years in a row, always upgrading, the idea of a staycation feels like punishment. And if you've gotten used to dropping $600 for a pair of shoes, why would you give a second thought to spending $300 on that pair of sandals? Relatively speaking, they're cheap.

Go ahead and give your quality of life a boost when you start making more money. You should enjoy the lifestyle that you're working so hard for. But make sure you give your goals a nod by reviewing them and perhaps setting some new ones. And keep a piece of all the new money you're making for the future by upping your auto-savings.

Spending more money consciously to have a more satisfying life is fine. Simply reacting to feeling richer by blowing gobs of dough on crap is stupid. If you let lifestyle inflation drive your spending, you'll rue it the next time you have a setback. Those $600 shoes will look like a pretty dumb move when you're staring into an empty fridge.

RULE #210: ALWAYS SHOP WITH A LIST

When you go shopping, go with a list. In the grocery store, use a list. (I keep a running list on my fridge and add things as I use them up.) In the home-decorating store, use a list. In the mall, use a list.

Using a list even applies to the things you're thinking about buying. My girlfriend Natasha showed me this technique. If she wants something like a new wallet or a new pair of sunglasses, she adds it to her wants list. If she finds a good deal when she's in a store, she looks to see where the item is on her list in terms of priority and whether she has the money to pay for it. If everything checks out, she buys. If not, she walks away.

Create a wants list to prioritize the things you'd like to buy yourself. The rules are simple. If what you want to buy isn't on the list, you can't buy it. You can put it on the list and go home, and then go back out again, assuming you have the money to pay for it. But you've got to wait a specific amount of time— 48 hours, two weeks, a month—so that the purchase becomes one that has been planned and isn't simply reactive.

Using a list means you're taking the impulse out of the shopping experience. You're planning what you're going to spend your money on. And you're weighing one need or want against the others so you're spending your money where it'll do the most good or create the greatest pleasure.

RULE #211: SELF-EMPLOYMENT IS TAX-SMART

Start a business from home, however small, and magically, expenses ranging from Internet access to plumbing repairs can become at least partly deductible. There are rules, of course. (See Rule #142: Know the Rules for Writing Off a Home Office.)

If you use your car for business, you can claim a slew of expenses, ranging from gas and insurance to maintenance and parking, as long as you deduct only the portion related to the business. Keep a record of kilometres used for business so you can show the Tax Man when he comes a-knockin.'

All kinds of things become eligible as a deduction if there's a business benefit. The obvious ones are things like telephones and Internet connections. Less obvious: If you must receive couriers and the odd business associate, you'll need to keep your driveway and walkway clear of snow for insurance purposes. That makes snow removal a business expense. Nice, eh?

Pay your bills by mail? You can write off your stamps; just get a post-office receipt. Have to take a client out for lunch? You can write off half the bill (the part the client was supposed to have eaten, regardless of who ate more!). Office supplies like pens, stationery, desks, and chairs are all legitimate expenses.

You can only write off those eligible expenses against the income you're generating from your self-employed activities. And you have to keep meticulous records to prove you aren't trying to write off "personal use" expenses. What skill, hobby, or talent are you going to put to use to make more money while saving on expenses?

RULE #212: IT'S NOT WHAT YOU SAVED —IT'S WHAT YOU SPENT!

People are always justifying their spending to me by describing how much they saved. (It seems that I instill this need for people to tell me about what they just bought. Hmm.) Hey, if you're justifying what you spent by what you saved, you're a bargain junkie.

Do you . . .

- hit sales and clearance racks when you're feeling sad or mad?
- spend more than you can afford?
- see sales as opportunities you just can't pass up?
- feel guilty about your shopping?
- walk out of stores with things you hadn't expected to buy?
- hide your purchases?
- forget what you bought?
- find things in your closets with the tags still on?

Who doesn't love a good sale? But when bargain hunting, coupon clipping, or mastering the deal becomes the objective, you and your budget are likely headed for big trouble.

If you're spending money you don't have—if you're putting a purchase on credit and not paying your balance off in full—it's not a deal. If you're buying something you don't need, it's not a deal. If it takes you three weeks, three months, or never to put what you bought to use, it's not a deal.

SMART SHOPPING

Some places are known for having deals, and people take the value they're getting for granted without actually checking the prices. Dumb! And there are people who will go to extremes to get a deal, lining up for hours to browse—and ultimately buy—in stores where they wouldn't normally shop. The newest of deals come right to your email inbox in the form of daily savings coupons. I know one chick who had $800 worth of these suckers piled up because she just couldn't resist the deal!

People who can't pass up a good sale even if it's on something they don't want, need, or even particularly like aren't smart bargain buyers—they're compulsive shoppers. Scoring deals helps them to ease their insecurities and feel more competent and in control. And they rationalize their purchases as something good they are doing for themselves or their families.

Loads of people can't resist a bargain. And heaps of people buy more because of a low price tag. Some people get such a buzz from bargain shopping that they are always on the lookout for the next hit.

Tell you what—you show me the money you "saved" by being such a great bargain hunter and I'll eat this page. Yup, show it to me in a savings account. If you can't, you may want to think seriously about whether you're a smart shopper or a spending junkie.

RULE #213: CLOSE CREDIT ACCOUNTS YOU'RE NOT USING

If you have credit cards or lines of credit you're no longer using, or if you've paid off a bunch of balances and want to do some trimming back, closing those accounts may make sense for three reasons:

1. As long as the account is active, there's the potential for ID theft.

2. Easy access to credit could be more temptation than you can handle. If your track record with revolving credit has been a little shaky, the temptation to spend could get the better of you down the road.

3. If you're planning on doing some "good" borrowing, you don't want to be overexposed credit-wise. Every piece of credit is taken into account when a lender is deciding whether to give you more credit. Lenders add up all your limits—LIMITS, not outstanding balances—and do their calculations as if you have borrowed all that money already. Why? Because you COULD!

But before you run out and cancel, there are a couple of downsides to closing a credit account if you don't do it just right:

- It can create a short-term dip in your credit score, which in turn can affect your cost of borrowing. So you have to time the cancellation so that either you do your "good" borrowing first, or your credit score has enough time to recover.

- It can affect your credit history. If the account you cancel has a long and lustrous credit history associated with it, as soon as you cancel the account, you could potentially lose the credit history because it may be deleted from your credit file.

Here's a safe way to close credit accounts:

1. Look back over your credit card and LOC statements to see which ones are the oldest and have the healthiest credit histories—read "no missed or late payments." Hang on to those accounts to keep your history intact until you've built a sparkling credit history elsewhere.

2. Choose the credit accounts that you want to keep.

3. If the accounts you want to eliminate have good histories, start by reducing the limits to reduce your credit exposure, but keep the accounts alive. Don't use those accounts (cut up the cards); just don't cancel them. In the meantime, focus all your credit activity on the card you plan to keep. After six months, you will have built up a solid history on your newer card and can close the old accounts.

4. Make sure you've redeemed all your rewards so you don't lose them.

5. Then call to cancel your card. If the sales rep promises you her first-born to keep the card, stand your ground. Remember, you've already chosen the accounts that you're going to keep.

6. Send written confirmation to the card issuer and keep a copy on file. Fax it if you can so you have a record of its receipt. Ask for written confirmation that the account was closed. I actually had a department store allow charges to go through on a card I had reported lost, so don't assume that because a creditor says a card is cancelled it's cancelled. Get proof.

Once you receive confirmation that the card has been cancelled, wait about six weeks and then check your credit report. Remember, it's your responsibility to verify that your credit report is accurate.

RULE #214: TAKE A SPENDING HOLIDAY

It's amazing how used we get to spending money. Whether we've been bitten by lifestyle inflation or we've just executed a bunch of buys we've carefully planned for, blowing through a bunch of money in a short space of time can leave us with a higher spending threshold. We've become so used to spending that every little thing we look at seems like a reasonable cost.

If you've just come through a particularly expensive period where you've laid out a lot of money—you just got married, you just bought a new home, you just got back from vacation—take a spending holiday to reset your money set point for spending (See Rule #40: Figure Out Your Money Set Point.)

Figure out what it takes to live modestly for a month. You'll need to cover your regular bills like mortgage or rent, utilities, car payment. Once you think you've got the bare bones covered, look at how much cash you think you'll have to spend. Planning to spend $600 this month on everything from groceries to gas to your sister's birthday present? Cut that in half and challenge yourself to live on less.

Before you throw your hands up and say, "Ridiculous," just try it. There's no failure here. You're resetting your spending threshold. Even if you miss by $150, you've still spent much less than you thought was possible and you've brought your spending threshold down.

RULE #215: IF YOU GET
BAD ADVICE, *COMPLAIN!*

Consumers can be a wussy lot. We're treated badly by our financial institutions and we grumble, we gripe—and then we keep going back. Changing institutions is just too much trouble. And complaining . . . who's going to even listen? Could that be why so many banks get away with giving bad advice and lousy service?

Whether you've been given bad mortgage advice, you've been cajoled (or was that bullied?) into taking out creditor insurance you really didn't want, or you've been shoved into an investment option that you neither understood nor felt comfortable with, you have recourse.

Your first step is to speak with the branch manager. Make sure you keep notes of whom you talk to, when, and any important details of your conversations.

If she or he cannot or will not help, ask for the bank's written complaint procedure. Write "COMPLAINT" in big letters at the top of your letter. Describe the problem clearly. Say what you expect as a solution. Make sure you have all the appropriate documents, such as brochures, account statements, and copies of contracts. Keep your originals and send only copies.

You may need to keep escalating the issue with more senior people at the bank to get heard. Don't take no for an answer. Many years ago when I was transferring my RRSPs from one institution to another, the original institution was dragging

SMART
SHOPPING

its heels. After three months watching the new institution fighting to get the RRSP transferred, I picked up the phone, called the president of the original company, and left a message: "Give me my frickin' money, or I'm going to go to the press and the Investment Dealers Association and tell them how long you've been dragging your feet." (I wasn't a big deal back then, just a girl with a LOT of attitude.) The money was transferred within two weeks.

Most banks have an internal ombudsman or compliance officer whose job it is to review issues that may be beyond a branch manager. This ombudsman or compliance officer will likely be the last step in the internal complaints process. Ask this person to provide you with a final letter outlining the firm's position on your complaint.

If the problem cannot be resolved internally, head to the Ombudsman for Banking Services and Investments.

Toll-free telephone: 1.888.451.4519
Toll-free fax: 1.888.422.2865
Website: www.obsi.ca
Email: ombudsman@obsi.ca
Regular mail:
Ombudsman for Banking Services and Investments
401 Bay Street, Suite 1505
P.O. Box 5
Toronto, ON M5H 2Y4

Again, make sure you keep copies of all correspondence and notes of phone calls.

RULE #216: STUDENT LOANS CAN BE
DISCHARGED AFTER SEVEN YEARS

There's a lot of confusion around the bankruptcy rules as they relate to student loans. Once upon a time, you could discharge your student loan debt through bankruptcy if you'd been out of school for 7 years. The rule changed and you had to wait 10 years. The rule changed again, back to seven.

But here are a couple of lesser-known facts:

- In cases of "hardship," a special rule will allow ex-students to apply to bankruptcy court after five years to have their student loan reduced or discharged. If you're living modestly and within your means (no, you can't have run up a whole whack of consumer debt), have done your darnedest to find work, or are working a minimum wage job and just can't make ends meet, you can apply for relief.

- Even if you've been out of school for seven years, if the government objects to the discharge, you could still end up paying some or all of your student loans back. The discharge isn't guaranteed. You have to have demonstrated a best effort in dealing with your student debt. A bankruptcy trustee will guide you through the process of dotting your i's and crossing your t's to stay on the right side of the rules.

If you have graduated and have had a hard time finding work in your field, if you're struggling with your student loans, if you've been diligent in trying to keep up with your responsibilities, but it's always a struggle, go see a bankruptcy trustee.

RULE #217: REPLACE IMPULSIVE ACTION WITH CONSCIOUS CHOICE

Are you blundering through your life, spending money without thinking about it and then crying about what you can't have? If you aren't aware of what you're doing right and what you're doing wrong, if you're not sure of the implications of what you're doing and you're just doing, how's that working for you?

If you are "sold" anything—if you buy because someone told you to buy, as opposed to because you purposefully decided to buy—you're using your money unconsciously. Every impulse purchase is an example of unconscious spending. Every fear-induced response—buy the warranty or you'll be sorry!—is an example of reacting unconsciously.

If you're operating unconsciously, you're at the whim of whomever you're dealing with at the moment. Without being conscious, staying focused on the big picture is pretty tough. Sure you're burnt-out and would love a vacation, or you've been studying your nuts off and would love a night out with friends, but if you're spending next week's rent money, grocery money, or telephone bill money to do it, you're going to be very sorry.

Pick something you do "religiously," without thinking about it, and figure out the long-term cost of your unconscious "small indulgence." Whether you're a "bottle of wine a week" girl, a "magazine at the checkout" chick, or a "doodad at the automotive store" dude, add it up. Actually add the buys up. Multiply the amount by 52 if you do it weekly, 250 if you do it every workday, or 365 if you do it daily.

Let's look at a small spend like an afternoon snack done daily at work over 30 years and you'll see what I mean. There you go, spending $1.67 each afternoon on your favourite treat (is it a cuppa tea, a chocolate bar, or a bag of chips?) to get you to the end of the day. That's $1.67 × 250 = $417.50 a year.

Once you figure out what you're spending in a year, multiply it by 30 to see what it's costing you long-term. (That $1.67 a day will end up costing $12,525.) Or better yet, put it into an online calculator with an average return of 5% and see what you're missing out on in terms of the return you could have on that money. (That $1.67 a day could grow to $28,415 in a TFSA.)

I'm not saying you have to eliminate all your treats. I love my treats. But your self-indulgence should be on stuff you truly appreciate, not just a knee-jerk reaction that has you spending money unconsciously.

Having a budget means you're making a conscious decision about how you really want to spend your money. My budget includes a line for "pleasures," and I decide exactly how much I'm prepared to spend on the things that bring me a little joy. Being conscious is about being aware of how much you have, and prioritizing thoughtfully so you can cover the bases on the things that are important to you. It isn't about "doing without." It's about "living within" your means.

Keeping a spending journal (see Rule #19: Write Down What You're Spending) means you hold yourself accountable for every purchase you make. Yes, you'll still do some dumbass stuff. That's life. You're human. But you'll make far fewer boneheaded decisions, because you are conscious.

RULE #218: COLLATERAL
MORTGAGES ARE A TRAP

Collateral is the asset you pledge as a guarantee that you'll repay a loan. If you don't keep to your commitment, the lender can sell the collateral—whatever you put up as a pledge—and take his money back.

Of late, some banks are offering their customers "collateral" mortgages instead of the typical "conventional" mortgages. It's a trap. Don't get caught.

A "collateral mortgage" is a loan attached to a promissory note and backed up by the collateral security of a mortgage on a property. Typically, a collateral mortgage is registered for a secured line of credit, allowing the balance of the loan to float up or down depending on the customer's use.

A "normal" conventional mortgage lets you establish a set amount you are borrowing, the rate for the term you have chosen (say, 4% for three years), and the amortization (the total amount of time you'll take to pay back the loan), so you'll know exactly when you will have the whole kit and caboodle paid off. You know what your payments will be for the term, and if you stay on track, the property is yours at the end of the amortization. Should you need to borrow more using a second mortgage or by registering a home equity line of credit, then you can. If you don't borrow any more money against the property, the principal balance on a conventional mortgage goes only one way: down. And Canadian major chartered banks will accept "transfers" of conventional mortgages from one to the other at little or no cost.

With a traditional mortgage, just the value of the property is used to secure the loan. However, with a collateral mortgage not only is the current value used, but lenders like to hook into the future value as well. The primary security on a collateral mortgage is a promissory note with a lien on the property for the total amount registered, so you can register far more debt against the property than the property is worth. Some banks are registering 125% of property value, even though that amount may not have been advanced to the borrower initially. (This is a very creative way to get around the government's new guidelines designed to stop lenders from overlending to clients on their mortgages.)

Since the collateral mortgage allows for the "re-advancing" of principal, like a revolving line of credit, the balance can rise, and very often does, with most people ignorant about the holes they are digging for themselves. Most chartered banks will not accept "transfers" of collateral mortgages from other chartered banks, so you have to pay a whack more fees to register a new conventional or collateral mortgage if you decide to move to a new lender because you can get a better rate or better service.

Collateral charges allow lenders to change the interest rate and/or loan more money to qualified borrowers after closing. All you'll likely have to do to trigger an increase in interest rate is miss a payment. That can't happen with a traditional mortgage. But since the collateral mortgages are being registered with rates as high as prime plus 10% (regardless of what they initially offer you), lenders will cover their potential losses by juicing the rates if they get a whiff of potential default.

Consumers are an easily led lot, and this is a product designed to lead you further and further into debt. Keep in mind that you don't have to be bad with money to fall into the trap. Just be married to a Money Moron and watch all your "equity" evaporate.

A **big** "uh-oh!" on collateral mortgages comes at renewal. Now that The Bank has a ring through your nose, it can offer you whatever rate it chooses and your options are to suck it up or pay significant legal fees (we're talking hundreds of dollars) to get the hell out of Dodge.

Another pile of poop into which you may step by signing up for a collateral mortgage involves the other debt you may have. Under Canadian law a lender may seize equity to cover other debt you have with the same lender. So, in essence, you're securing all your loans be they credit cards, lines, car loans, or overdraft that you may have with The Bank with your collateral loan. Yup, The Bank can take the equity in your house to cover those other loans, and if that means selling your house out from under you, that's what The Bank will do.

Think of a collateral mortgage as a mousetrap and the low rates use to attract you as the cheese. If you're considering a collateral mortgage, ask yourself:

1. Are you prepared to tie yourself to a single lender to the end of your amortization—25, 30, or 35 years?
2. If you want to switch down the road, are you prepared to pay hefty fees?
3. Do you trust your lender enough to believe you won't be screwed over come renewal time?

4. Do you intend to use your home as a constant source of credit, or do you actually want to get that puppy paid off?

Would I buy one of these suckers? Not on your life! Do I look like a mouse to you?

RULE #219: BUY INSURANCE WHEN
YOU DON'T NEED IT

If you think you don't need insurance because you're young, healthy, and have no dependents, you're operating under an old, short-sighted rule. Never planning to marry? Won't ever have assets to protect? No kids? You're sure?

I was dead sure I was never going to have kids. Two marriages in, I was still childless. So what made me get life insurance and disability insurance at 30? My mother. She nagged me and nagged me and nagged me until I did it. God bless her. I had kids at 34 and 37 and would have had to pay a pretty penny to get my insurance when I finally "needed" it.

The biggest mistake you can make when it comes to buying life and disability insurance is waiting until you need it. Not only may the price come as a big shock, but "insurability"—qualifying for the insurance—may also be a HUGE issue. The trick to buying life and disability insurance is buying it while you are young and healthy.

I'm not going to get into a discussion about permanent versus term insurance here. See Rule #13: Term Insurance Is Not Better Than Permanent, for that.

Here's a chart that shows the monthly premiums for a whole life policy worth $200,000 for a non-smoker, based on different ages.

	MONTHLY COST		PAID OVER LIFE OF POLICY	
	Male	Female	Male	Female
Age 25	$80	$70	$38,400	$33,600
Age 30	$100	$85	$42,000	$35,700
Age 35	$120	$100	$43,200	$36,000
Age 40	$160	$130	$48,000	$39,000

Buying the policy at age 25 means the premiums will cost you substantially less per month. It'll also cost you less over the long term. If you buy your insurance at 25 and pay $80 a month until you're 65, you'll spend $38,400 for your coverage. If you wait until you're 40, the coverage to age 65 will cost you $48,000.

You need to get your insurance early because you're likely to have far less wrong with you at age 25 than at age 45 or 50. Just go ask your mother about her aching bones! Waiting until you're older won't just mean a premium increase; it could also mean you're declined for insurance because of medical conditions that have arisen. A little high blood sugar here, a little high blood pressure there, some bad cholesterol, and BAM! You're declined or your premiums skyrocket.

Here are some numbers for disability insurance, which has even tougher qualifying criteria when it comes to being approved; if there's the least little thing wrong with you, you'll be turned down.

	Male	Female
Age 25	$57	$86
Age 30	$65	$104
Age 35	$80	$129
Age 40	$102	$152

Notice how life insurance premiums are higher for men and lower for women, and the exact opposite is true for disability insurance. That's because men die and women get sick. If you're a woman, you MUST buy your disability insurance as early as possible to get a reasonable rate and QUALIFY! Even a visit to a shrink to see you through a tough relationship issue is enough to disqualify you for disability insurance. Guys, buy your life insurance early and you'll win the premium game regardless of what kind of insurance you choose.

RULE #220: ADD UP WHAT YOU OWE

People like to play the "keeping it in different piles" game. When I ask a body how much it owes, it's likely to say something like "Oh, I have $7,000 on my line of credit and I owe about $2,000 on my VISA. Oh, yah, then there's the Sears card. I owe about $450 on that. Oh, and my student loans. Wow. I owe about $27,000 still on that. I took out $20,000 from my RRSP to buy a house, so I guess I owe that too. Do you count overdraft? Coz I'm about $400 into my overdraft."

Add it up.

If you've been keeping your debt in piles and haven't added it up, you're hiding behind those piles so you don't have to face the reality of what you owe. If you quote your debt in small chunks instead of adding it all up, you're in denial. If you look at only the minimum payment instead of what it would actually cost to pay off the debt, you're in denial.

It's much easier to think, "I only owe $2,000 on my VISA and $400 on my overdraft," than it is to say, "I owe a whopping $56,850!" That's a number big enough to make you wobbly in the knees.

Until you add it up, until you look your debt square in the eye, you can keep on deluding yourself by putting the word "only" before whatever small balance you're thinking about. Once you add everything up, "only" won't work—and you'll find the motivation to dig yourself out of debt.

RULE #221: DON'T BUY AND CHECK OUT

If you confused the "buy and hold" strategy with "buy and check out," this is your wake-up call. As an investor, you must keep your eye on what your investments are doing. Nothing brings this home more than the bait-and-switch of the mutual funds industry.

Mutual funds can change their management, merge and change investment objectives, or increase MERs at any time, leaving you feeling like your fund has mutated. If you're paying attention, here's what you would do next:

Find out about the new management. While a change in managers does not signal the demise of a fund, it can be pretty frustrating to buy into a fund manager's philosophy, plunk down your money, and watch as managers do a dance, switching portfolios, moving from one company to another. And if a good fund has swallowed an underperforming fund, know that post-merger, hot funds tend to cool off. If you were holding the crappy fund, you may have traded up.

Find out why the merger is happening. Sometimes it's because the fund you had was underperforming and the merger will create a strong fund. Sometimes fund companies do mergers just to hide the bad past performance of a fund they've been managing, since the merger makes the history disappear. In buying the fund, you would have analyzed its track record and its characteristics. (You did that, right? See Rule #200: Mutual Fund Averages Don't Mean Diddly.) If the management changes, you'll be looking at a different track record. Now you have to look at the performance history of the guys who are taking over, in deciding if this fund should remain in your portfolio.

Find out if the new fund fits with your asset allocation. Take a look at whether the new fund complements your current holdings in terms of your asset allocation. When mutual funds merge, they can create whole new funds you never expected to own. Let's say you bought a bond fund that invests in investment grade bonds—high-quality government bonds or bonds rated single A or higher. If it merges with another bond fund and the new mandate allows for lower credit quality, now the fund is aiming for higher returns, but it's also willing to take more risk. The question is, are you?

Find out if your fees are going up or down. Mergers could mean increases in a fund's management expense ratio (MER), leaving you out of pocket because your fund has metamorphosed. If your MER goes from 1% to 2.1% because the fund is now trading actively, you'll have to assess if you're happy with the return after fees or if the fund is just making money on the MERs without giving you anything more to sing and dance about.

If you're not happy with the merger, as an investor there's very little you can do about these changes except to get the hell out.

RULE #222: DON'T BORROW TO CONTRIBUTE TO AN RRSP

This replaces the old rule "Borrowing for an RRSP is smart!"

It's a trick. All those ads that tell you how smart you are to borrow to contribute to your retirement savings because of all the growth you'll get in the plan are designed to fool you into paying interest. Borrowing may make sense for a Tiny Tim small handful of folks. For the majority of people, borrowing is another case of instant gratification. Since you couldn't NOT spend the money you needed to save for the contribution to the RRSP, then the loan gets you the RRSP you should have planned for. The cost is the interest on the loan.

Okay, let's get who should borrow out of the way. You're smart to take out an RRSP loan if

- you are in a significantly higher tax bracket and need to do some tax planning, AND
- you can pay off the loan in one year or less, AND
- you can make your current year's RRSP contribution as well as pay off the loan.

You have to meet all three criteria. Two don't count.

As for those whopping catch-up loans—the ones for $30,000 to $50,000, offered so you can catch up on all the contributions you've missed making—run for the hills. If anyone tells you they're a good idea, they're straight out lying to you. I don't care what magic they do with the numbers to show you how you'll benefit. You're buying swampland. You'll be mired in debt and paying interest for ages. And your investments would have to perform miracles just for you to break even.

Oh, there's one more situation where you can use an RRSP loan: If you're trying to establish or re-establish your credit-worthiness, an RRSP loan is a great way to do it. But you're going to take out a small loan and you're going to pay it back in six months or less. In this case, the objective isn't to make money. The objective is to get back on track credit-wise. You should expect to pay for that!

RULE #223: OPEN AN RESP FOR YOUR KIDS

If one more person tells me that she had to pay her way through school, so she and her mate are leaving it up to their kids to do the same, I might get violent. Hey, if you don't have extra money to set aside for your kids, that's one thing. But if you have the wherewithal and you're not doing it because you don't think you need to, heads up.

Alex went to university in 2010. Tuition alone was $6,000, never mind books and lab fees, which added up to another $1,500. Residence was $6,300; a minimal food plan was another $2,000. We're up to $15,800.

Gone are the days when you could go to school and rack up $4,500 in student debt a year, and then graduate with under $20,000 owing. Now you're looking at spending pretty close to $18,000 a year, all in, if your kid lives away from home. Even though Alex shared a house with six other kids, her second-year costs were almost $18,000. If that were going on student loans, she'd be looking at $72,000 in debt for a four-year degree.

Do you want your kids to be buried in debt before they even get started?

When my children were born, I started socking away $100 a month for each of them for post-secondary education. As time went by and I made more money, I stuck away as much as I could to grab all the grant money the government was offering.

There is no maximum that you can put into an RESP each year, but there is a $50,000 lifetime limit. Every time you make a contribution, the federal government will give you some money in a savings-matching program called the Canada Education Savings Grant (CESG).

The basic CESG room is $400 per year from 1998 to 2006 and $500 from 2007 on. Let's say you made no RESP contributions for your Mini-Me who was born in 2005. The total CESG room your little mite would have accumulated would be $3,800 ($400 for the years 2005 to 2006, and $500 for 2007 to 2012). If you set up an RESP for your little beauty in 2013, and contributed $5,000, you could grab a grant of $1,000, which is the maximum grant you're entitled to in any one year. You read right: you'd put in five grand and the government would give you one grand . . . that's an automatic 20% return on your money, before it's even invested.

Since the maximum a child can receive in a calendar year is $1,000 (assuming grant room is available), don't be tempted to catch up too much at once. Each year you can catch up for roughly one year of missed contributions.

As for all the folks who aren't using an RESP because they don't have any money to save, did you know that the Canada Learning Bond provides $500 for low-income families to establish a RESP account and allows for an annual contribution of $100? Free money and yet the program only has about an 8% participation rate.

If you have a kid, open an RESP.

RULE #224: NEVER BUY A GROUP (OR SCHOLARSHIP TRUST) RESP

Risking the wrath of thousands of (commission-based) sales-people, I'm going to say it: Don't buy a group RESP.

Group RESPs—sometimes called "Scholarship Trusts"—have about 30% of the market despite being a crappy product, proving—once again—that if you build it, someone will buy. I've never been a fan of these options, and I've shouted far and wide. But don't take my word for it. A study prepared for the federal government on RESPs found that group RESPs have a number of drawbacks, including the fact that:

You must pay an enrolment fee and make contributions according to a preset schedule.

If you close a Scholarship Trust before maturity, you forfeit the enrolment fee plus any investment gains and government grant money. So if you can't keep up with the preset contribution schedule, you lose. And no, you can't simply transfer the plan. The government won't let you.

Some Scholarship Trust plans deny payments to students who are entitled to those benefits under government rules, because some Scholarship Trusts don't recognize all courses of study. If your child chooses something outside the plan's parameters, he or she won't be able to use the money in the plan. If the group scholarship plan is cancelled for any reason, you get your contributions back, net of fees and without the investment income. The grant money is also repaid to the

SAVING

government and cannot be earned back later if new contributions are made for the same beneficiary.

Scholarship Trusts have high fees. The report notes that in 2006, 20% of gross contributions went towards fees.

What if you're already in one of these plans? Only you can decide how far in you are and whether it's worth it to take your money back and start again with an individual or family plan. Find out what the limitations are on your plan (they are all different) and then make a black-and-white decision about whether to stick with the plan or cut your losses.

RULE #225: CONSIDER A MARRIAGE CONTRACT

If you're marrying someone who has significantly fewer assets than you do, if you've been the beneficiary of a divorce or insurance settlement or inherited money, or if you have children from a previous relationship, you might want to consider a marriage contract or cohabitation agreement the second (third, fourth, or fifth) time around.

While no one ever gets married with the intention of getting a divorce, each year thousands of couples call it quits. Most people would prefer an amicable separation, but anger and disappointment being what they are you might be disappointed. And while less than 4% of divorces are finalized by a contested hearing, the squabbling and messy confrontations of an out-of-court settlement are no less messy.

Want a way to clarify how the money would be divvied up before all the hissing and spitting starts? Negotiate and sign a marriage contract or cohabitation agreement and it'll be perfectly clear how your stuff will be divided if you and your partner go your separate ways. (While these are sometimes referred to as "pre-nuptial agreements," this isn't the terminology used in Canadian legislation.)

A marriage contract is a contract between two people who are going to be married or who are married. It organizes financial affairs in a way that is different from how they would be organized if spouses were to separate under current family law, which differs from province to province.

A cohabitation agreement is an agreement that is entered into by two individuals who are living together but not married. Since cohabiting couples have fewer rights legally (see Rule #147: Living Together Is NOT the Same as Married), when negotiating a cohabitation agreement the range of options is narrowed. A cohab agreement is used to set down support obligations with less focus on the division of property, unless the individuals plan to marry at some point in the future.

The number one reason people sign on the dotted line is to protect their assets. Custody or access issues are beyond the purview of cohabitation agreements or marriage contracts. Contracts also can't stipulate that if your relationship breaks down, you can boot your ex out of the matrimonial home. With a matrimonial home—defined as "property ordinarily occupied as a family residence at the time of separation"—married partners have special rights of possession. However, as far as all other assets go, you can set down how they will be divided in the event of a split.

Knowing what's what upfront can be particularly important if one of the parties is receiving spousal support. Let's face it, if you're receiving a very comfortable level of spousal support from partner number one, and you're contemplating hitching up with partner number two, you're taking a big risk financially. Should the new relationship not work out, you will have given up the income stream from your first ex—an income stream that might not be replaced by your second ex.

The biggest signal for a cohab agreement or marriage contract is usually if one partner has significantly more than the other, or if there are children on one side and not on the other. Then the partner with the mostest may want to protect assets accumulated prior to the relationship. Or Mommy or Daddy Dearest may want to ensure assets meant for their children go where they were intended.

Some people think the very idea of talking about a marriage contract or a cohab agreement is yucky. Aren't you supposed to trust the person you're hooking up with? I mean to say, if you're good enough to snuggle up with at night, aren't you good enough to trust?

Those are the same people who refuse to face the reality that they may get sick or die. All a marriage contract or cohabitation agreement means is that everybody knows from the get-go what's happening. Gone are the secrets. Instead, both partners enter the union knowing exactly where the chips will fall if they do.

When you buy insurance, you don't expect your house to burn down, do you? But you buy insurance anyway, right?

RULE #226: YOU WON'T GET RICH ON MATERNITY LEAVE

Maternity benefits suck. They're better than nothing, but if you don't make some significant changes to your spending while you're off with your wee one, you could end up in hot water.

You might be surprised at how little you'll get on maternity leave compared to what you're used to making. Hello. Maternity benefits are a social program. They aren't intended to keep you in the lap of luxury. And if you're making more than $500 a week from your job, you're going to have to learn to live on less.

There are rules to qualify for maternity leave benefits, and you can find out if you qualify by submitting an application for EI online, or going into a Service Canada Centre. Even though you won't be able to apply for benefits until you're actually on maternity leave, you should know the rules and make sure you meet the requirements.

There's a two-week unpaid waiting period before you start collecting, so have some money in the bank to bridge the cash flow gap. And know that it can take six weeks or longer before your first cheque arrives . . . yup, you need some money in the bank to cover your costs while you're waiting.

The basic benefit rate is 55% of your "average insured earnings"—a technical term for how much money you've earned—to a maximum of $468 per week before taxes. (This is at the time of writing. To check the most current numbers, go to www.servicecanada.gc.ca.)

Maternity leave income is taxable. If you're having your baby late in the year and earned a healthy chunk prior to maternity leave, you might be hit with a tax bill at the end of the year. Don't assume the system takes enough tax off your maternity benefits. Figure out what you should be paying based on your marginal tax rate and request the appropriate amount be deducted from your benefits. (See Rule #24: Calculate Your Taxes to Avoid a Tax Bill.)

If you think that you'll just get a part-time job to supplement your maternity leave income, think again. Earnings are deducted dollar for dollar from your benefits. If you are on parental leave, you can earn up to $50 a week, or 25% of your weekly benefits (whichever is higher). Above that and your benefits will be cut back dollar for dollar.

When you're doing up your mat leave budget (you ARE making a maternity leave budget, aren't you?) check with your benefits administrator at work or call Service Canada and clarify all the details so you know exactly where you stand. The last thing you want is to be dealing with the stress of not having enough money while trying to care for a new baby. The second to last thing you want is a tax bill at the end of the year.

RULE #227: SET A PET MEDICAL SPENDING LIMIT

Animal people will move heaven and earth for their precious poochikins. Nothing is too good for their sweet kittiboo. I'm a pet person without a pet, and I miss it like all get-out. But the timing isn't right and my current circumstances won't let me make the commitment to a puppy just yet.

In my last life I had a dog, multiple kitties, two horses, a pony, and a llama. I know what it costs to feed critters and keep 'em healthy. But I'm a pragmatist; I also had limits so that I didn't end up in the poor house.

Set a limit in terms of what you'll spend for medical intervention each year. Pet insurance can help defray the costs, with premiums ranging from as low as $15 to over $100, depending on the animal and the level of coverage you choose. You can be strategic about how you use pet insurance. Get it early in kittiboo's life so the premiums are less expensive. Start with emergency and accident care, which is generally inexpensive and covers most dogs and cats (no, you can't insure your snake or tarantula, since exotics aren't covered). Choose to use a deductible—an amount you're prepared to pay out of your own pocket each time you claim—to reduce monthly costs.

Not all animals and all ailments will be covered. Since German shepherds often develop hip dysplasia, and kidney disease is common in Persian cats, some companies won't insure breeds with hereditary diseases like heart defects, eye cataracts, or diabetes. Some companies have age limits for coverage. Some cover routine checkups and vaccinations, but this kind of "comprehensive coverage" is usually the most expensive. Since insurance may deny your coverage if you don't take your pet for routine checkups, make sure you read the fine print!

Avoid non-lifetime policies, which cover conditions suffered during the policy period, but then on renewal deny coverage for that condition going forward. And know the limits of your coverage. While a pet may be covered for an ongoing condition, there may be a "per condition" or "per year" limit on how much you can claim. Also make sure you know your "wait period"—how long the policy must be in place before you can make a claim.

As your pet ages, more will go wrong and the cost of all the medical interventions available could set you back a couple of mortgage payments. Know when it's time to put your pet down. Going into debt for a pet isn't going to make your life easier down the road. It's more likely to negate all the emotional and stress-relief benefits you're supposed to derive from pet ownership.

RULE #228: KNOW WHAT BEING AN EXECUTOR ENTAILS

When your sister asked if she could name you as executor of her will, you responded, "Sure," without any thought to what the role might entail. You should have thought about it a little longer!

As executor (sometimes called "estate trustee"), you'll be called upon to manage everything from the funeral arrangements to locating assets, paying bills and taxes, and divvying up the remains to the heirs. This job carries important responsibilities and demands attention to detail. If there are squabbles about who should get what, the whole thing can get pretty nasty. So it's nice to know that just because you've been named executor doesn't mean you have to take the job. If you don't feel you're up to the task, just say no.

If you decide to accept, you'll need to present the original will and swear an "affidavit of service," which you'll file with the court. About six to eight weeks later, you'll receive a certificate that gives you the authority to act, so that anyone who needs proof—the bank, the brokerage house, the credit card company—knows you're "legal." Your next job will be to notify all the beneficiaries under the will.

Part of your role as executor will involve taking an inventory of the deceased's assets and debts. You will be responsible for safeguarding and valuing the assets, dealing with banks, brokers, and insurance companies, and arranging for the investment or liquidation of assets. You can seek help from experts in managing the estate's assets, but you can never give up your discretionary responsibility for how those assets are handled. So if you do a terrible job and the estate suffers losses as a result, you can be held liable for those losses.

Don't rush to pay out bequests too soon, no matter how much pressure heirs are putting on you. If you do and then don't have enough left to pay debts and taxes due on the estate, the money will come out of your own pocket unless you can persuade beneficiaries to give back some money. (Fat chance!)

You'll have to file tax returns for any years for which returns have not been filed, both in Canada and wherever else the deceased may have held assets. You'll also have to file a return for each year the estate exists and earns income. Get a clearance certificate from the Tax Man to ensure he agrees with things such as property valuations and deductions claimed before you distribute the entire estate.

Make sure, as well, that you've done due diligence to uncover all the debts owning. If your sister was sloppy in her bookkeeping, or things got out of hand and bills have been lost, unpaid debts can come back to haunt you personally. Advertisements to creditors that include a fixed date for distribution a month or two from the advertisement date, followed by payment of all debts that have come to light, are usually enough to cover an executor's liability to creditors.

For your time and trouble, you are entitled to receive a fee from the estate (though you don't have to take it if you don't want to). Keep careful records of the time you spend and expenses you pay out of your own pocket, so that if you're challenged on the amount of your compensation, you can pony up your records.

If the going looks tough, you don't have to do it alone. You can hire a professional to step in and be your guide. A lawyer, estate administrator (available through your local trust company—most banks have a trust division), and accountant can help. While the estate pays these blokes, it'll be your responsibility to make sure their fees are reasonable.

Being an executor is a big responsibility that can eat hours and days and weeks of your life. If you're thinking of taking on the job, make sure you're prepared for what's involved. If you think you can't go it alone, ask for—and be ready to pay for—help.

If you're thinking of naming someone you love as executor of your estate, do this person a favour and keep everything in tip-top shape so no one ends up having to untangle a mess.

RULE #229: ASK YOURSELF, WOULD YOU PICK IT UP?

People can be very dismissive about what they consider "small change." I tell people to move their savings accounts from a stupid account paying 0.5% interest to one paying 2% interest. They do a quick calculation in their heads and say something like "On my $10,000 emergency fund that works out to just $150 a year." Hanging on the end of the statement is "It just isn't worth the aggravation."

So along comes my friend Victoria, who always has a quip that brings home the point. Her question would then be "So would you bend down and pick it up?"

People look at her oddly when she asks this question. She usually has to repeat herself. "So would you pick up the $150 if it was on the ground?" Everyone says, "Yes." And says it as if it's a no-brainer.

So now I'm asking you: If it was right there to be picked up, would you step over it? If it takes a little effort to achieve the same end, tell me you're not going to turn a blind eye to the free money!

RULE #230: KNOW THE LIMITATIONS ON RESP WITHDRAWALS

If this is your child's first year at university, you may be trying to figure out how to tap all that money you saved in an RESP. When Alex went off for her first year, I was surprised to learn that only $5,000 of non-contribution money could be withdrawn in the first 13 weeks a kid is in school.

"Non-contribution money" is the income earned (in the form of interest, dividends, and/or capital gains) and the CESG payments you received from the government. There is no withdrawal limit on contributed money. You'll need to provide proof of enrolment at a qualified school to get money out the first time. After that, you can take whatever you want to pay for books, rent, tuition, and the like.

Only the original contributions to the RESP can be withdrawn tax-free. Both income earned and grant money are taxed in your child's hands. Since you can direct your financial institution to withdraw contributions or earnings, withdraw as much of the earnings and grant money as you can as soon as you can, leaving the contributions in the plan the longest should your kid drop out, in which case you can take the money you contributed back but without tax consequences.

Since the life of an RESP is 36 years, unused RESP money can be transferred to younger siblings who have plenty of time to use the money. No sibs? Then you'll have to collapse the account. There will be a penalty on the non-contribution money if you don't transfer that money to an RRSP.

Keep in mind that no beneficiary is allowed to receive more than $7,200 in grant money during his or her lifetime, so watch those family accounts carefully. If you miscalculate, the government will take the extra grant money back.

RULE #231: UNDERSTAND HOW YOUR PENSION PLAN WORKS

While you might think that loads of people have company pension plans, the majority of us have to fend for ourselves even as we bemoan the fact. And yet, many of you who are enrolled (or eligible to enrol) don't understand how your plans work. Do you even know what kind of pension plan your company offers?

Pension plans fall into one of three basic categories:

1. defined benefit (DB) plans,
2. defined contribution (DC) plans, and
3. group RRSPs.

DB plans promise to pay out a regular income calculated according to a predetermined formula. You know exactly how much you'll receive at retirement, but until then the rest—what your plan is worth at any point in time, how much return your savings are earning—will be a bit of a mystery.

DC plans define the annual contributions required by the employer (and in many cases by the employee). The size of the pension depends on the amount of money accumulated through contributions and earnings in the plan.

Group RRSPs function a lot like regular RRSPs, except that your employer runs the plan and you make contributions by payroll deduction. Some employers match contributions, but that's not a given. If contributions are made by the employer,

SAVING

those contributions are taxable as income to you, and your total contributions can't exceed the annual maximum RRSP contribution limit.

If you belong (or could belong) to a company pension plan, figure out how the plan works. Here are seven questions you'll want to ask for sure:

1. **Will your company contribute to the plan?** With a DB and a DC, it's a given. Not so with a group RRSP. If your employer is willing to match your contribution and you're not participating in the plan, you're walking away from good money. What's wrong with you?

2. **How much are you required to contribute to the plan?** This is usually done by payroll deduction and you need to know how much less disposable income you'll have after the deduction. Keep in mind that this goes towards the "saving" component of your budget.

3. **What are the costs associated with the plan?** You should know what you're paying in fees and commissions. While you're at it, make sure you find out if some investment options come with higher costs, so you can take that into account when choosing how to invest your pension money, if you have that option. (You won't with a DB plan.)

4. **When are you eligible to keep the assets in the plan?** Pension plan money doesn't become yours until it

"vests." That usually means you have to be employed for a certain amount of time, or participating in the plan for a certain amount of time (or both). If you change jobs before the plan vests, you'll walk away from the employer's share of the money in the plan.

5. **Will your plan continue to pay your spouse an income after you die?** Some company pensions end with the death of the pensioner. Others pay a reduced percentage to the surviving spouse. If there is no continuation of income, or if that income will be reduced significantly, both of you will have to make some decisions about how you structure your other sources of retirement income.

6. **Is your pension indexed?** Inflation can eat away at your pension benefits. Check to see if your pension provides for full or partial indexing, and find out when that indexing kicks in.

7. **Is your pension integrated?** In other words, will your pension benefits be blended with CPP to provide your income? If your company pension plan is integrated, whenever you get pension income estimates from your employer don't double-count your CPP benefits.

If you can't answer all these questions about your pension plan, get thee to the pension administrator and learn the answers.

RULE #232: DON'T BUY NOW AND PAY LATER

I know the lure of new furniture is sweet and the ease of the Buy Now Pay Later (BNPL) plan is easy. Who doesn't want a new TV, new couch, new bed for nothing down and nothing for months to come. It's like Christmas!

The BNPL plan has become a common way to get what you want without having to figure out what else you have to give up. Take it home today and pay for it next week, next month, next year. Take two years to pay. Hey, you know what they say about too good to be true?

The best-intentioned people are like flies to a Venus flytrap. In they buzz, attracted by the sweet deal, and SNAP, they're trapped. They start off planning to pay the BNPL in full before the due date, but somewhere along the line the train jumps the tracks and they end up in a debt wreck. I've got a million stories. Here are a couple.

Suzie and Alan were determined to use a BNPL to their advantage. "Why wouldn't you keep your money in the bank if they're willing to let you take home the TV and furniture free?" Alan asked gleefully. So they put their money in a high-interest savings account earning 1.5%, with the intention of paying off the TV and living room furniture two months before the due date and pocketing the $67.50 in interest they'd earn. But then a funny thing happened. Since they had lots of money in the bank, Susie got a distorted view of their financial reality. Seeing that money sitting there made her feel richer than she actually was. Despite the fact that the money had already been "spent," it acted as a barrier to them saving more.

"You know, I couldn't believe how easy it was to spend money we should have been putting in our emergency fund because we kept saying, 'Well, if worse comes to worst, we'll just use that money we've set aside for the furniture.'"

Barbara-Ann planned to make the monthly payments that would get her BNPL paid off by the due date. She took her total amount of $2,150 and divided by the 11 months she had to make the payments interest-free, to come up with $195 a month; that was an easy amount to work into her budget. Barbara-Ann wasn't prepared when, out of the blue, the transmission on her car went and she had to defer a couple of interest-free payments to cover the cost of the car repairs. She promised herself that she'd catch up, but she never did. When the BNPL deadline arrived, there was no money to pay off the balance, and the rapacious interest rate kicked in retroactive to the date she took home the new fridge, stove, and dishwasher. She'd spent $3,600 on new appliances, but now she owed an additional $1,155 in interest, increasing her appliance cost by 32%. Wow!

BNPLs also snap shut with a wicked bite if you're even slightly off on your calculations. This is one reason I suggest that if people are going to use this to their advantage, they cut back their "repayment period" by a couple of months. So if you're entering into a 12-month BNPL, you actually base your repayment schedule on 10 months to make sure you're clear of the due date well in advance.

People are always messing up, making a payment late or not

having the entire balance paid in full by the due date, and their mistakes are usually very costly. That "No Interest" jumps to a whopping 36% overnight, making moot the 1% they've been earning by keeping their money in the bank.

The biggest problem with BNPL is the ease with which people can take home stuff they have yet to pay for, making it feel like they got a special deal, and leaving them with the euphoria of purchase without the pain of payment as an offset. BNPLs encourage people to spend more than they would if they were shopping with cash. Physiologically, we need the pain/pleasure balance to help us prioritize. Removing one side of the equation lets us delude ourselves.

If you don't have the money to pay for something, you don't have the right to take that something home. If you have the money, pay for it and be done with the transaction. Trying to "work the system" is breaking Rule #192: Don't Be Too Smart for Your Own Good.

RULE #233: NAME A GUARDIAN FOR YOUR CHILDREN

One of the biggest decisions you must make when children start arriving is who will care for them if you can't. Not knowing whom to name was a major deterrent to my husband and me making wills after our daughter, Alexandra, was born. We weighed the pros and cons of everyone in our lives and no one was healthy enough, old enough, young enough, strong enough, gentle enough. Sadly, we realized that if we didn't make a choice, we'd be casting Alex to the fates. So we picked someone. And we made a good choice because we made a choice.

Guardianship issues are particularly significant for single parents or sole custody parents who must contemplate child-rearing arrangements in the event of their own demise. The idea of leaving a child behind is traumatic. Most people refuse even to think about it. But if you don't and the worst does happen, the implications for your little one may be dreadful. If you haven't already done so, it's time to bite the bullet and start thinking about who you would want to raise your children if something happened to you.

Whom you choose as guardian will depend on what's important to you. Perhaps you want a person with the same religious beliefs. Maybe you want to maintain your child's continuity of lifestyle. In my case, I wanted someone who was pretty similar in terms of child-rearing values. I watched my cousin raise her two girls with a firm hand and loads and loads of love, and thought how perfect that would be for my daughter.

Thinking about naming your parents? Make sure they will be well enough to take on the job, even through the trying adolescence years. If you decide to choose a friend rather than a family member, discuss it with your family first. The appointment of a "custodian"—the legalese for a "guardian"—is not binding. A court can overrule your wishes if it feels your choice is not in the best interest of the child. Get your family onside so your kids don't end up in the middle of a custody battle.

Put some thought into the financial provisions necessary to ensure your children will be raised and educated without being a burden to their guardian. Integrating new children into their household will be difficult enough without the additional financial burden of having to upgrade a home, feed extra mouths, and educate extra minds. Insurance is a good way to build your child a safety net. If you've been actively working towards a secure retirement using an RRSP, you can designate your dependent children as beneficiaries.

Will you ask your child's guardian to also be the person who manages their inheritance? Consider appointing a more financially experienced someone to co-manage your children's money and provide a regular flow of funds to meet their needs.

Before you officially name your guardian, say please. And be prepared for that person declining if the prospect of managing your crazy brood is simply too overwhelming. When you find someone willing to step into the breach, have a talk about the values you would like to see in place, the financial provisions you have made, along with all the little details.

Hopefully, you will be able to choose someone who has an ongoing relationship with your kids. Regardless, make sure you check back periodically to ensure that your children's guardian still feels up to the job. Life changes and so can minds. Don't assume the status quo simply because you're unwilling to go through the guardianship appointment process again. Part of parenthood involves dealing with all the smelly, squishy, yucky issues. This is just one more of them. Hold your nose and jump in.

RULE #234: FIND THE BUDGET SYSTEM
THAT WORKS FOR *YOU*!

I receive hundreds of letters every month from people who say that the standard monthly budget won't work for them because, because, because. Hey, a budget is a tool. You have to make it work for you.

Whether you buy yourself an app so you can track your spending on your smart phone, or you get yourself a notebook and write down what you're spending, you need a system that you can live with, work with, learn from. High-tech or low-tech, it's got to be about what works for you.

I like a notebook and pen. I collect my receipts throughout the day and make notes in my spending journal at the end of the day (or couple of days, if I'm travelling). Then, once a month, I manually transfer the whole thing to my budget spreadsheet.

Oh. My. God! You have got to be kidding, Gail!

Some people imagine that such a repetitious task is arduous and the duplication of re-entering information onto a spreadsheet is a waste of time. Not me. The first time I record my spending in my spending journal, it is so I have a record of where the money went and how much I have left to spend. The second time I record the transaction on my budget spreadsheet, it is to see how much I ended up spending in the month. Do I spend less on groceries if I go once a week (four entries a month) or many times because I need fresh ingredients (I've had up to 12 grocery trips in a month)? I know because I watch the patterns in my spending and adjust accordingly.

If you're living on a tight budget, you might skip the spending journal completely and enter your daily transaction directly into your budget spreadsheet to see how much you've got left in each category and where you might have to steal from to make it through the month. Hey, if you blow a tire and your emergency fund doesn't have enough to cover it, some creative reassignment—moving money from clothing or entertainment—may be what it takes to stay in the black.

As for all the wonderful websites and applications available to help you track your money, do what works for YOU. (See Rule #71: Be Careful When Giving Out Your Info.)

RULE #235: CALCULATE THE PER USE COST TO DETERMINE VALUE

This replaces the rule "Always pay more for higher quality."

Sometimes spending a lot of money on something you will only use once or twice makes no sense at all. Instead, use the "how much per use" calculation to determine whether you'll go cheap or drop a bundle.

If you're buying a pair of shoes that you'll wear all the time—you'll get 365 or 730 uses out of the pair—you should be prepared to pay a little more so a) the shoes last and b) they're comfortable. But if you're dropping $800 on a pair of uncomfortable high heels that you'll end up wearing four or five times, you're looking at a $160 to $200 a wear cost. Dumb!

It isn't really about how much you pay but more about how much you pay by use. So if you're going to use something a lot, and you want it to last, hunt around for the best price on something that's of higher quality. If it's a "once and done" use (or there'bouts), cheap should do fine.

While the adage "You get what you pay for" is hauled out a lot to justify spending more, sometimes it's just an adage. I'd no sooner pay $500 for a handbag with a name on it than punch myself in the face. I'd have to use the same handbag day in and day out for about 1,000 days—almost three years—to see that as a good deal.

No matter how hard you try to convince yourself that the quality is better, if you do the per use calculation, you'll be dealing in black and white on the value, not just justifying your purchase.

SMART SHOPPING

RULE #236: WATCH YOUR VARIABLE MORTGAGE LIKE A HAWK

Variable mortgages hold lots of appeal. They're usually offered at an interest rate that's lower than a fixed rate mortgage. And they're sold on the basis that if rates go down, you'll benefit since more of your mortgage payment will go to pay the principal.

Hey, who wouldn't rather pay 2.3% than 5.7%? That's a no-brainer. And if rates are coming down and you aren't locked into a higher rate, you'd feel pretty smart, right?

What if rates are rising?

While you will be told this when you take out your variable rate mortgage, you likely won't hear it amid the excitement of everything that's going on, so pay attention now:

If interest rates go up, your payment will not change, but more of your payment will go to pay the interest. If your payment is less than the interest, the interest will be capitalized—added to your mortgage—and that likely means your amortization will increase because you will owe more money.

Okay, let's go through that step-by-step.

If interest rates go up, your payment will not change. It would be great if, in our efficient virtual world, your banker would send you a form asking you to decide whether to

a) pay more to cover the increased interest,
b) keep the payment the same and capitalize the extra interest, or
c) lock into a fixed rate mortgage now.

If you got this kind of notification obliging you to take action each time there was an increase, you'd have to think about what you were doing with your mortgage. Most people just ignore their rate increases. Hey, the bank didn't say it was a problem, so it's not a problem, right? And your house is going to increase in value anyway; you'll make it all up later. Ha!

More of your payment will go to pay the interest. That could mean that you're paying little or nothing against the principal. Or it could mean . . .

If your payment is less than the interest, the interest will be capitalized. Instead of paying down your mortgage, each payment will make your mortgage bigger because the amount not covered by the payment gets added to your mortgage. Yes, they do that.

Your amortization will increase because you will owe more money. So you get to what you think is your mortgage burning party after 25 years of payments, only to find that you still owe money. Instead of that variable rate mortgage saving you interest, it cost you big-time. Or worse, you sell your house and then discover that what you sold it for doesn't cover the cost of the mortgage because the mortgage has been growing. Yes, that actually happens.

If you decide to go with a variable rate mortgage, you've got to watch that beast like a hawk. Take your eye off your mortgage for a couple of interest rate hikes and you could find yourself upside down on it, owing more than your home is worth.

Remember, as well, that as the rate increases on your variable rate mortgage, so, too, will the fixed rate mortgage increase. All that blah-blah-blah about how easy it is to lock in later never mentions that if you do choose to lock in down the road, the five-year rate may be considerably higher.

I don't hate variable mortgages. I've had one. But it scares the crap out of me when I hear so many horror stories from people who are not prepared for interest rate increases and the impact on their mortgage payments.

If rates are in decline, by all means check out a variable rate mortgage. Keep your eyes open every step of the way. If rates are rising, that is NOT the time to go variable.

RULE #237: DON'T CONSOLIDATE TO YOUR MORTGAGE UNLESS YOU'RE SERIOUSLY SERIOUS ABOUT GETTING YOUR DEBT PAID OFF

Some people use the consolidation of debt onto their mortgages as a way of reducing their interest costs and paying off the debt faster. This is a smart move. Some people do it to give their cash flow some breathing room so they can get rid of their debt and have a life too. Not my fav, but as long as the consolidated consumer debt portion is paid off in three years or less in addition to the payments you would have made normally on your mortgage, I'll buy it. And some do it simply to fool themselves into thinking they have room to go shopping on their cleaned-up credit cards. Heaven preserve me from idiots!

If you're serious about getting your debt paid off, consolidate and make a commitment to carry no consumer debt ever again. Yes, you can use a credit card, but you cannot carry a balance. If you can't afford something, you don't buy it. If you don't have cash in the bank to pay for it, you don't buy it.

Consolidating doesn't mean you get to sit back and sigh with relief. You didn't just dodge a bullet. As long as that debt is stacked in your mortgage, you're paying mega interest. Not only must you stop racking up debt, but you must also make the principal payments you would have made to the debt to the mortgage so you aren't walking around with that debt strapped to your house for the next 20 years.

To calculate the extra repayment amount, take your consolidated consumer debt and divide it by 36. So if you have $47,000 in consumer debt that you've just consolidated to your mortgage, your calculation would look like this:

$47,000 ÷ 36 = $1,305

You would have to be putting an extra $1,305 against your mortgage every month to make this debt consolidation work smartly. You could do it by increasing your monthly payments, or by auto-debiting the $1,305 every month to a high-interest account and then using it to make your annual prepayment. If you can't manage the $1,305 a month, what are you going to do to deal with the debt, as opposed to just hiding it from yourself?

If all you accomplish by consolidating your consumer debt to your mortgage is to hide the debt, you're an idiot—and it's only a matter of time before you run out of equity.

RULE #238: STOP THINKING OF AN RRSP AS AN INVESTMENT

It's not your fault that you've got the wrong idea about what an RRSP is and you think it's an investment. This is totally the fault of all the advertisements you've been bombarded with for years that have encouraged you to "invest" in an RRSP before the deadline. You can't invest in an RRSP. It's a plan registration number, not an investment vehicle.

Putting an RRSP number on the paperwork signals the Tax Man to treat the money in a special way.

Imagine that you have a ball, a box, and an umbrella. The ball is your money. The box is the investment you're putting your money in. It could be a savings account. It could be a GIC. It could be a mutual fund, or individual stock or bond. Okay, you've put the ball in the box. Now slide the box under the umbrella. There ya go. You've just put the money into an RRSP.

Many people contribute to an RRSP before they decide how they'll invest their money. So they put the ball under the umbrella first to get it into the plan before the deadline. Later they choose the box that best fits their ball. What's important to remember is that until you choose a box, you haven't "invested" your money. While the money is under the umbrella, it's registered and safe from the Tax Man, but until you put that ball in a box, it's just sitting there earning sweet-diddly-squat. You've saved it. You still have to invest it to put those savings to work.

RULE #239: WATCH YOUR FOOD COSTS

One of the questions I'm asked most often is "How much should my family be spending on food?" I get this question three or four times every week.

How would I know? How big is your family? Where do you live? (Yes, location affects costs.) Do you have any special dietary requirements? All these things will affect what you're spending on food. But the most important thing is to be smart about your shopping.

The average Canadian family spends about $9,630 a year on food, which works out to be about $185 a week. Hey, that's a huge piece of your budget pie. You better be smart about how you're using that money.

That $185 a week . . . that's just food. It doesn't include personal care items like shampoo and deodorant; household cleaning items like laundry detergent and dishwasher soap; tobacco, alcohol, magazines, or lottery tickets—the multitude of things we often add to our carts as we stroll up and down the aisles, all the while driving up our shopping bill.

If you don't want your food costs to drive you into the poor house, shop with a list. Only buy what you've planned to use. And meal-plan before you head to the store.

Know what stuff costs, so that when you see a deal, you can buy in bulk. When salmon hits pennies a tin, or coffee goes on sale, or toilet paper is a bargain, stock up. If it's not going to spoil, buy on sale and save. (This is a good reason to build an extra $10 to $20 into your weekly shopping budget.)

SMART SHOPPING

Watch the per unit cost. Companies use different sizes and formats for their products, so it's easy to become confused about which is the better deal. And the most recent trend in dealing with rising food costs is for manufacturers to reduce the amount in the packaging while selling for the same prices. If you don't calculate the per unit cost, it's virtually impossible to tell what is a deal and what isn't. Just because the package is bigger doesn't mean the per-unit cost is lower.

If you set out to buy something advertised as "on special" and it's not in stock, make sure you get a rain check so you extend the sale and get what you wanted at the best possible price.

And shop where prices are lowest. So obvious. And yet, not always the way we go. Do you do your shopping at local markets or in ethnic stores? Would you be interested in saving up to 30% just by switching your supermarket? The place might not be pretty, but it would mean $45 in savings on a $150 food bill. Over a year, that'd be over $2,300. That sounds worthwhile, doesn't it?

RULE #240: EMBRACE SIMPLE PLEASURES

Have you ever noticed how much you enjoy your first glass of wine and how indifferent you are to your fourth? Or how great those first three or four chips taste, and then how irrelevant the last 30 are? Our lives have become so abundant that we often forget how to enjoy small pleasures. We exchange quantity for quality. And sometimes we totally miss out on great experiences just because we think they'd take big bucks.

You can drop a few hundred dollars at a spa, but a bubble bath, some candles, and a great-smelling body cream can leave you just as relaxed. A little lavender oil on your pillow, a wonderful cup of tea, a great book—those are all things that cost little or nothing and increase your pleasure enormously.

It may take a little planning to create small pleasures. Have a mani/pedi party, and while you sip a glass of wine, paint your BFF's nails. Sharing time, laughing together, and enjoying an evening of co-pampering won't cost a bundle but will put a smile on your face.

Get four or five friends together and have each bring a sublimely delicious "tasting" to your Epicurean Evening. They can be savory or sweet, whatever turns your crank. Turn off the lights and feed one another an offering at a time. The darkness will intensify the experience. Scared of the dark? Use tea lights. Revel in the smells and tastes. Draw out the experience.

Sometimes all it takes to make something simple special is a commitment to go slowly, a little creativity, and the willingness to experiment. Set your imagination free.

SMART SHOPPING

RULE #241: EVEN COMPANY PENSION PLANS HAVE RISKS

This replaces the rule "Your company pension plan is a sure thing."

Many people are under the impression that if you belong to a company pension plan, you've got a golden parachute. If your pension plan is well managed, you could have a sound plan. But there are no guarantees.

Hundreds of defined benefit pension plans (including one belonging to a bank) are underfunded in Canada: Read "not enough money to make good on the promises made." If you belong to one of these, wouldn't you want to know? It's got to be worth the time it takes to send a 30-second email to your benefits administrator to see if your pension is in the black. Group RRSPs and defined contribution plans can't be "underfunded." The proviso here is that there will only be as much pension as there have been contributions and return. In other words, if you put in a pittance, you'll get out a pittance.

Market gyrations can also have a huge impact on your pension plan. Pension administrators have to put the money somewhere to earn a return, and if the markets go into the dumper just when you're starting to pull your pension, you might find yourself with less money than you thought.

You've got to know your pension plan. And you've got to keep your eye on how your money in that plan is being invested. You may not be able to control where the administrators put your money, but you can decide how much you're going to rely on that money. If you think things look a little shaky, set some extra aside using an RRSP, TFSA, or an unregistered investment portfolio.

A company pension plan does not mean you can "set it and forget it." It just means you're catching a break and don't have to do it all on your own. Pay attention to what's going on with your plan so there are no surprises down the road.

RULE #242: IF CRAP HAPPENS, RENEGOTIATE YOUR STUDENT LOAN TERMS

One of the benefits of staying in the student-loan system as opposed to getting a consolidation loan at a lower interest rate is that there are several provisions available to help if you are struggling. That's why I only recommend consolidation once you've got some job stability. While most of the following aren't cures for student loan ailments, they do provide a salve.

If you're struggling to make the monthly payments, you can apply for a "Revision of Terms" to request that the amount of time it will take you to pay off your loan be extended. That will lower your monthly payments, but you'll pay more in interest. A $40,000 loan fixed for 5 years will cost you more than $10,000 in interest. Over the repayment default of 9.5 years, the payment will more than double to $21,000 in interest. So extend your term for only as long as it takes to get back on your feet.

Unemployed or stuck in a low-paying job after graduation? Apply for "Interest Relief." If you get it, you won't have to make any payments on your loan. If you do make a payment, will be applied directly to your principal. There are limits on how often you can do this.

Out of school for five years or more? Used up all your Interest Relief? Still struggling? Apply for "Debt Reduction." If you are approved, the amount of money you owe will be reduced, up to a specified maximum.

If you've been hit with a disability that is making it impossible for you to pay off your loans, apply for the "Permanent

Disability Benefit." If approved, your loan will be wiped out completely.

If you've got a whopping amount of student debt and you've been out of school for seven years or more, get thee to a bankruptcy trustee. Since you've been out of school for seven years, your student debt can now be discharged. It isn't automatic, but it is worth investigating. (See Rule #216: Student Loans Can Be Discharged After Seven Years.)

RULE #243: CO-SIGNED DEBT
IS 100% YOUR DEBT

If the primary borrower drops dead or defaults on the loan, you are 100% responsible for repaying any loans you have co-signed. It doesn't matter that you didn't get the money. It doesn't matter that the primary borrower swore you were off the hook. The reason you're co-signing is to guarantee repayment, and if the lender can't get blood from one stone, it'll come looking for your stones.

Co-signed debt is also factored into calculations that determine whether you'll get approved for any kind of borrowing, including a mortgage. Since you're on the hook for that $27,000 loan for which you co-signed, that's $27,000 less you can borrow for your own purposes.

So how do you say no to family or friends who see you as financially stable and a good resource for solving their problems? Try this . . . "Tonya, both Paul and I would love to help, but right now we're just not in a position to do so financially. We would be happy to sit down with you and Tony to talk about ways you could clean up the financial mess you're in. And we'd be happy to help in other ways, like taking the kids when you guys are working extra hard to get that debt paid off. But we can't co-sign right now. What else can we do to help you?"

People who need a co-signer for a loan can't qualify on their own because the lender believes they will default. I have heard of the odd positive co-signing experience like a young adult with no credit history whose parents sign on because they know their kid is a stand-up person who would sooner die than stick them with debt. But I've heard five times as many negative stories: parents who have been stuck with their children's irresponsible behaviour; families who watched as the primary signer went bankrupt, leaving them holding the loan. If a body can't qualify for a loan on his or her own merits, you have to wonder if you're actually doing this person a favour by adding more weight to his or her debt load.

RULE #244: KNOW IF YOU CAN "THOIL" IT

Alex and I are walking through a mall one day, when she tells me that she's got her eye on a new pair of shoes. "They're lovely," she says, her eyes gleaming. She's been on a clothing allowance since she was 12, so she's in charge of her spending decisions. She starts describing a very sexy pair of shoes. I'm nodding, sipping on my juice, when she says, "But I dunno." She hesitates for a moment and then adds, "I just can't thoil it."

The juice comes out my nose as I exclaim, "Thoil! Where the hell did you get that word?"

"I read it on your blog," she said. (Awww . . . she reads my blog.)

After I stop laughing and wipe up the mess that's dribbled down onto my shirt, we talk a little more about the shoes and about things we each can and cannot thoil.

So what the heck is "thoil"? It's a Yorkshire word that fills a hole in our language of needs and wants. It means to be able to afford something but not want it badly enough to spend the money.

While you may have taken care of all your needs and have the money sitting in the bank to buy a spiffy coat on sale, if you already have a perfectly good coat and just can't see yourself spending the money, you might say, "I just can't thoil it." You can afford it; you just don't want to spend the money. Sure, a new coat would be nice, but what you may have to give up— the money and what else the money could buy—isn't worth it.

I like a nice pair of shoes as much as the next girl . . . well,

SMART SHOPPING

maybe not quite as much, since I'm not prepared to spend $500 on any pair of shoes, no matter how beautiful. I can't thoil it. And while I love beautiful bedding and will spend big money on high thread-count sheets, a cupboard full of linen is more than I can thoil. Yes, I have the money to buy dozens of sets, but I can't justify spending more because I already have what I want, and keeping the money in the bank brings me more satisfaction than having yet one more set of sheets in the cupboard.

The next time you go shopping and get the itch to spend, weigh your desire against the comfort of having money in the bank, at the ready just in case. Think about your needs and your wants. Then decide if you can thoil that new whatever. It's an extra step that can help you decide if the impulse monkey is riding your back or if you're buying from a "good" place.

RULE #245: DON'T MAKE
YOURSELF HOUSE-POOR

Home ownership is NOTHING like renting. If you think you can afford a home because the mortgage payment is almost like rent, you're going into home ownership blind.

I can't believe the number of people who leap into it without a clue about the financial responsibility they're undertaking. You'll have utility costs. You'll have taxes. You'll have insurance. And then there's maintenance . . . . When the roof leaks, or the furnace gives up the ghost, will you be tapping your savings and whining "If only I'd known"?

Resist the urge to guesstimate what these costs will be. Ask friends in the area what they pay for heating, electricity, water, oil, whatever the house you're eyeing consumes. Look at real estate listings to see the taxes on comparable homes in the area. Get a quote on what it'll cost to insure your new nest.

Calculate your maintenance budget. Use the rule of thumb of between 3% (newer houses) and 5% (older houses) of the value of the home. Don't wimp out on this. If the property values in your area are horrendously high because of land costs, use the home's replacement value for your calculation.

If you aren't prepared for the costs associated with home ownership, you'll end up filling the gap in your cash flow by using credit, and your savings will go to hell in a handbasket. If you want to have a home and be able to save too, you've got to have a plan that is both realistic and achievable. There's nothing warm and fuzzy about being house-poor.

RULE #246: FEND OFF RETAILER INFLUENCES

Retail stores have a bunch of ways to make you spend more. From those huge shopping carts designed to carry every impulse you have to the checkout, to the placement of the most expensive product right at your eye line, nothing is by chance in a store.

Even if you run in for only a loaf of bread, a jug of wine, and an apple, you're likely to grab a cart on the way. Then they've gotcha. Ever found yourself at the checkout wondering how you managed to find so many things you needed? The empty cart did that to you. Skip the cart and carry the few things you intended to get. You're far less likely to browse and pick up as you go. Even if you do, you'll be limited in how much you can hold.

Have you noticed that all the staples like eggs and milk are at the back of the store? That's to make you walk through all the "want" stuff to get what you need. That's why you should never go into a store without a shopping list. Head directly to the back of the store, and work your way forward. Hopefully, by the time you've got your staples, you'll be tired of shopping and just want to get the hell out of there.

Know, too, that stores place the most profitable products at eye level, where they're most likely to catch your attention. Staples tend to be in the centre of the aisle, while the nice-to-haves are at the ends. Whenever something catches your eye, look a shelf above and a shelf below to see if a less expensive version is just a reach away. The best per-unit deals are usually on the bottom shelf, so stoop and save.

Even when an item isn't on sale, it can be advertised as if it were. I almost got caught by a pseudo sale on frozen pizza. A closer look at the actual price showed that although the store was highlighting the pizza, it wasn't on sale at all. The only way to battle this trick is to know your product prices. No, you can't expect to know them all—unless you shop with a price book—but even knowing the regular and usual sale price of the 25 to 50 things you buy most often will help you avoid being bamboozled.

RULE #247: NAME A "CONTINGENT SUBSCRIBER" ON YOUR RESPS

Most people don't realize that the money they put into an RESP does not belong to the beneficiary until it is paid out. All that money you're piling up for your kids or grandkids remains your money until you start doling it out. So says The Law.

Since kids who are beneficiaries have no legal interest in the plans, you'd be very wise to name a "contingent subscriber" for the RESP when you open it up. If you don't and you die intestate—without a legal will in place—the plan will likely be terminated and all the contributions and income earned put into your estate.

Since the plan has been terminated, the Canada Education Savings Grants would have to be repaid to the government. Whoosh! That's the grant money rushing out of your kids' hands and back to the government. Don't want that to happen? Make a will. Name a contingent subscriber; your children's guardian would be a natural choice. Sleep easy.

SAVING

RULE #248: CROSS CHEQUES
TO PROTECT YOURSELF

Once upon a time if you wrote a cheque and then decided to stop payment, the body who had the cheque couldn't cash it. With the growth of "third-party cheque cashing" stores like Money Mart, that's not true anymore.

According to the law, if a third party accepts a cheque that it doesn't know has been stopped, it can treat it as a valid cheque and collect the money from the issuer—the person who wrote the cheque. That'd be YOU!

If you are writing a cheque that may have to be stopped— to a supplier you're not sure of, or for postdated cheques you may have to cancel down the road, or to replace a cheque someone says is lost—cross your cheques. Draw two straight lines diagonally between the bottom left and top right corners of the cheque, and write "not negotiable" between the lines.

If a third party accepts a crossed cheque and then finds out the cheque was stopped, it can't come after you. It must seek recourse against the body that cashed the stopped cheque.

If you're the recipient of a crossed cheque, deposit it to your bank account and before you spend the money, check to see if the cheque has cleared once the hold period has passed. Sounds like a pain in the butt, doesn't it? Here's the upside: you won't get sued.

Don't be surprised if your bank does not accept a crossed cheque through an ATM. Despite crossed cheques being legal, sometimes the payment processing organization (the Canadian Payments Association, or CPA) rejects crossed cheques because its scanners can't read them. Once the cheque was returned to you as "not deposited," you would have to take it back in and insist on it being cleared and deposited to your account. Until people routinely cross their cheques to protect themselves, the banks will make this hard on you. But better a skirmish with your bank when you're right than a lawsuit you will not win with a cheque cashing company.

(Turns out that since the cheque cashing stores don't belong to the CPA, this is the very reason they cash stopped cheques. And since the law is on the side of protecting the ignorant cheque cashers—really? Money Mart needs protecting?—this leaves plenty of room for fraud.)

RULE #249: BUY THE INDEX

Over and over people write to me saying they want to get into investing but are overwhelmed with all the choices available. Should they go with a mutual fund or buy stocks directly? Then comes the inevitable question: "Which one?"

With so many choices available, new investors often feel as though picking an investment is tantamount to throwing a dart at a dartboard and hoping for a good score. Choosing is almost painful.

If you are relatively new to investing and want to get into the game but just don't know where to start, if you're learning, but don't want that learning to get in the way of investing in equities, the answer is simple: Buy the Index.

Stay with me now—it's about to get a little complicated. Here we go.

Since it would be very difficult to track every single security trading, a smaller sample of the market is used to represent the whole market, and that's called an "index." Charles Dow created the first index back in 1896, and at that time the Dow index contained 12 of the largest public companies in the U.S. Today the Dow Jones Industrial Average tracks 30 of the largest companies in the U.S.

There are many other indices, including the Standard & Poor's 500, the NASDAQ Composite, and the Russell 2000, all based in the U.S. The S&P/TSX Composite covers Canada. The Hang Seng is in Hong Kong and the FTSE 100 is in the U.K. There are also indices broken down by category such as transportation, financial services, and technology.

So how do you invest in an index? By using an Exchange Traded Fund, or ETF.

ETFs track an index, or a basket of assets like an index fund, but trade like a stock on an exchange. Since ETFs trade like stocks, their prices change throughout the day as they are bought and sold. ETFs also have expenses that are usually lower than those of the average mutual fund.

The beauty of buying the index is that you don't have to worry about how individual stocks will do, and you don't have to worry about managing a portfolio. You simply buy the index that mirrors the sector you want to invest in. You will do as well or as badly as the sector you've chosen. If you choose an ETF that invests in the gold index, you'll do as well as the gold does overall.

Since you're new to investing, you might simply choose to buy an ETF that tracks how the Toronto Stock Exchange (TSE) is doing and you'd be likely to beat more than 75% of the mutual funds from which you might have chosen.

Once upon a time the only game in town was iShares. Now there are dozens and dozens of choices, which can make choosing an ETF feel like the old dartboard game again . . . if you let it. Don't bother with all the new and improved options available if you're just getting started. The vanilla-flavoured iShares are strong and steady. Save the new flavours for when you've got a bit more experience under your belt.

RULE #250: TAX-PLAN IN JAN

Every April there are a slew of articles and consumer reports about how to keep more of your tax money. Hey, the tax year starts in January, and that's when you should be making your plans for the year. If you wait until you file last year's tax return in April, you'll have missed four months of working to a plan.

Tax planning may sound like something only Richie Riches need to do. But you'll pay a lot more tax than you have to if you don't know the rules and take full advantage of all the deductions available.

Get a copy of the last year's tax guide. (I'm not talking about the tax act . . . lord, that would give you years' worth of toilet paper! I'm talking about the guide that comes with the paper return.) Stick it on the back of your commode along with a highlighter or pen, and each time you sit, read a couple of paragraphs. Mark the stuff that you think applies to you. Perhaps you'll highlight the rules about how to deduct medical expenses. Or maybe you'll circle the rules about deducting child care expenses. Or the rules about student loan interest deductibility.

Go see a tax expert. Or, if you're determined to do your own return to save money, then you're acting as your own advisor and you better be giving yourself the right advice so you pay the least in taxes possible. If you don't know what your marginal tax rate or your average tax rate was for last year, get thee to an expert.

Either way, lay a plan to pay less tax.

RULE #251: DON'T GET SUCKED IN BY "FREE"

Can you imagine that anyone would be fool enough to sign up for a high-interest credit card because they were giving away a FREE T-shirt? A frickin' T-shirt? Seriously? It happens. All the time. The idea of FREE is so powerful that it can make even the most sensible person into an eee-jut.

Why does FREE work so well? First, when we get sumthin' for nuthin' we feel really smart. And since it's FREE, there's no downside. Having paid not a cent, we have nothing to lose.

FREE lowers our expectations for what we're getting. When Google Docs was introduced, if it had arrived with a high pay-to-access price tag, it would have begged comparison to a bunch of already well-established word processing programs. Because Google made the product FREE, our perception shifted from comparison to automatic acceptance, with a side of "Hey, this thing works well, considering it's free!"

In his fascinating book *Predictably Irrational*, Dan Ariely (a professor of behavioural economics at MIT) describes his chocolate-selling experiments to demonstrate the differences between social economics and classic economics with regard to things that are "free."

In the cafeteria next to the cash register, he sold Lindt truffles for 15 cents and Hershey Kisses for 1 cent, but you could only choose one. Seventy-three percent of the people chose my favourite chocolate: the Lindt. Then Ariely lowered the price of each chocolate by one cent, bringing the Lindt to 14 cents and the Kiss to 0. Under a classic economic model, since the price differential and opportunity costs of each option were the same, the results should have been the same. But they weren't. Nope. FREE won the day: 69% chose the Kiss.

FREE is so powerful we don't even have to see the word to recognize how good we'll feel following through. Think of the acronym BOGO . . . it's a word unto itself now. Buy One Get One has become synonymous with FREE even when it isn't. So now retailers are using "BOGO at half price," giving us a measly 25% off, and we rush to make the deal.

I've felt the twitch when I've seen FREE. And I'm smart and highly focused on being conscious about my shopping. But FREE pulls at me. If you aren't vigilant, FREE can make you do downright dumb things. So the next time you see FREE, think, "For Really Eager Eee-juts."

RULE #252: YOU'RE ALLOWED TO SAY NO

People have a really hard time with the word "no." Considering that it's practically the first word babies learn to say, it's funny how as time passes it becomes less and less easy to Just Say No.

We don't like to hear the word "no." And if we have reservations about seeming harsh, if we've been raised to accommodate, then "no" feels like the hardest word to say.

"Hey, we're going out for dinner Saturday. Wanna come?"

"Do me a favour and swing past the liquor store and pick me up some boxes for my move."

"We need you to work late again tonight because this is a really crucial stage in the project."

"Can you spot me $10 till payday?"

"Mom, I don't have any gas in the car, so I won't be able to get to school."

Some requests are implied, like the chick who used her mother's desire for her to finish university to get her to put gas in her car. Or the boss who uses the crisis of the day to keep you late again. Some are direct requests, like the loan. Some are assumptions that you've got nothing better to do than make the other guy's life easier. And some are genuine invitations to share time with you. But if any request—explicit or implied—puts you in the position of doing something you don't want to do, or spending money you don't have, no matter how much you love the person who is hitting you up, you've got to say no.

Perhaps the worst offenders of the "assumptive question"— which doesn't have a question mark and assumes a "yes" response—are adult children. Banking on the fact that their parents don't want to see them go without, these "children" continue to suck their parents (and sometimes other relatives and friends) dry.

I get letters all the time asking me what a thoughtful, responsible child can do to stop a parasitic sibling.

Nothing.

It's not your job to protect your parents from your sibs, or your siblings from each other. It's not your job to save anybody from anybody else. You can only be responsible for your own relationships. You cannot manage the relationships of others. You don't have to approve. And you don't have to be quiet about it. But you actually can't change it. The only person who can ensure that a body is not taken advantage of is that body. And "no" is the key.

If you are considered selfish because you say no, if you're yelled at or shunned because you choose to not give into the pressure to accommodate, you've got to be strong enough to know you are choosing to say no for good reasons.

"I would love it if you'd be my bridesmaid." How do you say no to that? "Sweetheart, I am so honoured, and I'll definitely be there to share your day, but I don't have the money to spend on a dress right now."

"Mom, it's a great opportunity. If you'd give me some money to do this, I'd be out of your hair for good." Tempting, isn't it? "Darling, I love you, but I'm not in a position to help right now. You're going to have to find a way to do this one on your own. I know you can do it."

"I'm desperate. I need to borrow this money. You're doing

so well. Please help us." It can be hard to turn away a plea for help from someone you love. And you can help, if that's what you want to do and you can afford it. If you can't, then say, "I would love to be able to help you right now. And if you want me to help you make a plan, I have all the time in the world for that. But I'm sorry, we've got our own commitments to meet."

BTW, when I use the phrase "I'm sorry," it is not intended as an apology. You have nothing to apologize for in saying no. It's a perfectly valid response. "I'm sorry" is an expression of empathy and goes a long way to soften a "no."

Saying no doesn't come easily. You have to practise. Start small. And don't start with the people you love the most. Start with the people who you would typically want to refuse but have never had the stomach to try.

Run through some scenarios in your head. Practise in front of the mirror. Learn to say no.

The next time a stranger comes to the door asking if you want work done, if you'd like to buy a chocolate bar, or if you want to sign up for magazines, say, "No, thank you." The next time people assume you'll be the one who buys the gift, figures out how the travel arrangements should work for the vacation, or drives everyone around, say, "Sorry, not this time." And when people hit you up for a loan, unless you're giving it as a gift (see Rule #115: Money Lent Is a Gift), say, "While I'd love to help you figure out a solution to your problem, I'm sorry but it won't be financially."

"No" is a liberating word. If you ever say yes with reservations, kick yourself later, or wonder why you always give in, you're the perfect candidate for lessons in saying no. Get busy liberating yourself.

RULE #253: GET OUT OF OVERDRAFT

CREDIT

Virtually every family I've worked with has been in overdraft at some point in the month. Some people spend virtually the whole month in overdraft, blipping into positive territory only on the days that the paycheque hits the bank account.

If you're serious about getting out of overdraft, it won't be easy. It will take some serious belt tightening. Here's how to do it.

1. Make a list of your monthly Fixed Essential Expenses. These are the bills that you must cover every month, like mortgage and car paymenst, minimums on your debt, and child care expenses. Add them up.

2. Make a list of your monthly Variable Essential Expenses. These are the costs that you simply can't avoid, like food and gas. I'm not talking fancy food and lots 'n lotsa gas. These are bare minimums to get you through the month. No clothes, no movies, no shopping at all on this list. Add them up.

3. Subtract these two totals from your income. How much do you have left? If you don't have enough to cover the unessential expenses in your life—the fancy cell phone, the uppity satellite service, and the like, you can see your problem. Time to cut back on the nice-to-haves until you're out of the hole. Change your services to the most basic you can get away with.

4. Commit to living on this very harsh, very tight budget for one month. Just one month. Take all the rest of the money you make and stick it in an envelope, a jar, or a high-interest savings account . . . just don't spend it.

5. And no, you can't use your credit during this process.

6. When you get to the end of the month, add up how much you've got left after your bills have been paid. Is it enough to cover your overdraft? If it is, then you'll have to live through this belt-tightening horror for another month as you build up the cash to pay off the overdraft again. If it's not, you may have to feel the pain for a few more months until you're in the clear.

7. Once you've paid off your overdraft, the final step is to create a buffer to forestall ever having to use it again. Do you have the fortitude to go one more month without the frills so you can have cash sitting in your account to take care of small missteps? Yes, you do! Just remember—once you've built up that buffer, whenever you have to dip into it for those minor shortfalls, you'll have to pay your account back so you keep that buffer in place.

Now you have a plan. The question is do you have the guts to execute the plan?

RULE #254: MAKE MORE MONEY

If you've cut your budget back to the bone and you still don't have the money you need to make ends meet, to get your debt paid off, to save for the future, your only option is to make more money.

Figure out how much you have to make to meet your needs. Can you work more hours in your current job? Does it make sense to get a different job? What extra training will you need? Can you get a second part-time job?

Think about starting your own small business on the side. Walk dogs. Drive elderly people to their doctors' appointments. Fix and repair stuff other people can't. Make stuff you can sell. Can you knit? Cook? Quilt? Paint? Compose music? Take photographs? Sit kids, wash cars, weed gardens, organize closets, mow lawns, rake leaves, clean out basements and cart away the stuff (which you can then sell on craigslist)?

Can you rent a room in your home?

Do you have a pile of stuff that you could sell? Kids' clothes can go to consignment shops. Furniture can go on craigslist. Figure out how eBay works and make it work for you. This one-time infusion of cash can be used to pay down debt or build up an emergency fund to take some of the pressure off your monthly budget.

The only solution to not having enough money is to make more money. People do it all the time. If you think you can't, you won't. If you are determined to, you will.

RULE #255: A LINE OF CREDIT IS NOT AN EMERGENCY FUND

Old Rule: "Get a line of credit for emergencies." This rule is so profitable for banks that they have spent millions of dollars selling it to us. And we have bought it hook, line, and sinker!

New Rule: A Line of Credit Is Debt Waiting to Happen!

The people telling you to get an LOC as an emergency fund are the same people who let you buy a house without enough money down, offered you ways to satisfy all your whims while spending money you hadn't yet earned (yah, I'm talking about your credit card balance here), and continually raised your limits until many of you had enough debt to bury an elephant.

A line of credit is not an emergency fund. If you hit a wall and end up racking up tens of thousands in debt on an LOC, how is that diverting disaster? You're simply replacing the lack of cash with a huge pile of debt. 'Course, substituting an LOC for a real emergency fund does mean you don't have to save anything, so you can keep spending all your money every month. Hey, if that's what you want to do, you'll keep doing it. But don't say you've got an emergency fund if what you've got is a line of credit. It just means you bought some bank's bullsh*t. You shouldn't want to admit to that! (It makes you look dumb.)

Cash in the bank is an emergency fund. How much cash? See Rule #8: Everyone Needs an Emergency Fund.

RULE #256: CALCULATE YOUR REAL MORTGAGE LOAN INSURANCE COSTS

If you can't come up with a down payment of at least 20% of the purchase price of the home you want to buy, you'll need a high-ratio mortgage: a mortgage insured through an organization like Canada Mortgage and Housing Corporation (CMHC). An application fee and insurance premium will apply. This insurance premium is a one-time charge calculated as a percentage of the loan amount. The percentage ranges from 0.5% to 2.9% of the mortgage amount and depends on just how much you managed to come up with for the down payment, along with your employment status, your credit score, the source of your down payment, and the length of your amortization.

The lower your down payment, the higher the premium cost. If you're self-employed and don't have a third-party income validation, you'll pay more. If your credit score is 580 to 600, you'll pay a premium. If you use non-traditional sources for your down payment—borrowed funds, gifts, lender cash back incentives—you'll pay more. And if you go with an amortization longer than 25 years, you'll pay more: 0.2% more for every 5 years you extend the amortization past 25 years.

You can pay this premium in cash or do what almost everyone else does and add it to your mortgage.

Before you go hiding your mortgage loan insurance premium in your mortgage, where you can forgedaboutit, figure out what that premium will end up costing. Let's say you're

CREDIT

buying the average home in Canada and paying $348,000. You've come up with 5% down, or $17,400, which means you're going to need a mortgage of $330,600. You're planning on amortizing for 25 years. Your mortgage insurance premium will come in at about $9,590. (To estimate your mortgage insurance premium, go to www.cmhc.com and use the Premium Calculator.) Add that to your mortgage and pay an average rate of 5.5% over the life of your mortgage and that mortgage insurance premium will end up costing you about $12,670 in interest. So you just added more than $22,000 to the cost of your home—more than your original down payment—before the interest on your mortgage.

Yes, Gail, but my home will be going up in value. Could be, but your house would have to increase in value from $348,000 to $630,754 just to break even on the interest on the mortgage because you chose a high-ratio mortgage and added the CMHC payment to your mortgage debt. And that's not taking into account property taxes, maintenance, and home insurance. (See Rule #83: Calculate the Real Profit on Your Home.)

RULE #257: STOP LOOKING FOR THE EASY WAY

People are lazy. Lazy can do one of two things:

1. It can make you more efficient. (This is me.)
2. It can keep you from achieving your goals. (Not me.)

I work like a dog. I shoot TV shows, write books, do a daily blog on my website, answer myriad questions, plus I blog elsewhere. I make public appearances, go to book signings, show up for interviews on television, radio, and in print. I take care of my family. I garden, cook, do laundry. I've got a lot going on, so I have to be efficient. What I'm not is the kind of lazy that's always looking for an easy way out.

The things you have to do to manage your money smartly aren't complicated. I'd go so far as to say they're pretty simple. But they're not easy. They require time, a commitment to doing the detail, and the perseverance to keep going. Managing your money isn't something you do once and you're done. Like cleaning the toilet or brushing your teeth, you have to do it all the time to keep the system sparkling clean and in good working order. Let it go a few days and you'll have to spend a little extra time catching up.

People are always telling me I should build an app for managing money. (You mean there aren't enough of these already? I actually created the anti-app, called The Gail Way, which is the way I manage my money. It isn't fancy, and it isn't for lazy people.)

Websites abound that promise to help you assess where

your money is going. You can buy financial software or use the stuff your bank will give you for free to keep you from using those third-party systems.

Here's the reality: **It doesn't matter what you buy to help you manage your money—there is no system on earth that can think for you.** There's no system that will make clear what you're doing right and what you're doing wrong. You're the only person who can decide if your money is going where you want it to, and what you're going to have to change if you want things to be different. There is no easy way. Sorry.

If you're too lazy to bother managing your money, you shouldn't be surprised that you're in debt, constantly in overdraft, or never have any money saved. If you're too lazy to track how you're spending your money, you'll likely squirm with anxiety or scream with frustration because you just can't seem to get what you think you want. If you're too lazy to make a budget, you have no plan for your money and you should be prepared for it to evaporate without a trace.

I'm all for the kind of lazy that makes you more efficient. But if you're the kind of lazy who is looking for The Easy Way, you'll never achieve your goals.

RULE #258: LEAVE $1,000 OF YOUR EMERGENCY FUND IN YOUR CHEQUING ACCOUNT

There are chequing accounts that waive all transaction fees when you maintain a minimum monthly balance of, say, $1,000. Take $1,000 from your emergency savings and stick it in your chequing account and it can do double duty: it'll be there when the caca hits the fan; in the meantime it'll save on bank fees.

The trick is to never touch the $1,000. It's a float that doesn't really exist in terms of what you have to spend. You have to be disciplined enough to not spend that money. In your spending journal—you are keeping a spending journal, right?—simply never count the $1,000 at the bottom of your cash pool. Since you don't have it in your "balance," you can't see it to spend it.

Living with a partner who is not as disciplined as you are? Make it very clear that the last $1,000 in the account is UNTOUCHABLE. There can't be any wavering on this issue. If the $1,000 is eroded at all and you have to top it up with more money from your emergency fund, your EF will have sprung a leak and it's only a matter of time before it's all gone. But if you have the discipline and the self-control to leave that money sitting in your account to save on bank charges, it could be worth between $120 and $350 in bank fees saved. That's a 12 to 35% return on your money . . . tax-free. That's gotta be worth a little self-discipline!

RULE #259: YOU DON'T NEED A TON OF CASH TO MAKE A PRINCIPAL PREPAYMENT AGAINST YOUR MORTGAGE

This replaces the misconception that if you don't have 10 to 20% in cash to put down as a principal prepayment against your mortgage, you can't benefit.

Just about every mortgage worth its salt comes with a principal prepayment option. This lets you prepay your mortgage by a specified amount—usually a percentage of the original mortgage—once a year. Sometimes it's at any time in the year. Sometimes it can only be done on the anniversary date of the mortgage.

If you took out a $200,000 mortgage and your principal prepayment option (yes, you have to read the mortgage document) lets you prepay up to 15%, you could knock $30,000 off your mortgage principal every year.

"Gail, there's no way I can come up with $30K."

I hear ya. But that doesn't mean you should come up with SOMETHING. The bank is giving you a free pass and you should be taking it.

How little is too little?

No amount is too small.

Let's say all you can come up with is $500 as a principal prepayment. Let's also say that your $200,000 mortgage is amortized for 25 years at an average interest rate of 5%. If you made the principal prepayment every year, you would save $10,697 in interest. So as little as a 0.25% prepayment saves you almost $11,000 in interest. Have I got your attention?

MONEY RULES · 483

Let's say you could come up with a 1% prepayment every year: $2,000. That would save you $34,637. See, it doesn't take a ton of money to make that principal prepayment pay off. But you've got to use it or you'll lose it. You can't carry it from one year to the next, so if you don't take advantage of it, you'll miss the boat that year.

Here's another way to use the principal prepayment to your advantage. Let's say you've sold your house and you're paying off the mortgage early. If you're breaking your mortgage contract, they're going to charge you a penalty (See Rule #81: Avoid Early Renewal Penalties.) But if you tell them to calculate the principal prepayment before they calculate the penalty, you'll save money since the penalty will be calculated on a smaller outstanding balance. Yes, it is as easy as that: just tell them to apply your principal prepayment before they calculate the interest penalty.

RULE #260: TAKE PLEASURE
FROM YOUR MONEY

I have a line in my budget called "pleasures." It's where I put the money I spend getting a massage, buying those delicious ginger/peach candles, and anything else that I want to splurge on. I guess I should put all the wonderful teas I buy in this category, but I put them under "food," leaving more space for self-indulgence (as long as I stay within my pre-set parameters).

I didn't always have a pleasures line. When my last husband and I split up, I blew through almost $70,000 in emergency fund money by putting a down payment on a new home, paying legal fees, and transitioning the kids with the least amount of disruption. With my emergency fund decimated, I went into austerity mode: I couldn't spend a penny on myself.

One day I realized that I'd eliminated all the fun stuff in my attempt to rebuild my emergency fund. With money in the bank I could now spend money, except I couldn't. I'd been in austerity mode for so long I'd forgotten how to take pleasure from spending. I was turning every purchase into an internal debate that would inevitably end with me not buying.

So I came up with the idea of the pleasures line. I looked at what I could afford to just blow on me and I put it in the budget. And I made myself spend it.

Here's the thing about money. It's for spending. Not all of it, but some of it. As long as you're not going into debt, and you've got all your bases covered—including long-term savings, emergency fund, insurance—you can spend your money on anything you want. Want to travel? Go. Want to drink expensive coffee? Do it. You work hard for your money and you should enjoy the pleasures it can bring you.

The only time spending becomes a problem is when you do it unconsciously and it interferes with your financial goals. You can't eat out four nights a week if you want to save up a down payment on a home. And you can't buy everything your heart desires if you have no emergency fund. Take care of the details and then you can go shopping guilt-free. It may take a little re-calibrating, but you can do it.

What if you're still experiencing pangs when you buy yourself the extras? Maybe you've been in austerity mode for so long you need to readjust to the idea that you can afford to splurge now, or maybe you shouldn't be buying what you're buying because there are other, more important things that should come first.

Keep in mind that for your pleasures to feel like pleasures, you can't indulge in them too often. If you love picking up a magazine at the checkout to enjoy with your Saturday morning tea, grab the mag. But if you aren't reading those magazines, or are just flipping through them because you bought them—so there's no real pleasure—stop buying. You need to go without for a while so you can reset your pleasure metre.

Being able to take pleasure from the things money can buy is part of having a balanced financial life. Don't take the desire to enjoy too far and you can keep enjoying for a long time. And if you have to forgo a treat for a couple of weeks because things are a little tight, your pleasure will be all the sweeter the next time you indulge.

RULE #261: DON'T TURN
GUIDELINES INTO RULES

Funny rule coming from a person writing a book of rules, no? Hey, I'm the girl who is always asking, "Does it work for YOU?"

When you think about the whole area of "personal finance," what pops to mind? Money, right? Hey, that's the "finance" part. But there's also the "personal" part. And that's the part so many people don't really get.

The finance part is straightforward: numbers are both concrete and absolute. But people aren't. And that's why, so often, people go through the process of doing the math, only to come out the other end with a plan they don't stick to. Sure, the math works. But they haven't put as much thought and effort as they need to into the "personal" part. In fact, folks have become so obsessed with the "finance" that some of them don't even acknowledge the "personal" part. Or is it that you're hiding behind the "finance" so you'll never have to come face-to-face with yourself?

Y'all know the Life Pie I've been drumming to death: 35% of your net income for housing, 15% for transportation, 25% for life, 10% for savings, 15% for debt repayment. The thing about the Life Pie is that it is meant as a guideline. While you're not supposed to spend more than 35% of your net income on housing, if you have no debt and you've got all your other costs under control (or you live in Vancouver!), you can spend more if you really, really want to. And if you've got a ton of debt and you've been saving sweet-diddly-squat, you may have cut way back on housing in order to get all your other ducks in a row.

Whether it's the 10% Rule for saving, or the 70% Rule for retirement income, you've got to weigh these carefully to make sure they're working for you. Sure, save 10% is a good guideline, but if you're already 42 years old and haven't saved a penny, it won't be enough. And the 70% Rule for retirement income is based on the fact that many pension plans pay out 60 to 70% of your pre-retirement income. But if you've got a ton of debt, a mortgage that isn't paid off, or young kids who are still dependent on you, you'll need more. But if you plan to sell your house and pay off the kids' mortgages while you live with them through your golden years so you can be close to the grandkids, you'll likely need less.

All the "rules" we use in personal finance are guidelines. They are not cast in concrete, nor should they be followed slavishly. Each of us has a unique set of circumstances, and the plans we make for what we'll do with our money must reflect those unique characteristics.

Whether we're using the Life Pie, a net worth calculation, or the 70% Rule for retirement income, these are guidelines. They help to show you where the trail is. But it is up to you to smooth that trail into a solid road to your personal destination. These guidelines are like averages, but when it comes to people, there is no "average." So you must begin by figuring out where you are and where you really, really want to go. Do the math. And don't forget the "person" in personal finance.

RULE #262: YOUR FINANCIAL LITERACY IS YOUR RESPONSIBILITY (PART 2)

There's a lot of buzz about financial literacy these days. Task forces have been struck. Literacy leaders have been named. But what exactly does "financial literacy" mean?

I define financial literacy as what you have to do to move from being dependent to being independent. Whether you're dependent on your parents, dependent on an employer, or dependent on clients, each step you take towards no longer needing their co-operation to live your life is a step in the right direction.

Part of being independent means knowing enough to ask the right questions and sniff out when you're being bamboozled. Sure, it would be easier if there was somebody we could count on to help us make good decisions about our money. But that, my darlings, is wishful thinking of the most dangerous kind.

The financial marketplace is full of scam artists. You might be surprised where some of those scam artists live. They're not all dressed in checkered suits, with slicked-back hair and greasy smiles. Some of them look pretty much like you and me. Some of them work for companies you've come to think of as having your best interests at heart. You couldn't be more wrong!

We have a love-hate relationship with our banks. We love 'em so much that we let them steer us in any direction they like. We hate the fact that we feel so powerless in their presence. That's our fault. We've given them way more control than they deserve.

Would you walk onto a used car lot and say to the salesman,

"Sir, please tell me which car to buy and how much I should pay?" Sounds ridiculous, right? Yet every day, people do just that when they walk into banks and ask, "How much can I afford to borrow?" and "Which investment is right for me?"

If you're still following the old rule that banks are looking out for your best interests, you're woefully behind the times. (See Rule #7: Your Banker is Not Your Friend.) If you're waiting for some federal, provincial, or local can opener to pry open your skull and make money make sense to you, you're going to be old and broke. If you want to make good decisions that move you from dependence to independence, you've got to step up and accept that your financial literacy is your own responsibility. And if you want your children to be smart about money, that's your job too. (See Rule #49: Your Kids' Financial Education Is Your Responsibility.)

Canadians spend 28.5 hours a week watching TV. I just want you to take one of those hours back to manage your money. Just one. Only one. Simply one. You can do that, right?

There is no magic to money management. So much of what you see, hear, read about money makes it sound far more complicated than it really is. The experts sent to guide you only make it sound hard, look hard, feel hard because they want you to feel out of your depth. Here's a case in point: if you have ever read about mutual fund investing, no doubt you've heard of "management expense ratios." Frequently, the term is reduced to its initials: MERs. When I speak to groups about financial literacy I ask, "How do you spell MER?" The audience looks at me as if I'm nuts. "C'mon," I say, "spell MER!" Someone will. Or not. Then I spell it: "F-E-E."

You see, the management expense ratio on a mutual fund is the fee the people managing the investments charge the fund to do the work of managing it. So why did we need to create a seven-syllable term—plus an acronym—for the word "fee"? Could it be that the smarty-pants want you to feel out of your depth so that you give up control of your money to them? STOP IT! Don't let them do that to you.

There are some areas of financial planning that can get very complicated: investing, estate planning, some insurance stuff. For those, you'll likely need an expert's help. Finding that expert is a matter of shopping around, just as you would when you're buying a car. Ask friends and family for references. Set up a meeting and assess how you feel about the person's communication style. (See Rule #187: Hire Good Help.)

The majority of what you have to do to make your money work for you is pretty straightforward: don't spend more than you make, know where every penny is going, save some, pay as little in interest as possible, and cover your butt so that if life screws with you, you have options.

When I'm asked why people are so unwilling to pick up the reins of their money, I usually say there are two reasons: because folks are lazy or stupid. But at a recent presentation I gave at a college, one perceptive young woman said she thought it was because folks are afraid. And that gave me pause.

You don't have to be afraid. You don't have to feel overwhelmed. Most of the stuff you need to know is dead simple. But what you have to do, while simple, won't be easy. It'll mean changing how you behave. It'll mean weighing what you hear against what you know. If you're not sure about something, it'll mean asking questions. Lots and lots of questions. And it'll mean not being willing to take the first answer to whatever question you're asking about money.

You've heard me say, "Money isn't rocket science, it's discipline." Most of what you need to know to move from being dependent to being independent you already know. Now you just have to do. And what you don't know, you need to figure out for yourself. You work damn hard for your money. Spend a little time to figure out how to make it work for you.

RULE #263: DON'T SETTLE FOR CRAPPY RETURNS ON YOUR SAVINGS

I know that it seems as if our interest rates have been in the low zone forever. But I'm still surprised at how willing some folks are to accept less interest than they could get on their savings if they were willing to shop around.

If you have $10,000 in a regular savings account at a brick-and mortar-bank, you're probably earning 0.75%, or $75 a year. If you have it in a high-interest savings account, you could be earning 2%, or $200. Why would you turn your back on that extra $125 a year? If you saw a $100 bill lying on the ground, would you step over it?

Once upon a time the way to get more interest on savings was to lock that money up in a guaranteed investment certificate. But with some high-interest savings accounts paying more interest than GICs, why would you restrict your access to your money?

Most of the best rates available are offered by companies you've probably never heard of. You'll have to do some digging on the Internet to find them. Look to the credit unions and their online spinoffs in particular for some of the best rates going. Less well-known companies tend to offer more return to lure in your dollars. And many are smaller, with lower overheads, so they can afford to offer higher interest rates. Does that mean they're riskier? Not necessarily. Some are insured by Canada Deposit Insurance Corporation, just like the big banks. Some are insured by provincial agencies,

SAVING

like Deposit Guarantee Corporation of Manitoba. Do your homework, but don't settle for less than you could be getting on your money.

There are some financial companies that made their name by offering decent rates of return. They were then acquired by larger banks and now their rates are only marginally better than their parent company's rates. Don't let loyalty or laziness keep you tied to lower rates. If you want your money to work as hard for you as you did for it, put some effort into finding the best rates.

Beware the transfer-in or "new deposit" bonus offer. There are companies that offer very attractive interest rates for new deposits, but those offers are only for a limited time, after which a much lower regular rate kicks in. You can use these bonuses to your advantage, but if you let your money sit languishing after the special rate has expired, you're a sap.

RULE #264: SHARE EXPENSES PROPORTIONATE TO INCOME

When couples decide to combine their lives, their initial excitement often means they don't stop long enough to have the money talk. Later, one or the other thinks that the way their mate is managing their money isn't working particular well, and I get a Dear Gail letter that goes something like this:

Dear Gail,

What's the best way for us to handle merging our money? Should we just put it all together? And what if my mate makes twice as much as me? Is fifty-fifty really the fairest way to divvy up the bills?

I'm a big believer in both partners in a relationship building strong individual financial identities, so I don't suggest just jumbling the money all together. I much prefer the "mine, yours, ours" approach, where you share your joint expenses (shelter, food, utilities, whatever you agree on) and manage your individual lives separately (retirement savings, investments, credit cards).

For partners who each have a vehicle, your cars are an individual expense; if you are sharing a vehicle, costs come out of joint expenses unless one of you is a vehicle hog! A mortgage is a joint expense, but no other form of credit should be shared. And no co-signing! (See Rule #243: Co-signed Debt Is 100% Your Debt.) Retirement savings and consumer credit should

CASH MANAGEMENT

be handled individually, but keep in mind that if one guy goes deep in the debt hole, that could very well affect their ability to pony up their share of the joint expenses.

As for how to contribute to that joint account for sharing those expenses, so many people default to fifty-fifty only to find it doesn't work, particularly if one person makes substantially more than the other. Sharing your expenses proportionate to your income works well to split the bills and still keep some money in each mate's pocket for personal spending.

To calculate your expenses proportionate to your income:

1. Add your net incomes together. If you bring home $2,000 a month, and your mate makes $4,000 a month, when you add your incomes together you get $2,000 + $4,000 = $6,000 as your family income.

2. Figure out the proportions. Divide your income by the family income and then multiply by 100 to get a percentage: $2,000 ÷ $6,000 x 100 = 33.33%.

3. Do the same for your mate's income: $4,000 ÷ 6,000 x 100 = 66.66%.

This means you'd split the bills for your joint living expenses with you paying 33.34% and him paying 66.66%. So, if you have a mortgage payment of $1,800 a month, you would pay $1,800 x 33.34 ÷ 100 = $600. Your mate would pay $1,800 x 66.66 ÷ 100 = $1,200.

This, of course, only applies to the bills you agree to split. If you've run up a whole bunch of debt, your mate may not want anything to do with fixing your mess. And if your mate loves to travel and you like to stick close to home, travel would be an individual expense. You should also talk about how you'll build your emergency fund, since you'll likely use most of this money to cover joint expenses.

If your mate earns considerably more than you and balks at splitting expenses proportionately, you'll have to make it clear that if you're spending all your money on needs, while your mate covers needs easily and has lots left for wants, it's only a matter of time before the resentment you feel boils over. If he or she sticks to their guns about splitting things fifty-fifty, know that their commitment to themselves may be greater than their commitment to you.

RULE #265: RENOVATIONS ARE
NOT AN INVESTMENT

If one more person tells me that their new kitchen is an investment, I am going to pour a bucket of cold water on 'em. Consider yourself warned!

People are under the impression—the delusion, really—that their renovations are investments. People use this train of thought to rationalize why that the man cave in the basement and the spa bathroom are must-haves. Investments are things that increase your net worth over time.

If you're renovating your home for a quick flip, that's when you have to make sure your reno dollars are going to come back to you. Some renovations pay back well, some not so much, and you should know which are which.

If you plan to stay in your home for five years or more, your renovation is not an investment. Hey, you know that fabulous new fridge you put in, those lovely new cupboards, that exquisite crown moulding? In five years it won't be new. And if you went with what was in fashion when you did your update, you'll have to stay in the home for 25 years to catch the retro rebound.

The renovations you make to your home that you will live with for five years or more before you sell are consumables. You're getting the benefit from them; the next owner is just as likely to say, "Blech!"

A brand new hardwood floor will look great for years to come, but it'll hardly produce a big return on investment after

INVESTING

six years of kids dropping toys and dogs scurrying to the back door to be let out. And it doesn't matter how neutral you keep your paint or floor coverings, even a year later their newness will have worn off.

If you're planning improvements to your home and you're going to spend some time enjoying them, stop justifying the money you're spending as an investment and focus instead on how much pleasure you will derive from the changes. Just make sure you have the money in the bank to make those changes, just like if you were buying a new TV or a swishy pair of shoes.

If you want to upgrade your home and you've saved the money to do it, have fun. If you're justifying putting your upgrades on credit because they're "good investments," I have a slap right here waiting for your forehead. Be healed, idiot!

RULE #266: CALCULATE YOUR BURN RATE

People are always telling me they don't have any money to save for the future. Sure, there are some folks who just barely make ends meet when it comes to their essential expenses. But for a lot of people, unconscious spending means they burn through their money with nothing left to save.

Maybe you're one of those dopes who blithely shops themselves into the financial dumper. Or maybe you simply haven't got a clue where your money is going; there just never seems to be enough. If you want to become fully conscious of how you're using your money, it's time to calculate your burn rate. It'll take about a week and here's how you do it.

1. Make yourself a tracking sheet. Write the days of the week across the top and some typical categories down the left-hand side. Include stuff like coffee, snacks, lunch, cigs, gas, magazines, newspapers—anything you spend money on in a day.

2. Leave lots of blanks on the left, because you'll be amazed at what you'll add when you see all the things you're pulling out cash or your debit or credit card for.

3. As you go through the week, write down what you're spending. You're going to add it up, so there should be a column on the far right for Total Spent during the week in each category you've included on your tracking sheet.

4. Identify the point at which you spent $100 on non-essentials. (No, your morning cuppa is not an essential.) That's your burn rate. Did it take you a whole week? Five days? Less than three days? What were your biggest areas of weakness? Eating out? Kids or grands? Ciggies? Booze? Your passion for fashion?

Now that you know better, it's time to do better. Take even half of the money you're burning through each week and set up an automatic transfer to your retirement savings for that amount.

But Gail, I can't live without my coffee in the morning. And besides, what's $5 a day going to get me anyway?

Sure, $5 a day on coffee or snacks may not add up to a whole helluva lot in five or ten years, but the more than $75,000 you'll have after 30 years (assuming just a 2% return) is much better than the alternative: zilch.

Manage even 1% more in return over the 30 years and you'll have almost $90,000. That'll go a long way to making your life more comfortable in the future.

Still not convinced? Here's some more motivation. The average Canadian receives about the same amount of money from the Old Age Security and the Canada Pension Plan, so if you don't save for your future you can look forward to an income of about $12,000 a year (in today's dollars). Imagine living on $12,000 a year right now.

Did you just shiver?

RULE #267: CMHC INSURANCE
DOESN'T PROTECT YOU

People think that buying a home with less than 20% down is fine because, well, there's that insurance from CMHC (Canada Mortgage and Housing Corporation) that'll let you do so. While you may be paying the premium on that insurance, you're not the one being insured. It's been a pretty sweet deal for lenders, and people are only just waking up to the reality that despite having paid CMHC insurance, they're still on the hook for the full amount if they default on their mortgage. Then I get letters like this:

I have a judgment against me by CMHC on a mortgage that was foreclosed. The property, which was sold for $205,000, was originally insured for $238,000. CMHC got a judgment against me for the difference of $33,000, plus interest, for a total of $51,000. What do I do now?

A lot of folks are under the impression that if their property goes down in value or interest rates go up and they can't keep up, they can just walk away from the property because CMHC will cover the lender's ass on the mortgage and everything will be hunky-dory.

Nuh-uh! While it's true that banks aren't on the hook for loans that have been CMHC insured, that doesn't mean that you are off the hook.

But Gail, what about that big, fat insurance premium I paid when I took out the mortgage?

You mean the one you rolled into your mortgage and immediately started paying interest on? That was just to get CMHC to cover the bank's butt. You didn't think the bank would have given you all that mortgage money without CMHC's guarantee, did you? Not on your life. Not if you couldn't come up with a 20% down payment.

But paying that insurance premium doesn't mean CMHC won't come after you for the difference between what a property had to be sold for and what its insurance coverage was originally. Here's how the process works.

Once your mortgage has been in default for three months, legal proceedings are started through power of sale and the bank takes possession of your property.

The bank sells the property and submits a claim to CMHC for any shortfall. This isn't just for the difference in what the home was worth and what it sold for; it may also include outstanding interest, legal and real estate fees, and unpaid property taxes.

CMHC gets a judgment against you as the defaulted mortgagor for this shortfall and tries to collect. CMHC can garnish your wages or government pensions like OAS and CPP. They'll do whatever they have to in order to recoup their losses.

If their attempts to collect are unsuccessful, your account will be forwarded to one of CMHC's collection agencies. There goes your credit history and your credit score.

Your alternatives: pay up or visit a bankruptcy trustee for advice on a consumer proposal or bankruptcy.

Avoiding the CMHC completely should be the goal. If you can't save 20% for a home down payment, using CMHC to squeeze yourself into the real estate market can have big downsides, and you may be putting yourself behind the eight ball.

RULE #268: DO AN ANNUAL FINANCIAL REVIEW

You've probably read and heard this before: Stupid is doing the same thing over and over and expecting to get a different result. If you want to be smart about money, you've got to take some time each year to look at how you're doing and what you have to change.

It's so easy to ignore the details of our financial lives when everything is rushing past us like a sped-up movie scene. You've got to slow things down and have a good look. It doesn't matter if you do this as a year-end review, a spring cleaning, or a back-to-school update, but at least once a year, you want to review everything.

1. Create or update your net worth statement. How do you feel about what you've accomplished financially this year? What's your biggest financial concern? What one thing do you want to accomplish before another year rolls past?

2. Review your budget. How did the numbers shake out this year, and what should you tweak? It's easy as we get comfortable living on a budget to become complacent even as costs start to rise. Look at your last six months' spending to see if it is still in line with your planning. Is it time to do some trimming? Have prices risen in some areas of your budget, indicating that you need to trim in other areas to rebalance? Are there

other changes that have taken place since you did your budget that you need to incorporate officially?

3. You don't have a budget? How's that been working for you? If you're sick and tired of not knowing where your money has been going, it's time to grab a calculator, six months' worth of credit card and bank statements, and an Excel spreadsheet (a pen and pad will work too). Do the spending analysis. Make a budget.

4. Recalculate your debt level. If your consumer credit payments are eating up more than 15% of your budget, you've got too much debt. Some people find that it's hard to even imagine being debt-free. But you can be. It may take another job to earn the extra money to get out of debt, but if that's what it takes, you can do it. Are you on target to be debt-free by a specific date? (See Rule #9: Calculate Your Own Debt Repayment Plan.)

5. Assess your emergency savings. It takes small steps to get to where you want to be. Having six months' worth of essential expenses socked away isn't a nice-to-have, it's a gotta-have.

6. Check your retirement plan. Did you meet your savings goal this year? No? How will you eat when it comes time to hang up your work gloves? How will you keep a roof over your head? If you think your kids are going to take care of you, how would you be doing right now if your mom and dad showed up on your doorstep?

7. Quantify your investment return. Are the investment choices you made still working for you? Are you well diversified? Diversification helps you weather investment volatility because all your money isn't tied up in one sector, type of investment, or geographic location. If your advisor hasn't reviewed your portfolio with you yet this year, get on the horn. This would be a good time to adjust the investments that may have fallen out of whack with your goals and tolerance for risk.

8. Review your insurance coverage: car insurance, property insurance, life, and disability insurance. If you think insurance is a waste of money, how would you cope if the worst did happened? How would your family cope? As if a life disaster isn't bad enough, would it be fair to them to be wiped out financially at the same time?

9. Do you need to review your will this year? How about your powers of attorney for both personal care and money? And have you named a guardian for your children? Have you reviewed this documentation in the last two years or since your last major life change (marriage, divorce, moving, birth of a child)? If not, time to dig out the paperwork and have a look to see if it still meets your needs.

It's easy to put off looking at your money. Put it off. Put it off. Put it off. But you'll get no peace of mind from NOT knowing where you stand. Buckle down and do the detail.

RULE #269: KNOW THE COSTS
OF BUYING A HOME

I didn't buy my first home until I was 30. It took that long to accumulate the 20% down I needed to avoid CMHC insurance. In my day, taking a high-ratio mortgage was a risky thing; it meant you were squeaking into home ownership. Then it became all the rage, and now people don't think twice before they do it. But you should (See Rule #267: CMHC Insurance Doesn't Protect YOU.)

Part of the problem is that people don't take the time to calculate the costs of home buying before they make the leap. Instead they quote nonsense like, "Renting is a waste of money! Why would you pay someone else's mortgage off when you can pay your own?" Then they rush to join the up-and-comers who own their own property, even if they don't really!

There's nothing like an example to prove the point. So let's say you and your mate have saved a down payment of $25,000. You take home $4,000 a month after taxes. Your mate's take-home is $2,000. The bank has qualified you for up to a $325,000 mortgage. You're going to try to get something in the $250,000 range, because property values are lower where you're looking to buy.

First up, CHMH mortgage insurance. If you put less than 20% down on a home, you'll have to buy insurance from CMHC so that if you can't make your payments, the bank is off the hook for the loss. The premiums for mortgage insurance are calculated as a percentage of the loan and depend on your down payment.

If you're buying a $250,000 home, amortized over 25 years with 10% down, your CMHC premium would work out to $5,400. Hey, what's another $5,400 if it gets you into a new home lickety-split, right?

Well, actually, it won't be $5,400 if you do what most people do and just roll that premium into your mortgage. Over the life of the mortgage, at just 5% for the total amortization, that premium will end up costing $9,421 when you add on the interest.

Next, it's time to head over to an online mortgage calculator to see how much of your monthly mortgage payment would go to interest in those early years. If you put in the mortgage amount (house price – down payment + mortgage insurance) of $230,400 at 5% for five years, with a 25-year amortization, a payment will pop up: $1,340 a month. Hey, that's totally doable, right?

But hang on now, how much of that is actually going towards your principal? If you look at how much interest you'd pay over that five-year period, you'll see it's a whopping $53,922.35. So, of the $80,400 in payments you'd make on the mortgage in the first five years, 67% or $899 a month would go straight to interest.

But your mortgage payment is only the beginning of your costs. You must then add on the cost of property taxes (let's say $200 a month) and home insurance (estimate $75 a month) and you're up to $1,174 a month in money spent that does nothing to pay off your new home. (Home maintenance is another cost people like to sweep under the carpet!) Whether you're renting property or renting money, it's still RENT!

Then there are all the costs associated with home buying that most people don't think about, costs like the appraisal fee, home inspection fee, land transfer fees, water or septic tests (if you're outside a major city), reimbursement of pre-paid property taxes, costs to set up new accounts, and legal fees. This can be anywhere from 1.5% to 4% of the price of the home you're buying.

Home ownership should not be seen as a badge, something you measure yourself and others by. Home ownership is a life-style choice. Home ownership is great if you do it right. Buy a home you can't afford, commit to payments that stress you out, and you'll rue it. Your home won't be something you can enjoy, it'll be an albatross around your neck.

RULE #270: KITCHEN TABLE SEPARATION AGREEMENTS ARE DANGEROUS!

Divorce is expensive. The average cost for a divorce in Canada runs between $15,000 and $25,000, depending on whether the courts have to get involved. And while we're willing to spend on average about $32,000 to get married, we want our divorce to cost as little as possible.

While you might be tempted to take matters into your own hands because you're trying to save money, please don't. Even if you don't think your case is particularly complicated, even if you mistrust lawyers and the legal system's penchant for making everything more complicated than it needs be, don't DIY your agreement.

I've been divorced enough times to know that if you don't know what you're doing—and if you're not a family lawyer, you don't—you could miss important things that will screw you later. I'm not saying you have to hire a gunslinger. I'm saying that if you don't know what you don't know, how will you avoid stepping in the poop?

Family lawyers have a name for these documents that people create for themselves as they are separating; they call them kitchen table agreements, because they're often signed in the kitchen over a cup of coffee. And their eyes flash with delight because they know that untangling the mess made will be profitable for them. Very profitable.

Sure, you'll save some money if you work out the details of your separation agreement amicably. That's common sense.

But if you don't get independent legal advice to ensure that all the i's are dotted and the t's crossed, lawyers and court costs may be in your future.

Just because you agree to a thing doesn't make it stickable. Just because you execute it, have it witnessed, and follow through religiously, doesn't mean it won't come back to bite you in the butt. Kitchen table agreements can be tossed to the curb as soon as any weakness in them is uncovered.

Witness the kitchen table agreement that was thrown out by an Ontario court because child support had not been implemented according to Ontario provincial guidelines. Or the one that was nullified because full financial disclosure wasn't made, so one spouse didn't fully appreciate what she was giving up when she waived her claim to her partner's pension. And then there was the agreement in which one partner tried to pull the wool over the other's eyes. Courts booted these agreements to the curb, leaving them not worth the paper they were written on. And because the courts got involved, those cheap kitchen table agreements became very, very expensive.

If your desire to get out of your current relationship has you rushing to sign an agreement, that agreement won't do you a lick of good if it doesn't stand the test of time. So do it right the first time.

Creating a legally binding and long-lasting separation agreement doesn't mean you have to go to court. Nor does it mean that you have to escalate matters. And you don't have to give away all your assets to the legal system, either. It does mean spending enough money to ensure that your separation agreement is consistent with your province's family law act and that everyone involved fully understands what it is they are agreeing to and signing. You're probably looking at spending $4,500 (which is less than 15% of the average wedding).

No matter how tempted you may be to keep the lawyers out of it, please, please don't put your faith in an office-supply-store separation agreement kit. Spend enough money to do it properly the first time.

RULE #271: KEEP VEHICLE LOANS UNDER FIVE YEARS

In the best of all worlds you'll pay cash for your vehicle. If that's just not an option, second best is to have the vehicle paid off in three years or less. But under no circumstances should your vehicle loan run for more than five years. If you're considering buying a car, a truck, an SUV, a motorcycle, anything that gets you from point A to point B, and you're thinking about extending the loan beyond five years so you can manage the payments, think again. That's not your vehicle, because it's simply more than you can afford.

What is it with people and their cars? Why would anyone think it's okay to finance a vehicle for 72, 84, or 96 months just because that makes the monthly payment manageable? Heavens to Betsy, have you calculated the cost of these long, long, long loans?

"But Gail, it's only $230 biweekly." Have you taken the time to add up what the car will end up costing you over the long haul?

Let's say you buy a vehicle for $26,000, take the loan for 96 months, and make monthly payments of $440. At the end of the loan you will have paid $42,240 (96 x $440) for a vehicle that was worth $26,000 just before you drove it off the lot.

The biweekly or weekly payment is the latest trend in payment positioning in the car biz. You can make just about any payment amount palatable if you break it down enough. The salesman looks at you, a twinkle in his eye, and says, "If you

SMART SHOPPING

take the loan for 84 months, you can have that beautiful vehicle for just $125 a week. You can do $125 a week, right? C'mon, it's just $125 a week to drive this beauty!"

Assuming, of course, you drive that puppy for seven years.

Car salespeople have another nifty trick up their sleeves when it comes to making you feel better about being a car kook. If you run out of car before you run out of payment, they're happy to roll what you owe over to the new vehicle they're selling you. They call what you still owe "negative equity." Translated into English, "negative equity" equals "debt." (See Rule #159: Negative Equity Is an Oxymoron.)

So, what if you've inked a deal and then realize you made a mistake?

You signed a contract, so you can't just ask to opt out. You can sell the vehicle for what remains outstanding with a plan to recoup all, most, or some of what you had to spend. Whatever the shortfall, it'll come out of your pocket. Alternatively, you can find a way to make more money so you can make extra payments against the loan and get to debt-free faster.

RULE #272: STAY OUT OF PAY
ADVANCE LOAN STORES

When people write to me to tell me that they've availed them-selves of the services of a pay advance store and now don't know how to get the hook out of their mouth, I just want to scream. Pay advance loans shouldn't even exist. If our government was doing its job, they wouldn't. But by continuing to turn a blind eye our lawmakers have, in effect, legalized usury.

The pay advance loan people say they're providing a service: helping people who can't find help anywhere else. Really? Well, if they're so interested in "helping" people, then what's with the fees and outrageous interest rates?

The terms and conditions of each payday loan vary by province since the federal government offloaded the responsibility of monitoring these companies to individual provinces.

In Ontario, the maximum amount that can be charged for interest and fees is $21 for every $100 borrowed. But that doesn't mean that payday companies follow the rules. In fact, in 2013 these companies appeared on the Ontario Ministry of Government and Consumer Services' top-ten list of consumer complaints and inquiries.

In B.C., the most a payday lender can charge is $23 for every $100 borrowed, unless you haven't paid the loan back in time, in which case they can charge 30% on the outstanding balance. Ditto Alberta. In Manitoba, it's just $17 for every $100. In Nova Scotia, it's $25 per $100. In Newfoundland and Labrador—where there are no rules—when I checked, one pay advance lender was charging $30 for every $100 borrowed. Quebec has effectively banned payday loan stores. Yeah, Quebec!

Have you taken advantage of the "cheap money" being offered by a pay advance store? Twenty dollars for a $100 pay advance may sound like pocket change, but it's the first step to a dreadful cycle of borrowing and re-borrowing. Whether you did it as an act of desperation, or you were just dumber than a sack of hammers, your decision to go to a pay advance loan store is costing you big time. Wondering how the hell to get off the treadmill?

Perhaps your rent is due. Or you have to take several days off work with a sick child, for which you're not going to be paid. Or you're just crap with handling your money and think this is an easy solution. Don't do it!

So you borrow $600 and write a postdated cheque for two weeks later, when your next pay hits your account. Your cheque will be for $720 to cover the interest and fees charged. That's right, in just two weeks, you'll pay $120 in interest and fees. How much of your next paycheque will that wipe out? What'll you do then? Borrow again? That's what the pay advance stores count on.

A rate of $23 per $100 borrowed for two weeks works out to an annual interest rate of 598%. According to the Canadian Criminal Code, the criminal rate of interest is anything greater than 60% per year. So, the pay advance stores are charging ten times the amount allowed and getting away with it. Makes me scratch my head and say, "Hmm." So much for all the government consumer protection agencies out there, right?

So, what do you do if you're in the cycle and are desperate to get out? You're going to have to suck it up and either be short for a couple of weeks—while you repay the loan and DON'T borrow again—or find a way to make more money so you can get the life-sucking debt off your back.

There ain't no other way, kids. You've just got to get serious about getting out of debt and do WHATEVER IT TAKES to break the desperate cycle of borrowing and then borrowing again to make up for the cash flow shortage caused by the outrageous interest and fees you had to pay.

It'll be hard. It'll hurt. But, hopefully, you'll have learned an important lesson and you won't do it again.

CONCLUSION
Money Is Just a Tool

Once upon a time we measured ourselves by "the content of our character." Most recently we have taken to measuring ourselves (and others) by how much money we have and how much stuff we can buy with all our money. Money isn't supposed to be a yardstick of our self-worth. Money is a tool.

When money was devised as a medium of exchange, the money itself represented a way to trade that was easier than hauling around sacks of corn to be bartered for lengths of material. Money was convenient. It was efficient. And it used the value of some underlying commodity like beaver pelts or dried corn to establish its worth.

Over time, the commodity most often used to establish the value of money was gold. That lasted until the 1970s, when the U.S. dollar came off the gold standard. This did away with the idea that money represented the value of some commodity or another. The new money—"fiat money"—took on a value of its own based on people's perception of its worth and a solid dose of faith.

Money's value is a constant interaction between the things that money can buy and your desire for those things. Enter the Unholy Trio: greed, credit, and the inability to defer gratification. Each represents a push to use money in perverse ways.

Greed is all about more, more, more. It's the inability to register when you're full, when there is enough, when you've been sated. And I'm not talking about food here. I'm talking about enough house, sufficient shoes, ample tools in the tool box.

Credit is a useful tool if you want to increase your net worth or your ability to earn a higher income over time. For every other purchase, using credit to buy what you can't afford to pay for in cash is a foolish case of scratching a consumer itch.

If you have been handed more and more credit without really understanding the implications of using it, you may have grown accustomed to scratching your itches. Ever scratched a mosquito bite? Notice how scratching only makes the itch worse? That's exactly what's happened as you've used credit to fill the gap between what you want and what you can afford.

Wanting isn't a bad thing. It is wanting that drives you to be more efficient, to work hard, to strive. But when you equate wanting with getting, regardless of your ability to pay for what you want, then your immediate gratification has outstripped your common sense.

Gratification of desire used to hang out with patience and anticipation. If you're in debt, at some point you lost hold of the idea that you could have what you wanted given enough time and effort. Having chosen to embrace the Gimme-

Gimmes, deferral has become a dinosaur, helped along in no small way by your access to easy credit.

Money is a tool that can get you the things you need and want. If you use it wisely and with care, you can have enough of what you need to live a comfortable life. You can use your money to buy you time: If you can pay someone else to cut the lawn, you can take the kids swimming. You can use money to achieve a goal: Think home ownership or going back to school. You can use money to smooth out your life: an emergency fund means you have options if the crap hits the fan; a retirement savings plan means you can look forward to not working; a car means you don't have to commute for an hour and a half to get someplace you could drive to in 20 minutes.

There are people who like to compare the length of their screwdrivers or the width of their wardrobes as affirmations of their rank in the social hierarchy. When you use money as a measure of your success, or when you use the stuff money can buy to feel good about yourself (or degrade others), you're giving money more power than it rightfully should have.

If you allow money to become the standard you use to gauge your worth, you're playing on a slippery slope. Hang out with people who are higher up the mountain, and you can be convinced you're a loser. Hang out with folks who are at or close to the base, and you might think you're superior.

Money is the tool you can use to make your life what you want it to be. Or money is the tool you can misuse—like taking a saw to cut butter—to create huge problems for yourself down the road. Use it wisely—you're a craftsman. Use it foolishly and . . . well . . . you know what they say about a fool and his money.

ACKNOWLEDGEMENTS

As always, to my favourite editor, Kate Cassaday, who brings clarity and a vision to everything that I write for her. You are a gem. I hope you realize how much I treasure you.

Thanks to Curtis Russell, agent extraordinaire, who is not only a fabulous negotiator but persistent beyond belief.

Thanks to Glenn Cooke for the chat about insurance.

Thanks to Casey and Sylve Duchaine, Megan McCoy, Michael Sheehan, and Jasmine Miller for scribbling on the manuscript. You guys gave great feedback. I know how busy you are, and I thank you from the bottom of my heart for taking time to read for me and tell me your "aha!"s.

To my very good frined Victoria Ryce, who has a huge brain and loves to share it. Thank you for your time and generosity. I can't tell you how much I love playing with you in the ideas sandbox. I want to write another book just so we can keep doing it.

LIST OF RULES